"Her experiences are exciting, portrayed here with a great deal of honor and respect, and her writing is compelling. The result is a fine addition to the growing genre exploring indigenous spirituality . . . Highly recommended."

—*Library Journal*

"Although [Jenkins] concedes that silencing the critical mind and allowing intuition to guide her were prerequisites for entry into the spirit world, in this well-written account of her adventure . . . she employs her rationalist, academic background to evaluate her paranormal experiences."

—*Publishers Weekly*

Initiation

*A Woman's Spiritual Adventure
in the Heart of the Andes*

ELIZABETH B. JENKINS

BERKLEY BOOKS

New York

All Quechua spellings are taken from the 1996 edition of the
Quechua dictionary published by the Higher Academy of
the Quechua Language, Cuzco, Peru.

INITIATION

A Berkley Book / published by arrangement with
the author

PRINTING HISTORY
G. P. Putnam's Sons edition / August 1997
Berkley trade paperback edition / August 1998

The Penguin Putnam Inc. World Wide Web site address is
http://www.penguinputnam.com

ISBN: 0-425-16476-4

BERKLEY®
Berkley Books are published by
The Berkley Publishing Group, a member of Penguin Putnam Inc.,
200 Madison Avenue, New York, New York 10016.
BERKLEY and the "B" design are trademarks
belonging to Berkley Publishing Corporation.

PRINTED IN THE UNITED STATES OF AMERICA

10 9 8 7 6 5 4 3 2 1

Acknowledgments

First, I thank my mother and father, who gave me this body; my brothers, who helped make me who I am; and my Peruvian family, the Machicaos, for their endless love and loyalty. All my heartfelt gratitude and love to Cyntha Gonzalez, without whom this story could never have come to pass. Undying thanks to my "reader" friends, especially Carol Adrienne, whose constant encouragement and support are life-sustaining. All my thanks and admiration to my intrepid groups of Peru-goers and all students of the Andean Path. To my stunning and brilliant agent, Candice Fuhrman, my deepest gratitude for first seeing the potential in this book and in me, and the same to my magnificent foreign agent, Linda Michaels, for giving this book legs to travel. Thanks to my editor, Susan Allison, and all the people at Putnam for making this dream real. To all my teachers, including Don Manuel Q'espi and the Q'ero Nation of Peru, and especially to Juan Nuñez del Prado, for his incredible love, wisdom, and guidance throughout, an enormous thank you. And of course, although I never met you, thanks to Don Benito Qoriwaman, whose wisdom and teachings run throughout these pages. I love you all.

This book is dedicated with all my heart to Pachamama,
the living spirit of Earth and Mother of us all.

Contents

One day, when Don Manuel and I were out for a walk at a ruin called Moray, we were watching many men repairing an Inka wall. They were working on the restoration of that archaeological site. I asked Don Manuel what he thought about their work, and he said simply: "They are preparing the house of the Inka for the time when he will return."

These workmen knew nothing of the Andean prophecy; they thought they were carrying out the task assigned to them in order to earn their daily wage. But from the perspective of Don Manuel, an Andean priest, they are carrying out a mystical task.

"We shall have to wait," he said, laughing, "to discover who is right."

—Juan Nuñez del Prado

PART I

Pachamama Calls

I

The Mountain Spirit

"ELIZABETH! *TELÉFONO!*" SEÑORA CLEMENCIA CALLED ME down from the second floor of her enormous Spanish-style house. I struggled out from under the heavy alpaca blankets and threw on a sweatshirt and sweatpants, gasping as my skin met the freezing morning air. Stuffing feet into tennis shoes, I shuffled down the hall and half slid on my untied laces down the creaking wooden steps toward the phone. "Oof," exclaimed Panchita, the señora's dark round Indian housekeeper, as she rebalanced the tray of fresh bread and *café con leche* she was carrying in to the señora, the tray that I had nearly toppled as I rushed past her, rounding the corner at the bottom of the stairs.

It was a Peruvian acquaintance on the line, informing me that one of the local healers, a "psychic herbalist," would be performing a special kind of treatment called an egg diagnosis that very afternoon. Now my seemingly impetuous move to Cuzco, Peru, was beginning to make sense. Months of poking around had finally yielded something. I was going to have my first visit to an authentic local healer!

Ecstatic, I raced back up the stairs to inform Carlos, my cool-blue-eyed Argentinean friend and partner in spiritual adventure, certain that he would want to come with me. Carlos, a psychology student from Buenos Aires, had also been drawn to Cuzco because of its reputation as a center of magnetic and mystical power.

Securing Carlos's assent to our two-o'clock appointment, I headed back down the long outdoor terrace that led to my apartment and stopped, mesmerized by the view of Ausangate Mountain, a 22,000-foot ice peak at the east end of the Cuzco Valley. "Okay, destiny, I'm here," I whispered to the towering peak, "now what do you want with me?"

This was the question that had threaded its way through my thoughts day and night for the last three months, weaving a seductive web of doubt, apprehension, and tingling excitement. The pull to Cuzco had been so strong that I had left everything behind in California—job, family, fiancé, doctoral studies—and moved to Peru in response to an intense spiritual urging, a knowledge that the key to my future, and perhaps my past, lay here in this ancient landscape, this ancient city. I didn't know a soul in Cuzco and I didn't speak a word of Spanish. I had never done anything like this before in my life.

I quickly discovered that Cuzco—once the proud southern capital of the Inka empire, the city the Indians called "the navel of the world"—was now a sprawling metropolis of over five hundred thousand people of mixed Spanish and Indian blood. Some five hundred years after the arrival of the Spanish conquistadors, Cuzco remains a beautiful shining city lying in the lap of enormous mountain peaks. The narrow twisting cobblestone streets, whitewashed walls with red-tile roofs and ornate wooden balconies that leaned out over them, like the one I was now standing on, had captured my heart. Gazing out at the architecture that gave the city its cultured feel, I realized that, except for snow peaks, I could have been looking out onto a street in any little town in Spain.

But Spanish red-tile roofs sat atop an ancient and mysterious past. Foundations of perfect Inka stonework were visible everywhere. Was that what gave Cuzco its exalted quality? Or was it simply the two-mile altitude? On a clear day the skies were royal blue, and the still air hummed with a palpable magic. It was as if the land itself had a richness, a power that had made it the Inkas' choice then, and now kept it a magnet for spiritual seekers from all over the world. Certainly it had been a magnet for me. Now I was impatient to discover why. What was it that had uprooted me from my career as a psychologist and lured me more than five thousand miles from my home?

As a doctoral student in clinical psychology I had found my professional calling highly satisfying. I loved my friends, my studies, and my life in San Francisco; however, recently, I had become bored with the dry academic learning. I knew there was more to the puzzle of human beings than my textbooks were telling me; and I had a feeling the mystery lay somewhere within the spiritual dimension of our human nature. Therefore, I had come to Peru in search of information on indigenous healers and healing. At least that was the reason I gave to my friends and colleagues; and it was a plausible cover story for those to whom I could not explain my deeper, irrational spiritual calling. Certainly I could barely explain it to myself. I had been raised in the Western tradition of the rationalists, and to most of my fellow psychologists the word "spiritual" referred to an inchoate realm of nonreal experience, or hallucinations. The truth was I didn't know why I was in Cuzco. I just knew that I had felt compelled to move here.

It *was* true however, that since I had arrived in Cuzco, I was having the time of my life. I felt truly free for the first time; out from under the watchful eye and expectations of my family *and* culture. Or perhaps I was simply trying to escape my own expectations of who and what I should be and do. As a native English speaker I quickly landed a teaching job at the Institute of Peruvian and North American Culture for pocket money. But my true passion came unleashed when I began playing music in the local nightclubs. It was during one of my first local gigs that I had met Carlos, a fellow psychology student also interested in the spiritual world. Curiously, I found that indulging my artistic longings—something I had never had time for in graduate school—allowed a whole untapped aspect of my being to come forward, my intuitive voice. And I made a conscious decision to use this unique time and place to cultivate my intuition and live in a different way, letting my intuition lead me, rather than my rational mind.

In fact, one of my first intuitive experiments had led me to Señora Clemencia's house. Rather than look in the paper for a rental, I had decided simply to stand on the main square of the city and let myself be guided by an inner sense of direction. Almost immediately, the high ground above the square, and the road toward the archaeological ruin of Saqsaywaman, caught my attention. I began to climb a street called "Puma's Shoulder," and the señora's house was the second door I knocked on. I had been living with the Machicao family—Señora Clemencia, her husband Juan, her children Rosario and Pepe—and the housekeeper, Panchita, for three months now. The eldest son, Luis Carlos, lived in Lima.

The señora was a true matriarch and a nurse who spoke perfect Quechua, the language of the Inkas. She was one of the few upper-middle-class Peruvians who was proud of her Indian heritage and the Inka culture. As Señora Clemencia put it, she didn't have "complexes" about her mixed-blood ancestry. Her husband, Juan, a banker by trade, a painter by soul, played watercolor symphonies on the weekends in the courtyard of their eighteen-room, old Spanish-style house. She was a sharp staccato to his soft mellow tones. After thirty years of marriage, they still held hands as they walked down the street together. I glanced down into the courtyard to see the señora and her husband sitting in the sun on folding chairs, and chatting with the sweet intimacy that only many years of happiness can bring. I groaned inwardly, wondering if I would ever experience that, then shoved the longing aside as I contemplated my afternoon appointment for the egg diagnosis.

My best girlfriend, Cyntha Gonzalez, was the person who had

first introduced me to shamanism; and it was she who told me that the Andean people, the mountain people of Peru, believe that a fertile egg is a very sensitive receptor of energy. When it is passed over the human body it can receive an energetic imprint of the physical health of that person.

I met Cyntha in graduate school in San Francisco and we immediately became fast friends. In 1987 she left her academic career to go and study with two Peruvian shamans in the town of Moche, near Trujillo, Peru. It was Cyntha who had convinced me to escape the rigors of my doctoral studies for a few weeks; and in May 1988, I traveled to Peru for the first time, to join her in her research of the all-night healing ceremonies of these coastal shamans. Cyntha had learned that the coastal shamans, guided by beliefs similar to those of the mountain shamans of Cuzco, pass a guinea pig over the body of the patient, then cut the animal open while it is still alive. The organs of the guinea pig are supposed to reveal the illness of the patient. If the neck of the guinea pig snaps during the diagnosis, it means the patient is possessed. Somehow using an egg seemed much more humane.

Clearly Cyntha had paved the way for me to break away and begin to follow my inner guidance, and it was on that first trip, when Cyntha took me to Cuzco and Machu Pikchu, that I knew I had to move to Peru. But now that I was here, only *I* could discover the reasons behind my intense attraction to Cuzco and the Inkas. For months now, a gnawing impatience had been growing inside me. I knew there was something here for me to uncover, something for me to learn. I was not here to be a tourist; that much was undeniably clear.

Perhaps that was why I had leapt so excitedly from my bed when the phone rang—some part of me sensing that this would be the phone call to end the months of waiting, and my days as a tourist. Abruptly. Forever. As I stood gazing at the mountain from my balcony, the roiling in my blood told me that my visit to the local healer would be extremely important. The inexorable movements of destiny were at work here. What I didn't know was that that phone call marked an event that would change the course of my life irrevocably and put me on a path of unprecedented adventure.

AT ONE-THIRTY SHARP, I PUT MY READING AWAY AND pulled the wrinkled piece of white paper out of my pocket, glancing at the sketchy directions to the healer's office that I had hurriedly scribbled down. From what I had written, I wasn't at all convinced we would find the place. When I knocked on Carlos's door he popped his head out. "Ready," he said, blue eyes all fire. Like me, he was curious about the local customs, curious to penetrate the mysteries that surrounded us like solid Inka walls. In fact we were just two of hundreds of foreigners, attracted to Cuzco's mysterious magnetism. Señora Clemencia, well aware of the tourism market in Cuzco, was converting her overly large home into a Peruvian *pensión*. She had asked me to bring a few handpicked tourists to rent the extra rooms, and Carlos was my first recommendation.

Carlos and I had gotten to know each other well over the past several weeks, as we toured the sacred Inka ruins of Cuzco together. During our travels, I was impressed by Carlos's open curiosity and his easy conversation with strangers. Rather than being put off by the poverty of the local Indian people, he was particularly generous and affectionate toward them. He was a very levelheaded and down-to-earth traveling companion, yet he operated on intuition as well as common sense, something I was just learning about. What I liked most about Carlos was his good sense and practicality, yet there was a richness to his being that told me he was not closed to life's mysteries. So, as we set out to find the healer's office, it was all the more disconcerting when he told me the extraordinary story of how, just before coming to Cuzco, he had been initiated with an ancient power object.

"My teacher, Señor Martinez, told me that when he was seventeen years old, two Tibetan monks came to his house and took him to a mountain in the north of Argentina," Carlos said. "They pointed to a certain spot and told him to dig. After a while he unearthed a two-foot-long staff of basaltic rock. The monks told him that he was to become the keeper of the staff. They also said there was a prophecy that when this staff and the Holy Grail are brought together again, it will be the signal of a new era." He related the information matter-of-factly, his sea-blue eyes a study of intelligence and concentration.

"And that was the staff you were initiated with before you came here?" I asked.

"Yes. They call it the *bastón de mando*, the staff of power."

In California, I thought to myself, I would have shaken this off as some wild fantasy. But here in the southern continent, in this ancient land where reality felt much more malleable, it didn't seem impossible. And Carlos was no New Age flake. I didn't know why, but I sensed his story was important, and I was certain I would not forget it.

However, the more immediate mystery was how to find this healer. We made our way up the steep grade of San Blas, the artist's quarter of Cuzco, trying to follow the confusing directions I had been given. There were few street signs in Cuzco and almost no numbers painted on the blue and green doors, so we had to find our way almost by intuition alone. We climbed up cobbled walkways, more stairway than street, past rows of yellowing whitewashed houses that were easily hundreds of years old.

Some of the houses showed large, perfectly cut stones, the remains of original Inka stonework that had been used as a foundation. In others, two massive stones inclined at the top and capped with enormous stone lintels were actually original Inka doorways. These houses could have been up to five hundred years old!

I had heard stories that the Inka priests had retired to Machu Pikchu and lived there in hiding from the Spanish. Then the Inkas inexplicably disappeared. All that was left of their culture were descriptions by Spanish chroniclers of a vast and glorious empire that stretched from southern Colombia all the way to what is now central Chile.

"This must be it!" Carlos announced triumphantly as we came

to a house with fresh white paint on the walls in the general vicinity that our directions indicated. A wooden balcony extended out above the street. The shutters were open and there were people moving about. We climbed the creaking wooden stairs.

"Is this the office of Patricia Alvarez?" I attempted in broken Spanish, hoping my gringa accent didn't render the words unintelligible to the man with the serene smile who greeted us at the top of the stairs. He was slim and dark, of medium height, dressed from head to toe in white, with long hair and a salt-and-pepper beard. His clothing and demeanor were of a sort that I associated with the ashrams of India. He led us through the inner office to an outside patio.

"*Sí*, this is Patricia's office," Carlos translated, as the man nodded and gestured for us to sit down and wait.

A large wooden vat was propped against the inner wall of the building. A dark liquid bubbled at the top and clouds of vapor wafted into the air, giving off an herblike medicinal smell. The man in white reappeared several different times and calmly carried out the same operation. He brought a tall glass of water with a raw egg sloshing around in the top over to a sink in the corner, threw out the contents of the glass, rinsed it, and refilled it with the steamy brown liquid from the vat. I shuddered, hoping I wouldn't have to drink that.

Finally the man came back and spoke to us. "I am William, Patricia's husband. Are you here for the egg diagnosis?" We nodded. "Did you bring your eggs?" he asked in Spanish.

"No," Carlos told him. "We were not aware of this." William clucked his tongue and shook his head at us, gesturing again for us to wait.

We were the only nonnative people in the waiting room. Everyone else was Peruvian, and this appeared to be their regular healthcare visit. I had been told that more than ninety percent of the Peruvian population still use the indigenous healers as their treatment of choice, even though Western medicine is more or less available. Because of our clothing, Carlos and I stood out like sore thumbs. I was embarrassed, feeling that everyone must have known we were there mostly out of curiosity and not because we were sick. Still, we had to follow the same procedure as everyone else.

As William disappeared into the office, a plump teenage Indian girl with long black braids and a shy smile came out onto the patio, carrying a basket of eggs. She sold us each a large, warm, fertile egg for about ten cents, and instructed us to hold it in our left hands only.

Shortly William reappeared and escorted me to a small, bare room divided by two cotton partitions. In each "room" was a cot and a little desk with a tall glass of water on it, like the ones we had seen him emptying on the patio. He gestured for me to lie down on my back on the cot. He confidently plucked the egg from my hand as I lay down nervously on the creaky old cot, which seemed barely able to support my weight.

My eyes closed, my body tense with suspicion, I planned what I would do if his hands strayed to the wrong places. Silence. I squinted open one paranoid eye to see him holding my egg with both hands to his forehead, his lips moving in silent prayer. Embarrassed, I relaxed and then watched, fascinated. With his eyes closed he began to move the egg over my body in a series of complex motions. Starting at my feet with some figure eights, he worked his way up around the circumference of my body. The egg seemed to be directing his movements.

At last he opened his eyes, and I squeaked involuntarily at the tickling sensation as he rapidly rubbed the egg firmly against each of my armpits, then at my groin, stomach, heart, and forehead. With a flourish he broke the egg into the glass of water. As he surveyed my egg, he began shaking his head and clucking his tongue again.

"What? Is it serious?" I asked nervously in my broken Spanish.

"A little mucus in the lungs . . . and a few other things, but we'll wait for Patricia to give the real diagnosis. Don't worry," he said, laughing at my frowning expression.

A few minutes later Patricia, a professionally dressed, vibrant Peruvian woman in her early forties, with thick shoulder-length brown hair, came striding in. She was humming lightly under her breath, and energy and confidence entered the room with her. She introduced herself to me with a warm smile.

"Now, let's see, hmmm . . ." she said, eyeing my egg glass. Suddenly her buoyant manner dropped. She ceased humming. "Oh, my!" Patricia exclaimed. Oddly, I did not feel afraid; the change in her manner had only caused me to become more alert. I felt an adrenaline rush of excitement through my body, and my heart started to beat faster before she began to speak. "You have been feeling very strange lately and crying a lot without knowing why. No?" I was surprised at her words.

"Yes . . . but how did you know that?" She was absolutely right, yet I hadn't mentioned this even to Carlos.

"The egg shows your physical, emotional, and spiritual status," she informed me. "You're not a tourist, are you," she stated, flatly.

"No, I've come here to live, I . . ." I stuttered.

"And you're here to do some spiritual work," she said knowingly. I gulped and nodded.

Patricia looked me fiercely in the eye. "Then you must speak with the *apus.*" I regarded her blankly. She took a deep breath and patiently explained, "The *apus* are the mountain spirits, the guardians of this land. You see, your problem is that you have come here responding to an invitation, no?" Again I was amazed at how she verbalized my innermost feelings. "Let me explain it like this. It's as if you were invited to someone's house for dinner, and you've spoken to the cook and the gardener but you haven't greeted the owners, the ones who invited you."

Oh, my God, I thought to myself. How stupid! Here I was in a powerful and mysterious land, yet I had not made any greeting or acknowledgment to the spirits of that land. I had heard that one was supposed to do this, but after all I *was* a gringa. Nothing in my education had prepared me for this.

"Patricia, I think I understand. Thank you for telling me this, but how do I greet them? What do I do?" I asked.

"You need to find a priest who can help you," she replied.

"A priest?" I asked, bewildered. "How can a Catholic priest help me with this?"

"Not a Catholic priest," she corrected me. "An Andean priest." I looked at her, confused. "Andean priests can speak directly with nature," she said simply, as if explaining to a child. "They are the ones who talk with the mountain spirits, the *apus*. To work here, you need to work with the permission and help of the *apus*. Anyone who works in healing works with the *apus*. I have twenty or thirty *apus* that I work with myself," she explained.

"*Ahpoos,*" I said, trying out the word.

Patricia kept talking. "I'm going to give you some herbs for the mucous in your lungs. Your astral body is looking cloudy."

At that moment William ushered Carlos into my cubicle and set his egg glass down next to mine for Patricia to see. None of the North American formality or confidentiality here. "Oh, how great!" she said, looking at Carlos's egg. "Look." She pointed to his glass. I was surprised to see that his egg appeared very different from mine. The white of my egg looked like wispy, scattered clouds, while his was clear and uniform. "Your friend's astral body is very clear and strong. In fact, it has been protecting yours." Again, what she said matched my feelings. I hadn't thought of it before, but now I realized that I *had* felt distinctly protected and safe since Carlos had come to Cuzco.

"You," she said, looking at Carlos, "will receive a different herbal formula because you are a tourist. On the other hand, she," Patricia said, pointing to me, "is living here, so I will give her herbs to help her adapt to this place." She began busily filling two small plastic bags with various herbs from her shelves. She gave us instructions on how to prepare the herbs and when to take them. We thanked her, paid her, and left.

As we walked home I asked Carlos what he thought of Patricia. "I am always skeptical about these things," he said. "She did not tell me anything that I did not know already. But for you, I think it may have been important," he replied. I was elated by her reading of me and her instructions. I vowed inwardly to find the priest right away.

As we walked on in silence, I kept thinking about the "invitation" Patricia had mentioned. It made me recall something that had happened back in the States, almost a year before. I had been standing on the Santa Cruz boardwalk, calmly contemplating my upcoming trip, my first visit to see Cyntha in Peru, when a strange feeling overcame me. I heard an inner voice, a commanding voice that said, "If you go to Peru, your life will never be the same. Do you still choose to go?" Not being one to back out of a challenge, I immediately answered "Yes," then laughed at myself for responding to my own inner dialogue as if it were a conversation. Besides, listening to voices, feeling scared of going on a vacation, for God's sake! To my rational mind it all seemed silly, ridiculous even. Now I wondered if that voice I had heard, before I had ever set foot in Peru, had something to do with the "invitation" Patricia was talking about.

A week later I was getting frustrated. I had been trying for days now to find out how to get in contact with the Andean priest, but I was getting nowhere. No one I asked seemed to know anything about Andean priests. When I said the word *apu*, the locals nodded their heads and pointed to the mountains, but I got no further than that. And I was running out of time *and* money.

I had been traveling around South America and living in Cuzco for a total of eight months now. I felt a need to go home, back to California, if only for a brief visit. Aside from the fact that I was nearly out of money, I was missing my friends and family, not to mention hot showers! I made a reservation for the following week. But I kept thinking about what Patricia had said about "greeting" the *apus*. I couldn't leave without having truly arrived.

I spent the day shopping for gifts to take back to the States, and by the time I returned to my apartment, it was already late. Since I seemed to have no other alternative, I decided I had better "talk" to the *apus* myself. I *had* to do some kind of ceremony to greet and honor them before I left Peru. It felt wrong in my heart to delay this long, but I had been hoping to find the priest.

I sat down on the bare wooden floor of my room in a meditative posture with nothing more than an intention in my heart. The sun had gone down hours before and the doors and windows of my room were bolted shut against the freezing night air. I sat facing in the direction of the 22,000-foot ice peak that I had heard the locals call Apu Ausangate. On a clear day I had a perfect view of the mountain from my bedroom window. "Monday, March 13, 1989," I wrote in my journal. I looked at my watch as I crossed my legs, adding, "9:25 P.M."

Moments later, I was lying face down on the cold wooden floor, stretched out in the direction of the ice peak, weeping hysterically. A freezing wind blew over my head. I could not move my body. "Well, what did you expect from an ice peak . . . a warm wind?" I heard a deep, commanding male voice. It was a voice I recognized. The same voice I had heard that day on the boardwalk in Santa Cruz!

Reality melted as I was at once awake and in a strange, dreamlike state:

A large man with long hair and a beard, of an imposing combination of red, white, and black hair, sits on top of the ice peak. He wears a golden sandal on the right foot and a silver sandal on the left. His expression is fierce and powerful and at the same time kingly. "Lord Apu," I tell him shaking and weeping, "please forgive me for not honoring you sooner. I am just a stupid gringa and I don't know the customs of your land. I want to thank you for inviting me and ask your permission to live and work in this sacred place." I cower before him. The stern expression on the apu's face softens and he reaches out to embrace me, giving me a warm kiss. Warm lips touch my forehead. My body relaxes and I stop crying. I sit up. I have been accepted. I know it with my body. Instinctively and without opening my eyes I turn my body toward the huge Inka ruin of Saqsaywaman. An older gentleman appears. "I think we already know each other," he says. Without hesitation he embraces me. I turn physically toward another peak at the opposite end of the valley from Apu Ausangate. A lovely green peak that looks like a pyramid. I see a beautiful woman with long black hair. She welcomes me, smil-

ing warmly, and puts her arms around me, stroking my head and back, and calling me "daughter."

As suddenly as they had come, the images and sensations disappeared and I opened my eyes to find myself in my room once more. It seemed as if only a few minutes had passed, but my watch read 10:33 P.M.

2

Andean Priest

A S I LAY IN BED THE NEXT MORNING, MY EXPERIENCE OF the night before seemed like a strange dream. Yet the physical reality of it had been undeniable—the cold wind, the warm kiss—and I did not feel afraid. On the contrary, I felt much better. Curiously, I felt a deep sense of satisfaction, as if I had gotten something done that really needed to get done, like cleaning the kitchen. Besides, it wasn't the first time in my life that I had experienced a vision.

When I was about six years old, growing up in Minnesota, I saw a little bird fly into the freshly cleaned plate glass of our living room window and fall to the ground. I rushed outside to see if I could help. I remember picking up the bird, trying to feed it some of the apple I was eating. A trickle of blood came out of its beak, as it heaved a sigh and expired right in my hand. As I held it, I watched a tiny circle of luminescent light come out of the bird's body and float upward, against the deep blue of the sky, until it disappeared, merging into the sunlight. At the time, it struck me as a perfectly natural occurrence, and it took me a while to realize that not everyone saw what *I* saw. Soon I had learned to keep these experiences to myself.

Yet I suppose it was because of these "visions" that I had always secretly believed in another, subtler world behind the material one, and my current interest in traditional healers probably sprang from these early experiences. But, without any cultural context for my visions, and because my culture demanded tangible proof, I had eventually dismissed the notion as a product of my vivid childhood imagination. That's why last night's "meditation" with the *apus* had been so powerful. The cold wind had tousled my hair, and the kiss on my forehead . . . I had actually *felt* warm lips! There was no denying that something completely extraordinary was happening here; and although I tried to rationalize it away, I simply couldn't.

Because I was trained in psychology, my explanation until now, for people who heard voices and saw people who weren't there, was that they were probably coping with severe emotional problems. I knew of many cases, especially in instances of abuse, in which people who felt powerless in their relationships left consensus reality behind to speak with invisible beings. I understood it as an attempt to exert some control over an impossible or chaotic situation, and in many cases this type of exit from "reality" actually allowed for psychological survival.

Knowing this, I examined myself for psychological trauma. I felt great! In fact, I had never been more relaxed in my entire life. The schedule I had left behind in the States some eight months before, stretched between my two half-time jobs and a full-time Ph.D. program, had been infinitely more taxing than my current lifestyle. It occurred to me that perhaps I was not traumatized, but rather that my psychological theory was somehow lacking.

Perhaps it was overly simplistic of my profession to assume that all "visionary experience" was the result of trauma. Certainly the most recent writings in transpersonal psychology were suggesting another possible interpretation through studies carried out in traditional, or "shamanic" cultures. Was there an invisible world? Had I just touched it? And if there was, how did it work? These were the very questions I had come here to pursue, but for the moment I shelved these stimulating ideas and got up to go about my day in Cuzco.

As I ran my errands in town, I accomplished everything with an ease that was almost uncanny. Several people I had been trying to contact for weeks found *me* in the main square. And, more impressively, the doors to the Qorikancha Temple, once the central Sun Temple of the Inkas, but now the Catholic monastery of Santo Domingo, magically opened for me.

Over the past two weeks I had been trying to get into the Sun Temple, but the guards insisted that I buy an expensive tourist pass to fourteen sites. When I told them I was not a tourist, that I lived in Cuzco and only wanted to go into the Sun Temple, they laughed and insisted I buy the ticket. Stubbornly I refused. Why was it that on *this* morning, I was able to enter the Temple of Qorikancha, meaning "golden field," like an invited guest? I spent hours there, and although the guards seemed to look right at me, they never asked me for an entrance ticket. Things were clicking, as if some invisible barrier between me and what I wanted to do had been removed. I couldn't help but think back to my experience of the night before. Were the *apus* helping me?

A FEW DAYS LATER I WENT TO THE INSTITUTE OF PERUVIAN and North American Culture (IPNAC), where I had been teaching English, to tell my friends and colleagues that I would be leaving in a couple of days. I arrived just between classes and as I stood in the office chatting animatedly with several friends, a slight but handsome man, another teacher, approached me. Although I had seen him in the IPNAC for months, we had only once been formally introduced.

"*Hola*, Elizabeth," he said. I was surprised he remembered my name. "I am Antonio," he reminded me.

"*Hola*, Antonio, how are you?" I replied as we exchanged the traditional kiss on the cheek.

He looked at me rather intensely, and said, "Elizabeth, I hear that you are interested in esoteric things."

"Yes?" I answered, wondering what he was getting at.

"Elizabeth," he hesitated, weighing his words carefully before saying, "I am part of a group that works with the *apus*—"

"*Apus!*" I nearly shouted, interrupting him in my surprise. I caught myself and continued the conversation almost in a whisper. "Can we go somewhere and talk?" I asked. "I've just had an experience with the *apus* that I feel I must tell you about."

As we moved away from the crowd, I described to him as quietly as I could the visionary experience I had had only nights before. It was a tremendous relief to be able to tell the story to someone because the experience had been so powerful, so out of the realm of my ordinary experiences, at least my ordinary North American experiences.

As I spoke, Antonio's eyes grew wider and his face even more serious. When I finished, he paused a moment. "Elizabeth, some of my colleagues and I are deeply interested in our native traditions. We have been meeting with an *altomisayoq*, a person who calls the *apus*. I would like you to come to our group."

I was delighted, "Yes, of course. I'd love to come," I answered. "But what is an *altomisayoq*?" I asked.

"The word means 'high priest' in Quechua." Antonio explained. My heart jumped. This seemed to be exactly what I had been waiting for.

"When is your next meeting?" I asked enthusiastically.

"Well, it's not that easy. You see, we've never had a white person attend one of our ceremonies. I will have to talk to the group. I think maybe in three or four weeks I could arrange something—"

"Oh, that's too bad," I said, cutting him off. "I leave for the States on Monday."

"Then," he said decisively, "you must come tomorrow!" I was taken aback by his sudden resolve. Why was it so important to him that I come? At the same time I was thrilled by the opportunity that was presenting itself.

"Okay," I agreed, and we shook hands.

"Meet me at San Francisco Church tomorrow morning at ten," he told me.

"Great," I said, thoroughly excited by this turn of events. "I'll be there."

The next morning I arrived at ten o'clock sharp and waited the obligatory thirty minutes for Antonio. Even after all these months of living in Cuzco I was still on time for appointments, but I had come to accept that Peruvians probably would not be. It was a beautiful morning, and after Antonio arrived we walked and talked through the San Pedro marketplace and down a long dirt road that followed the railroad tracks out of town. We headed toward the northwest corner of the city, into a very poor section where the buildings were made of mud bricks, with straw for roofs. We saw several dead animals along the tracks. Life was very raw here, and death was not hidden.

As we walked, Antonio explained to me that the *apus* performed healings and astral operations and were consulted on the whereabouts of lost belongings. "Even the doctors from the hospitals in Cuzco send their patients to be healed by the *apus* when they can't do any more for them," he told me.

"So who performs the operations?" I asked, somewhat familiar with at least the concept of psychic surgery. "Does someone channel the *apus*?"

"No," replied Antonio. "Ricardo the *altomisayoq*—the Andean priest—*calls* them. He is known as one who can *call* the *apus*." Antonio told me the *apus* knew everything and that they were really more like angels. I was baffled. I began to feel more and more intimidated. What did he mean by "call"? Was I going to meet angels? What would I say to them?

We finally left the railroad tracks and climbed up a long crumbling cement stairway to a small scarred wooden door at which Antonio stopped. He knocked twice, paused, and knocked three more times in rapid succession. Immediately the door opened and we had to crouch to step through the doorway and into the muddy courtyard, which was surrounded by a barbed-wire fence. The strong smell of animal dung wafted into our nostrils, and a number of pigs and chickens ran loose. We walked in the direction of the six or seven native Indians, sunburnt cheeks and dark leathery hands and feet, who lounged on benches outside a small building in the hot morning sun.

Obviously, these people were not expecting to see a gringa on their turf. They all stared at me, some with curiosity, some with animosity. I barely knew Spanish and I didn't speak a word of Quechua, the dominant language in this small corner of the world. One of the benches was unoccupied, and Antonio gestured for me to sit down. We waited uncomfortably outside, until the doors of the small building opened, and Antonio motioned for me to follow him in.

We ducked our heads to enter a small square room made of mud bricks with a corrugated tin roof and a dirt floor. In the far corner of the room, a small dark man with shining black eyes sat on a chair, surrounded by Quechuan women wearing traditional multi-petticoated skirts and long black braids. The women had removed their tall stovepipe hats to enter the inner chamber, where this priest held his *mesa*, or healing ceremony. Ricardo himself was clearly Indian. He had a kind face, with a ruddy complexion, short blue-black hair, and a classically hooked Inka nose. He appeared to be in his late thirties, which seemed young for what I supposed him to be, some kind of medicine man.

"Ricardo is an Andean priest, at the fourth rung of the third level. That is the highest-ranking priest of the area," Antonio told me in a whisper. It sounded like an impressive credential, but I hadn't a clue what it meant.

When the crowd of people began to clear around Ricardo, Antonio took my hand and pulled me toward the man in the chair. As we got closer I could see that, like most Peruvian Indians, he wore a frayed pair of corduroy pants and an old polyester warm-up jacket, but his eyes danced with a quick aliveness, like the eyes of a bird.

As we moved through the crowd of people who were exiting the small room, the hair raised on the back of my neck as once again I sensed fear, animosity. I became increasingly aware of my bright white Nike tennis shoes, clean Northface down vest, new Levi's, and Ray·Ban sunglasses; my skin seemed to glow white. I felt excruciatingly North American. I could sense envy for my apparent wealth and that odd admixture of curiosity, disdain, and admiration that many Peruvians feel toward North Americans. I had only recently learned that I was *North* American, not simply American. "South Americans are Americans too," my Peruvian friends let me know.

This was probably my first palpable experience of being a minority, a white minority, in a majority of indigenous people. The sense that I or what I represented to these people was hated and feared was extremely distressing to someone so emotionally thin-skinned as I was. *What the hell am I doing here anyway?* I thought to myself. Part of me wanted to turn and run out of the room.

Antonio extended my hand toward Ricardo. For a moment I saw Ricardo surrounded by a dark yellow mist, but when I blinked my eyes, the mist was gone. We shook hands. Antonio flushed, embarrassed at not having had the time to alert his teacher to the fact that he was bringing a gringa to the *mesa*. But Ricardo accepted everything in a state of complete calm. He welcomed me with a shy, almost childlike smile, brushing aside Antonio's hurried explanations, and gestured for us to sit down while he got on with his preparations for the ceremony.

The room was small, about ten by twelve feet, with uneven crumbling walls that were painted an off-green color. I looked down at a dirt floor. The roof, made of rusty corrugated tin, looked as if it barely kept out the rain. The scent of clean earth was refreshing after the strong animal smells of the courtyard. Ricardo stood in front of a long rectangular table that appeared to be some sort of an altar.

On a white cloth in the center of the table lay several large quartz crystals, some paper bundles, a bell, a leather whip, and a bottle opener. I eyed the whip fearfully. Lined up along the back edge of the table, against the wall, were bottles of soda and Peruvian beer. A large wooden cross hung above the table. As I looked around the room I noticed there was either an icon of Jesus or a cross on each of the four walls.

About thirty people sat on the rough wooden benches that surrounded the altar table on three sides. Mixed into the crowd of Indians in more traditional clothing were six or seven Mestizos. Although their faces looked Indian, their clothing—mostly jeans and T-shirts—was more Western. This must be the "group" Antonio had told me about. We settled on a bench to the left of the altar. I was glued to Antonio, feeling extremely vulnerable and unwelcome by everyone except Ricardo. I had no idea what was going to happen next. I had been nervous because I barely spoke Spanish. Now I realized that not even Spanish was going to help me here, where only Quechua was spoken. I was completely dependent on Antonio for translation.

When Ricardo finished his preparations at the altar, the room suddenly became silent. A tall, dignified Peruvian man motioned stragglers into the room and closed the doors. A burly man with a black mustache began hanging heavy alpaca blankets over the small dirty window and the double doors. Another man pulled over a stool and, climbing on top of it, began to loosen the lightbulb. I gulped. Whatever was to happen, it was going to take place in total darkness. I elbowed Antonio furiously. "What's going on? Why are they making it dark?"

"Quiet," Antonio commanded in a whisper.

Ricardo was seated in a chair to the right of the altar. He spoke to the crowd in Quechua and there was immediate silence. Another sentence in Quechua, and he seemed to be asking if everyone was ready. When the silence affirmed his answer, he nodded to the man holding the lightbulb. With a final twist of the bulb, the room was plunged into total darkness.

Ricardo immediately began intoning a rapid-fire prayer in Quechua. I understood nothing. He prayed three times and then whistled three long notes, as if he were calling something. The group sat silently. It was only then that I realized we were waiting. But for what?

We waited several more minutes, and again Ricardo spoke into the darkness. Antonio whispered to me that Ricardo was asking the group for help. They began reciting the Our Father in Spanish, and then, also in Spanish, Ricardo asked permission to make the "opening of Jesus Christ." I extended all my senses into the darkness, trying desperately to perceive what was going on.

Suddenly a noise like a small explosion came from above. The flapping of large wings stirred the air of the enclosed room; I could feel the breeze. Something seemed to fly rapidly across the room and land with a loud thud on the altar table.

"*Muy buenos días, Señor Pampahuallya de Abancay Prima,* at your service," pronounced a young male, almost falsetto, voice from the center of the altar. This was strange. How could Pampahuallya, a mountain terrain outside Cuzco, be "at my service"? As I heard the voice, an odd image appeared in my mind. I saw the body of a large bird, but somehow the head and face had human characteristics, like some long-lost mythological creature.

"*Ave Maria Purísima,*" the people in the room replied simultaneously.

"*Sin pecado concebida,*" responded the voice. It sounded like a phrase from a Catholic mass. Small footsteps, walking back and forth across the altar table, sounded throughout the silent room. The voice seemed to belong to the footsteps.

"A very good morning to you," said the voice again, and I heard the sound of someone, or some*thing,* opening a bottle. "To your health!" came the voice from the table, and then came the sound of a carbonated liquid being poured onto the earth in front of the altar.

"To your health, *Papito,*" replied the group. When we first came into the room, I had noticed a circular depression in the dirt floor, just in front of the altar, and I assumed now that the drink was being poured into this depression.

"Antonio," spoke the high tenor voice, as the footsteps sounded nearer to our side of the table.

"*Ave María Purísima,*" replied Antonio obediently. It seemed to be some greeting of respect and I was angry that Antonio had not informed me of the proper way to address the *apus* before we arrived— if these were indeed the *apus.* My mind was racing. Could Ricardo be faking all this?

"Approach the table," said Señor Pampahuallya. Antonio stood up and walked closer to the altar.

"Yes, Father," he said, addressing the being in the darkness.

"You have brought a guest . . . Elizabeth." My heart froze as the being on the table spoke my name. "This is very good, Antonio. We are happy she is here," the voice continued.

"Thank you, Father. She is a psychologist from North America, here to visit you," Antonio said in simple Spanish, so that I could understand.

"Daughter Elizabeth . . ." the high-pitched voice came again.

My throat stopped up and I strangled out the greeting. *"Ave María Purísima."*

"Very good, daughter, very good. Approach the table," came the command in Spanish. I understood, but I hesitated, feeling shy and afraid.

Just at that moment, there was another explosive sound from above, followed by the same flapping of wings and a loud thud. Something else landed on the table and announced itself. *"Muy buenos días,"* came a deep basso, gravelly voice that I found rather frightening. "Señor Sollacasa, at your service." Once again, everyone greeted the newly arrived deity, and then the two creatures on the table set about discussing something in Quechua.

"Daughter Elizabeth, we are glad you are here. What can we do for you?" the high-pitched voice asked me. I was tongue-tied, stymied, and I wanted to crawl into a hole.

"Antonio, tell them I am feeling very shy, that my Spanish isn't very good, but I am very honored to be here and I want to ask their permission to live and work here." Antonio grunted his assent and translated for me. Contrary to my nature, a tremendous fear and awe had left me stuttering.

"Aha, permission," the deeper voice said. "For this we need to call Señor Potosí from Bolivia. He can give permission. But it takes him a while to get here because he has to come all the way from Bolivia. In the meantime, do you want to call your *santa tierra*?"

Antonio translated for me but still I didn't understand. Perplexed by my ignorance, Antonio finally asked me, "Where do you live?"

In my anxiety, I mistakenly answered, "Mariscal Gamara." This was actually the neighborhood I had just moved from to stay at Señora Clemencia's house. I didn't know the name the local people gave to my new neighborhood. It didn't seem to be a problem.

"*La Mamita Mariscal Gamara, Papitos,*" Antonio told them.

One of the creatures on the table picked up the bell and rang it, calling out loud, "*Mamita Mariscal Gamara, Mamita Mariscal Gamara.*"

There was a pause, and then the two creatures seemed to forget about me and began asking Ricardo about the business of the day. There were many pleas for help and healing, and many more *santa tierras* were called to the altar table, with the same ringing of the bell.

I slowly began to understand that a *santa tierra* was the earth spirit of the street on which a person lived. In this ceremony the *santa tierra*, or holy earth spirit, was called upon to answer any personal questions or resolve any problems of the families that lived on that particular street. Each *santa tierra* seemed to have jurisdiction over her street. I imagined the *santa tierras* were only part of an elaborate hierarchy of earth spirits. I was fascinated. Finally, the bell was rung and Señor Potosí was also called to the table.

This time, a smaller explosion sounded from the dirt floor in front of the altar, and the flapping wings rose up from the earth. There was a softer thud on the table, and a very high-pitched female voice that spoke only Quechua announced herself as the *santa tierra* of Mariscal Gamara.

Again Antonio translated for me. "The *santa tierra* of Mariscal Gamara says that you are a strong person and you have strong sight. You also know telepathy, and you saw the *apus* on the street, but didn't recognize them." I felt flattered and special, but totally confused. What did they mean, I had strong sight? Clairvoyance? My mind was racing. What does one say to nonphysical creatures that materialize in a dark room? Antonio continued, "*La Mamita* says you are strong, but you need more power. They are going to give you more power."

I wanted to scream "Wait! Stop! I don't understand what's happening!" Not knowing what else to do, I became extremely polite.

"Tell them I am asking permission to live and work here," I told Antonio, feeling the need to assert some control over this crazy experience. I was reeling. Somehow these beings were saying that I was important. The fact that they had addressed me at all came as a complete surprise.

"They have to wait for Señor Potosí to get permission," Antonio reminded me.

The beings spoke in almost pure Quechua and they had many people to attend to. I was grateful when the focus of attention was off me and they began once again to attend to others in the room.

There were many requests for help from the *santa tierras*. One woman had lost her wheelbarrow and wanted to know if they could help her find it. Another woman asked for her six-year-old son to be cured of his fever. The *apus* promised to visit the boy and take his fever away. A man who asked for help with his cancer was invited up before the altar table to be blessed by the *apus*.

Soon another very loud explosion came from the ceiling and a flapping of what seemed like huge wings as an *apu* that was bigger and heavier than the others landed on the table. A gentle voice spoke into the silence. It came from higher up, as if this *apu* were taller. "Señor Potosí of Bolivia, at your service."

The room responded with the customary greeting: *"Ave María Purísima."* With the arrival of Señor Potosí, the atmosphere in the room changed and everyone seemed to soften. He was clearly in charge.

He spoke to a woman who was receiving a healing at the table, saying in Spanish, "I am an angel, don't be afraid of me."

As the *apus* responded to the different problems and illnesses, Antonio's colleagues, the university professors, busily wrote down the herbal recipes that were dictated by the *apus*. I could hear their pens scratching in the darkness.

As time passed I hoped that I had been forgotten. My heart was pounding, my mind was going crazy searching for explanations. I was certain this was some sort of hoax, but I was unable to explain how they could fake something so elaborate. They would have needed very high-tech equipment in a country with almost no-tech.

"Daughter Elizabeth," the voice of Señor Potosí suddenly addressed me, breaking the wave of my rampaging thoughts.

"*Sí, Papito,*" I addressed him as I heard all the others respond, trying to follow the protocol.

"We are very glad you are here," Antonio translated. "You have permission to work and live here. Your work is good, but you need more power," continued Señor Potosí of Bolivia.

What did they mean by I "need more power"? I wondered, feeling a little insulted. "Do you know who we are?" Señor Potosí asked me.

"No, *Papito,*" I honestly replied.

"We are the mountain range seraphim angels of God," Antonio translated. Somehow when this *apu* spoke I felt better, more reassured. He seemed kind and gentle, instead of scary or pompous, the way the other two struck me. I felt embarrassed by my thoughts; did they know what I was thinking about them? On cue, Señor Potosí spoke, "We know you don't believe in us yet, but you will. You think we are some kind of trick. We are not. Come, approach the table. We will give you more power," he commanded.

Just as I began to wonder if I wanted more power, the people around me started shoving me toward the table. This was apparently a real honor, perhaps something they all wanted for themselves, but it was happening to me. Did I want this? I had no time to make a choice. I was already standing in front of the altar.

For the past ten minutes or so I had noticed a strange scratching sound coming from the altar, like pieces of glass being rubbed together. The only objects on the altar that could produce that sound were the crystals. When I first heard it I had imagined that one of these "bird people" had picked up one of the crystals in its claw and was worriedly rubbing it against the other, like a sort of nervous habit. The rubbing sound stopped.

"Look at the table," commanded Señor Potosí. I looked toward the voice. Suddenly there was a loud crack and a blue flash of light, as if two stones had been struck together with a great force. The crystals? I waited to see if I felt something. I felt nothing, but the flash of light in the darkness and the sound had made an impact.

Again Señor Potosí spoke to me. "Now, daughter, we have given you more power. You have permission to work with our group, in fact you must work with our group," the *apu* told me.

"*Gracias, Papito,*" I replied, not knowing what else to say. "But I am returning to the States tomorrow," I continued, feeling that if I was getting a job I should at least let them know about my availability.

"Very good," he replied. "When you get to the United States, send our regards to the North American *apu*s. Go to the highest mountain in the West, near where the president lives, and offer prayers. But before you ask for anything from the *apu*s, offer a Cuzqueña [a Peruvian beer made in Cuzco] with our regards. Then take pictures of the highest mountains. The *apu*s will appear in the pictures."

I didn't know what to say. "Thank you, *Papito*, thank you for everything."

The ceremony ended as each earth spirit saluted the group with its name and exited in a flapping of wings. The *santa tierras* flew down into the earth, and the *apu*s flew up into the roof. During the ceremony, the altar must have held at least eight or ten *apu*s at any given time. The last one to go was Señor Potosí. "*Señor Potosí, ciao,*" he said, and the wind from his large wings filled the room as he exited through the ceiling.

"Open the doors," the tall man commanded. The blankets were removed and the doors were flung open. Fresh air and morning sun came streaming in. I was never, in all my life, so happy to see the light of day.

I grabbed Antonio by the arm and pulled him aside, whispering furiously, "Okay, now you and I are going to have a long, long lunch and you are going to explain *all* of this to me. Right?"

Antonio looked at me and laughed. "Calm down," he told me. When he noticed my expression had not changed he added, "Okay, okay, you may take me to lunch."

Antonio kept laughing at my seriousness, then he pointed to the crowd: all the previously hostile faces were now smiling and beaming at me. Apparently the *apus* had shown me a very favorable response and this seemed to grant me immediate acceptance into the community. "I didn't know it was this important, but I had a feeling," Antonio told me.

I eyed him suspiciously. "Antonio, will you please stop being so cryptic? Just exactly what do you mean?" I asked. The events of the last hour had scared me down to my bones and I was reacting angrily out of fear and shock.

"I'll explain at lunch. But first we must go and pay our respects to Ricardo."

Okay, here it comes, I thought. During my three months in Peru I had already experienced instances in which people tried to "get money out of the gringa." As a natural reaction, I had become rather cynical. Peru was a very poor country, and I, although a "starving student" in my own country, undoubtedly seemed rich to Peruvians. And by their standards, I was. I paid about forty dollars a month for room and board. I could afford to stay on in Cuzco for a while, where an excellent three-course meal cost about fifty cents. But now I was certain this was where the sting of the operation was going to come in; Ricardo was going to ask me for a lot of money to participate in his group. I braced myself.

Ricardo shook my hand and smiled at me. "It seems the *apus* are in favor of our Elizabeth," Antonio said, winking at Ricardo.

Ricardo only laughed. "No accounting for taste," he kidded. "Come back and see us when you return from the United States," he told me. "You are welcome anytime."

"Thank you . . . er . . . *gracias,*" I said, still too dumbfounded to find words. He never mentioned money.

"OKAY, ANTONIO, NOW YOU ARE GOING TO EXPLAIN TO ME exactly what that was all about," I demanded, as we sat across from each other at a small local restaurant. I was still in shock. A chicken walked around under our feet, pecking at scraps that had fallen onto the dirt floor.

"A few months ago . . ." he began, but his voice trailed off. Antonio appeared to be overcome with emotion. He began again, slowly, "the *apus* told us that a psychologist from North America would be coming to join our group. Naturally we assumed it was going to be man. Then you showed up," he said, his serious countenance breaking into a sunny smile. "For some reason I had a strong need to speak with you at the IPNAC only last week, even though I had seen you there for months. Then you told me about your experience with the *apus.*" He left a few moments of silence, waiting for me to catch on.

"Yeah? So?"

"Don't you see the significance of the events?" Antonio asked earnestly. "When I first met you, hearing you were a psychologist, I wondered, but I never spoke to you until last week, until after you had had your own experience." My heart started to beat faster as I realized that this was connecting to the sense of mission I had had when I was first drawn to come to Peru.

"Why did they think this person was coming?" I asked.

"When the *apus* told us of the North American, they said that together with this person the group would be given the power to call the *apus.* This has never happened before in the history of the tradition," he said. "I wasn't sure at first, but now, because of the way the *apus* responded to you, I am sure. That North American is you!"

I gasped. I felt flattered and humble, almost embarrassed. "But Antonio, what can *I* do? Why me?"

"The *apus* work mysteriously, in ways that are hard even for us Peruvians to understand," he replied. "But you should know this: Many people come here looking for the *apus*, but few find them. If your heart tells you to work with us, then do it. You are free to decide."

"Something else you should know," he said, pausing briefly for the impact. "Some of the high priests have painted pictures of the *apus.* They have the bodies of condors . . . but with human heads." I started.

"Antonio, this is what I saw in my mind's eye, when the *apus* materialized!"

He smiled at me, "Then why do you ask *me* why it is *you* they choose? I have been working at the *mesa* for one year, and I have never seen such a thing."

I sat completely bewildered. I felt as though I were in an adventure movie that was actually happening. It was my life!

"Okay," I answered, "in some crazy way this all fits together. But I can't pretend to understand it. Antonio, if I was asking the *apu's* permission to work here in Cuzco, then why did they call a Bolivian mountain spirit?"

"Ah," Antonio answered thoughtfully, "that is an interesting thing. The Andean priests do not work in your modern geography. They cling to an older identity and an older geography, one that perhaps corresponds more closely with the Inka empire, or with the hierarchy of nature herself . . . I am not sure. But one thing is certain, each priest must work with the permission of his head *apu*, and for Ricardo that is Señor Potosí.

"Elizabeth, you are leaving tomorrow, yes?" Antonio asked. I nodded. "The *apus* have given something to the group. It is an Inkan artifact, what you would call a 'power object.'" I was intrigued and urged him to go on. "It is a stone plate of unusual properties. It's kept in a place not far from here. I would like you to see it."

I felt like a child who had gone out in the rain puddle jumping. I was already soaked to the skin in strange experiences, so at this point, what was one more puddle? Besides, if I wanted to work with Antonio and his group I might as well find out more about them, I rationalized.

"All right," I answered, "let's stop there on our way home."

After a short walk, we arrived at a storefront and were invited into the back room. The store, a fabric shop, was owned by the father of one of the group members. Antonio introduced me to three people that I recognized from the *mesa*: Felipe and Maria, a young couple who were both physics professors at the University of Cuzco, and Raul, their longtime friend. "We are glad you could join us, Elizabeth," Felipe said as we greeted each other.

"The *apus* told us where to look to find this," he said as he picked up a heavy-looking object wrapped in a burlap sack. He unwrapped the burlap and produced a large stone plate with two stubby handles. The plate was about two and a half inches high and made of a dark greenish white stone that looked like granite. The inner surface was smooth but the dish was not very deep. In the bottom, at the center of the dish, three white dots formed a triangle.

As I gazed at the dish, I experienced a strange sensation, as if I were falling. I was immediately moved to put my hand into the plate. I gasped as my hand disappeared into a cloud of stars. I closed my eyes and reality melted.

The stone plate, circling end over end, breaks free of the earth's atmosphere and is shot into outer space. As it floats free in space, I see its molecules coming apart, rearranging, and coming back together in a new configuration. Something is added. A rarified metal. Gold! The plate begins to spin again and is shot through space and back down to earth.

As I removed my hand from the plate, the world slowly returned to normal. I looked into the expectant faces around me. "What did you see?" Antonio asked me gently.

"The plate, it has something extra . . . transmuted gold," I answered sleepily, not really knowing what I was saying. Felipe, Maria, Raul, and Antonio were nodding their heads. They did not look surprised. In fact, all this seemed like a normal afternoon's activity for them.

"Run your hand over the top of the plate, you can feel the energy," Raul told me. Being careful not to touch it, I passed my hand about a foot above the plate. I could quite clearly feel a surge of energy, warmth, and tingling when my hand passed over the top of the plate. I tried it several times with the same result. At that moment I sensed that this stone plate and I would share a story, and that somehow I would be connected to it in the future.

Antonio and I walked home together in silence. I was looking forward, with relief, to my long plane ride tomorrow. I had a lot to think about.

3

Ritual at Ojai

I STARED AT THE MOUNTAIN PEAKS OUT THE WINDOW OF the airplane, tears streaming down my face, grateful that I had a whole row of seats to myself. I felt like a baby leaving its mother. Of the many places I had lived in my adult life, including the home where I grew up in Minnesota, I had never once cried in leaving. For people I had wept, but a place, a land? Never.

That was all changed now, but many things had now changed. After I recovered from the initial shock of my meeting with the *apus*, the significance of this event hit me. There *is* an invisible world! I knew it! My child self had always known it, but now I had a real experience. I had proof! Providing, of course, that the *apus* were not a trick.

But if the events at the *mesa* had not been a trick, then the *apus* were real. This called for a serious revision of my worldview; from one in which the "spirit world" was a tantalizing possibility to one in which it became an actual fact. Had I just witnessed a doorway to this other world being opened and closed? Could this be what Ricardo meant by the "opening of Jesus Christ"? The *apus* came from somewhere and went somewhere. But where? A whole new world had suddenly opened up for me, a world that included magic, and this made going back to the States, the land of the mundane, all the more painful.

In leaving Cuzco, I left the only place on earth where my soul had ever felt completely at home. I let the tears flow freely. In Cuzco, the inner and outer worlds had come together for me, and I knew that my guts and my heart, my very flesh, belonged to this part of the earth. Although it was painful to be torn away, I knew beyond all doubt that I would be back. It was my trip to the States that was a vacation from my new home. I dried my eyes and stared out at the mountains feeling the visceral contact with the land. In my mind's eye, it seemed I could see three creatures waving good-bye. The *apus*?

"Fasten your seat belts, please. Flight attendants, prepare for takeoff," ordered the captain over the airplane loudspeaker. I looked down to fasten my seat belt and gasped in surprise. Three silver spinning disks floated a few inches out in front of me, one in front of my heart, one at my belly, and one at my genitals. The thought came to me plainly, *These are the energy centers of my body.* I wondered if the blast of energy I had received from the *apus* to "give me more power" was responsible for this effect, somehow opening my subtle vision.

The flight attendant came by and put my seat into the upright position. I looked down again and saw only my wrinkled white shirt, the edges of my new Peruvian wool vest, and the top of my pants. My ordinary vision was back, but was this momentary glimpse of the energy world a harbinger of what was to come in the States? I had assumed that because I was leaving Peru, the strange experiences would stop. Now I wasn't so sure.

I HAD BEEN BACK IN SAN FRANCISCO FOR TWO WEEKS AND was still catching up with old friends when Rusa called, inviting me out to Greengulch Farm for tea.

My first priority on returning to California had been to find a job that could make me some good money over the summer, so that

I could return to Peru to pursue my research on healing with the *apus*. I had had some interviews, but no job offers yet. The *apus* had told me to speak freely about them, so I arranged to give a free lecture at my graduate school. It was exciting to imagine speaking publicly about my experiences. But first I needed to tell my friends privately. I needed support from the most levelheaded people I knew. Rusa, a doctoral student in clinical psychology, was one of them.

I had known Rusa for more than five years. We studied together in graduate school, but she had gone on to complete her doctorate. I respected her perseverance. Rusa, a petite and exquisitely graceful Chinese woman, was extremely intelligent and had a will of iron. This tiny woman swam almost every day in San Francisco Bay, saying "a mantra for the sharks." Both she and her husband, Reb, were long-time practitioners of Zen meditation. During graduate school I had lived with them for a year and taken care of their daughter, Thea.

Over tea I told Rusa my story and then waited anxiously for her reaction. "If that is what you tell me happened, Lizzie, even though it sounds wild, then I know that is what happened." Her simple honesty and deep belief in me were relieving, to say the least.

A moment later, the phone rang. Rusa got up to answer it, and I wandered into her husband's library and began idly surveying the books on the shelf. One book in particular stood out from the rest. It almost seemed to glow or pulsate. Strangely magnetized, I reached up, pulled it off the shelf, and looked at the cover. *Parzival: A Romance of the Middle Ages*, by Wolfram von Eschenbach. It was published by Random House in 1961. I opened the book randomly and read:

10. The Grail

... this second treasure was a platter (Welsh: *dyscyl*): "whatever food one wished thereon was instantly obtained." The word *dyscyl* was, as has been mentioned, the semantic equivalent of Old French *graal*, and around 1240 the Helinandus defined *graal* as "a broad and slightly deep dish" ... thus a semantic blunder led ultimately to the creation of the supremely poetic symbol of the Middle Ages, the Holy Grail.

The book went on to say that the *dyscyl*, or platter, was not made of metal, but rather that it was probably fashioned out of stone. A broad and slightly deep dish fashioned out of stone! Immediately my mind leapt to the stone dish, or "cosmic plate," that Antonio had shown me before leaving Peru. Why had I turned to this page? Could the cosmic plate *be* the Holy Grail? "No!" my rational mind shouted. "This is beyond absurd!"

My stomach was trembling and once again, I felt that uncanny sensation of destiny, as if I had been doused with a bucket of cold water, but from the inside out. Goose bumps stood out thick on my upper arms. Certain that I must be suffering a severe attack of psychological grandiosity, I kept my mouth shut, telling no one about the experience.

Shortly thereafter I received a phone call from my very dear friend Jennifer, and we made plans to get together for dinner. We decided to meet at a restaurant in Noe Valley to exchange stories over a good meal. I arrived early and sat down at a more secluded table, so we could have some privacy. Jennifer was one of the few people I knew I could speak with freely about my more unusual spiritual experiences, because she had had a few of them herself.

I thoughtfully chewed on warm buttered bread, wondering how I was going to explain what had been happening to me, when Jennifer appeared. "Hi, there!" she spouted cheerily. I looked up at my dear friend, a beautiful woman, dressed from head to toe in black, making her rich golden mane shine even more brightly. "Ha! Look at us," she said, "You, all in white, and me, all in black. Well, I suppose this is going to be an important meeting." I only then realized that I was indeed dressed in pure white: the jumpsuit my mother had given me the summer before. I hadn't worn white for eight months; in Peru, no traveler would.

"How are you?" I asked, giving her a bear hug. We sat down.

"I'm well. And I can see you've been having some adventures," she said, looking deeply into my eyes. She had always had a facility for reading me, and I depended on her for it. This, along with our mutual interest in the spiritual, had bonded us together as friends long ago, soul friends. "I want you to tell me everything, but first, let's order." Jennifer's practicality put me at ease.

We ordered, and I quickly began to unfold the tale, starting with my visit to the egg doctor and ending with the ceremony in the dark, and the *apus*. "I just don't know what to think, Jennifer. You know, I feel like I've stumbled into something really important, but I just don't have all the pieces yet."

I could feel Jennifer listening very intently, her eyes locked onto mine. Just as I finished speaking a strange sensation overcame me. I felt my awareness shifting. The restaurant became suddenly remote, unreal. My heart began to beat quickly and a throbbing sensation ran through my heart and down my right arm, as if a flow of energetic force were passing through me and collecting in the palm of my right hand.

Spontaneously, I raised my right hand and held it out toward Jennifer, palm facing her, fingers pointing up. Instinctively she raised her left hand to meet mine, but suddenly self-conscious, put it down again. "Yes, yes!" I said, encouragingly, "I think this is for you!"

Unsure of what we were doing, we tentatively put our palms together. Immediately, magnetic force began to pump through my hand into hers. I had never felt anything like it. I looked up at Jennifer and in an instant her face and hair, that fabulous hair, melted into pure light. I gasped, blinking at the radiance. Jennifer's head had suddenly been replaced by a thousand-watt lightbulb. My whole being shuddered with the bliss of this contact. It was sensual *and* spiritual, a kind of energetic ecstasy.

By some act of heaven, time and space had disappeared and all at once I was able to behold the great luminosity that *was* Jennifer. Her soul was revealing itself to me. My eyes welled up with tears. I blinked and the light dimmed just enough so that I could see the outline of her facial features. In that moment, I became aware that that blinding light was the *real* Jennifer, and her face was simply a limited projection of that brilliance. Against that light, her face now looked like a cartoon, a caricature. I could see lines of pain etched there, a deep sorrow.

All at once, I understood. She had forgotten. Tremendous alarm ran through me and it seemed I had to travel across a great distance to reach to her. "Jennifer," I urged her passionately, "Remember . . . remember. You *must* remember who you *are!*"

Precisely what I said and for how long I spoke, I cannot say. My soul spoke to hers, repeating the same urgent message. Then, from my strange perspective, her head seemed to divide and a fountain of sorrow gushed forth, covering the world in tears and weeping. It was the sorrow of forgetting.

Just as suddenly as the vision had begun, it was over. We let go of our hands. "Did you want anything else?" the waitress asked, suddenly able to approach the table. The restaurant quickly regained its normal appearance.

"No, thanks," Jennifer said with her practiced nonchalance.

After a long silence, I spoke. "Jennifer . . . what *was* that?"

She looked thoughtful for several minutes. "You were *seeing* me," she said simply. "Thank you."

THUS BEGAN MY CAREER AS A PSYCHIC, A CAREER THAT would last throughout the summer, and earn me the money I needed to return to Peru. Shortly after my dinner with Jennifer, I met a psychic reader who told me that I was very psychically gifted and offered to teach me to do readings. For the next two months I worked almost full-time, in a city full of psychics, sometimes giving up to six readings a day. In a short time I had miraculously gathered together enough money to fund the next leg of my research. There was just one thing left to do. I had to complete the mission given to me by the *apus.*

We bulleted past the other cars on the freeway in Claudia's new red Honda. We were in a hurry. We had a date with a mountain spirit. Since I had returned to the States, I had been trying to decipher the message of the *apus.* Señor Potosí had said that I must perform a ritual at the foot of a mountain in the West near where the president lives. "But the president lives in the East, in the White House," my logic argued.

It took another old school friend to make the connection for me. I was having tea with him, relating this mystery about the mountains and the president, when suddenly he looked at me and said, "Ojai." The word popped out of his mouth as if it had been under pressure, then it rang like a bell in my head. "They mean Ojai. That's near Reagan's ranch," my friend insisted.

"But he's not the president," I protested.

"Once a president, always a president," my friend said, winking at me.

Much more than his logic, it was the effect the word "Ojai" had had as it shot out of his mouth like an arrow and landed deep inside my body. My mind may have doubted, but my body was absolutely convinced—this was the place. Further confirmation came later, when I telephoned my friend Cyntha in Detroit immediately on arriving home. Within two hours she had arranged for her friend Claudia, a beautiful young Argentinean woman who lived in San Francisco, to drive me to Ojai. She had even arranged a place for us to stay overnight in Ojai, with a woman who was very much in support of rituals. It was green lights all the way!

Because Cyntha had negotiated my introduction to shamanism in the first place, when she had dragged me to one of the shaman's all-night healing ceremonies in the coastal town of Moche, she had now become my confidante in shamanic adventure. Our phone bills were outrageous. With my arrival to Peru, Cyntha completed her study in Peru before destiny called her on to live in Europe. It was pure luck really that she happened to be visiting her family in Detroit at the same time I was in California. But not even Cyntha could explain the strange *apu* phenomenon.

"If the *apus* are angels," Cyntha had asked me during our phone conversation, "then why do they need you to do a ceremony in order for them to talk to the North American *apus*?"

"Good question," I had answered. "I think that maybe they are a kind of 'earth angel,' and perhaps they are relegated to certain areas, but that still doesn't explain why they couldn't communicate with one another. Unless—"

"Unless they were estranged," Cyntha finished my sentence with a tone of certainty. Again, the information registered a bull's eye on the truth target inside of me.

This was a unique but exciting way to move through the world. I was having to deal with events and situations about which there was no way to objectively confirm their truth. I *had* to rely on my intuitive body-sense of truth in order to act. I had been taught all my life to use my rational mind, to think and reason out situations and act by logic. In this new world of the soul, logic had little power. Or should I say logic was not primary as it always had been in the past. I was moving and responding to some larger, organic structure, a universal order in which logic and linear thinking played only a small part.

But logic still had a powerful hold on me. I was trapped in my own cage of rationality, and as I strained against those bars, they bent and buckled as they began to break open. It was at once terrifying and exhilarating to be free. However fearful, I knew there was another world beyond the cage, and, greedily, I wanted it.

To live in this new world, I had to be receptive, attentive to my inner body sensations, and use these as my guiding force. I could no longer rely on the outer world, the dictates of culture, society, or even my own logical or psychological interpretations. All that was suspended until further notice. I was following the undulating, sensate, organic urging coming from within. It made me unbelievably happy . . . to pay attention to and follow this subtle inner urging rather than overriding it with logic as I had always done in the past. There was something deeply feminine about this way of being.

After seven hours of driving we arrived in Ojai and found a map and key to our overnight lodging waiting for us, all arranged by Cyntha in advance. As we drove to our accommodations Claudia laughed, shaking her head. "You and Cyntha are the witchiest witches I know. It's amazing how you get things to work out for you. I'm hoping some of it is going to rub off on me. That's why I came with you, you know."

"Don't worry, Claudia, you've got plenty of witch in you. And don't forget, you are the official photographer for this expedition," I reminded her. The *apus* had said to photograph the mountains during the ritual and that the North American *apus* would appear in the pictures. If they did appear in the photographs this would be concrete proof of the reality of the *apus*. In Cuzco, Antonio had told me the *apus* appear in pictures, but that after several months they fade from the photographs, leaving only the background. I wanted to see this for myself.

The next morning we woke up late. My mind, a mishmash of dreams and reality, made it hard for me to awaken fully. It had been a long time since I had slept so soundly. Claudia grabbed my bag as we walked out to the car. "I'll be in charge of this," she said as we packed our gear into the car, "you have other things to carry." We laughed, but she was right.

For this ritual I had collected a number of items: a small Peruvian blanket to use as an altar cloth; two bottles of Cuzqueña, beer from Cuzco that I had smuggled out of the country wrapped in my underwear; Peruvian tobacco from cigarettes called Inkas, and a shell in which to burn sage. I knew that North American Indians offered sage and tobacco during their ceremonies, and because I was now in North America, I figured I had better cover all the bases.

We headed down the main drag of the town, toward a tall peak in the distance. "That must be the sacred mountain of Ojai," Claudia said, pointing to the peak dead ahead of us.

"Yeah, but you can't even really call these mountains," I teased. "The Andes . . . now those are real moun—" I stopped talking in midsentence. Claudia turned to stare at me.

Suddenly an image of the Cuzco Valley had superimposed itself over the landscape I was currently seeing, making me instantly aware that the Ojai Valley was the exact same shape, almost a replica of the Cuzco Valley, only in miniature. The sacred mountain of Ojai occupied the same position as the Andean holy mountain of Ausangate. When I got my tongue back, I told her what I was seeing.

"Good, good," Claudia said. "You're getting tuned in."

"Yes," I answered. "The ritual must take place at exactly ten minutes before two." I was in a kind of trance.

"Perfect," Claudia replied. "That'll give us just enough time to sightsee and then have lunch."

It was about one-thirty by the time we had finished our lunch and taken the long bumpy road that led up to the Ojai Mountain. I wanted to be on time. Claudia parked the car at the gate and we walked into the Ojai Center, passing two octagonal buildings that appeared to be offices. I knew that the Ojai Center had been started on this sacred ground as a place to support shamanic beliefs and traditions and to hold conferences with indigenous people. I thought they would be interested to help with the ritual I had been sent here to perform, but their office had never returned my telephone calls. Quickly I realized I would have to do this one on my own.

"This way," I told Claudia, spotting a small trail that led upward in the direction of the peak. I was following my nose. I needed a site where I could see the peak and still have some privacy. We took the right-hand fork in the road and headed uphill. Tall underbrush covered the ground on both sides of the path, but off to the right of the path, I noticed a small open area. We crashed through the tall underbrush, heading straight toward the tiny meadow. "Perfect," I pronounced, laying down my bundle and surveying the area. It was more or less hidden from the road by the tall brush, yet we had a good view of the mountain.

Not knowing quite what to do next, I opened my bag and began taking out all the items I had gathered together for this moment. "Before you talk to them, offer a Cuzqueña from us," the *apus* had told me. I set out the altar cloth and put the shell in the center and the Peruvian beers along the back edge, as I had observed on Ricardo's altar. Luckily, I hadn't forgotten the bottle opener.

I lit a match and burned some sage, cleansing myself and offering the sweet smoke to the mountain. Next, I opened the bottles of Cuzqueña and poured the first drink onto the ground, offering it to Pachamama, the spirit of the earth. Then I poured some beer onto my fingers, flicking the drops toward the mountains, as I had seen Ricardo do. I took a sip and had Claudia take one. As I worked, I began to slip into a trance.

I lit a cigarette and took the tobacco smoke into my mouth as I made a prayer to the mountain spirits. I blew the smoke to the mountain, to the earth, and to the four directions. I could just barely hear the click of the camera as Claudia snapped shot after shot. I felt my consciousness merge with the mountain.

"I bring you greetings." *(I seemed to be looking down on Ojai Mountain from the peak of Ausangate, and I said the words out loud.) He ... I ... Ausangate ... was a beautiful green-gold shimmering light. She was angry, silent.* "Come, let us forget this ancient quarrel and live in harmony as we once did." *Ausangate Mountain spoke through me. All at once I sensed a need to shift my position. I turned my body facing south, taking on her side. She ... Ojai ... emanated a lovely red-gold color.* "Why should I forgive you?" *She spoke defiantly, and if a mountain could have stamped her foot, she would have. My awareness merged again with Ausangate.* "Because I love you, daughter." *Overwhelming pain and sadness coursed through me. Tears streamed down my face. Suddenly two currents of energy opened—and a rush of green-gold energy enveloped me. The red-gold of the daughter and the green-gold of the father. They merged together in my body. I felt bliss, bliss ... love ... and the rush of energy. ... Two energy fields that belonged together, but had been long parted, were once again reunited.*

All at once, I was thrust back into my own consciousness. I felt the mountain personalities recede from my awareness. Still in a trancelike state, I made the sign of the cross, and I heard myself say, "As it was in the beginning, so shall it be again and unto ages of ages. Amen." I felt like a priest who had just performed a ceremony.

As suddenly as it had begun, it was over. It seemed as if we'd been there for hours. I took a deep breath, and, shaking my head to clear it, I walked over to where Claudia was standing and hugged her, as much to thank her as to feel my own physical body again. Then we gathered up our things and headed back to the car. It was two o'clock. A grand total of ten minutes had passed.

I was exhausted. The ceremony had been intense, powerful, painful; I had felt strong emotions. I psychoanalyzed myself, wondering if my desire to resolve my own anger with my father made me project these feelings onto the mountains, shamelessly anthropomorphizing them.

"Elizabeth," Claudia said, breathless from our walk to the car. "I have to tell you something."

"What?" I answered, suddenly self-conscious. I wondered what she had witnessed.

"The Ojai Mountain, I think it's his daughter. You know, the daughter of the mountain in Cuzco."

"What?" I exclaimed. Claudia had been standing at a respectful distance, at least ten feet away. Could she have heard me muttering?

I took her by the shoulders. "Claudia, this is very important. Did you hear what I was saying?" I asked her.

"No." She looked at me surprised. "I just felt like I was watching a father and daughter talk to each other."

"Yes," I mused, "I actually felt like I was doing family therapy, but with mountains." Could that be the meaning behind the similarity of the shapes? Were there families of mountains? Yet I didn't even know what this family quarrel had been about. It had been resolved purely energetically.

One week after our return from Ojai, I went out to get the mail. There was a letter from Continental Airlines. I had received a free travel voucher, although I could not remember signing up on their mileage program. It read, "Good for one free round-trip ticket anywhere within the continental United States. Must be used before June 16, 1989." This incredible stroke of luck meant that my flight from San Francisco to Miami would be free, and that covered more than half my fare to Peru!

I hadn't planned on returning to Cuzco quite so soon. But as I thought about it I realized that I had already completed everything that I had come back to do. I had made money, renewed contacts with old friends, made new friends, developed a new talent, and completed the task given to me by the *apus*. It was indeed time to return to Cuzco, and this travel voucher only sealed the deal.

4

The Birthday Party

I HAD BEEN BACK IN CUZCO FOUR DAYS BEFORE ANTONIO showed up at my door. "The *apus* want to see you," he said. "They told the group that you are one of their 'special daughters.'"

"Let's go," I said, tying up the laces of my hiking boots. I had been waiting for him, and I hoped his comment meant that I had done well at Ojai.

This time, I was ready to face the *apus*. In fact, I had a list of questions to ask them. Claudia and I had developed the film she shot at Ojai, but not one *apu* appeared, only a strange mark that looked as if it had been made by a tear in the negative. I was disappointed by the photos, but still very excited to begin the next stage of my research.

As we walked, Antonio told me more about the *apus*. "Each *apu* has a different ability. For example, Señor Volcán Misti, a volcanic mountain in Arequipa, he is known as the postman."

"The postman?" I asked, raising an eyebrow.

"Yes. I am told that you can place a letter on the *mesa* of the masters that call on this *apu*, ask *apu* Volcán Misti to deliver it to any-one in Peru, and it will show up in that person's room."

"Incredible," I said, thinking that this mystical mail system was probably much more reliable than the regular Peruvian post.

"Señor Potosí performs astral operations. There is a woman who needs a kidney transplant. She will be at the *mesa* today." I looked at him in surprise. I couldn't imagine how this was going to take place. Antonio laughed at me, saying, "That is only the begin-ning. There are many stories about the abilities of the *apus*. You will learn for yourself. They are very powerful."

Antonio also told me that there had been trouble while I had been away. One of Ricardo's students had stolen the crystals from the altar. Unfortunately, he was a policeman who carried a gun and no one knew how to get the crystals back. "*Los Papitos* say that the crystals are really powers because they have living energy. They say we should call things what they are."

"Do you have a plan to get the crys—I mean the 'powers' back?" I said, wondering if I could help.

"No. We must wait and see what the *apus* command," Antonio told me.

Something about what he said had irked me. Why should the *apus* command them? I had never liked being told what to do by peo-ple, never mind spirits in the dark. I reminded myself that I was here to learn from this unusual situation, not impose my value judgments on it.

We arrived at the *mesa* and were ushered directly in to see Ri-cardo. Ricardo shook my hand and congratulated me. He did not speak, but began preparing the *mesa* for the arrival of the "angels." The other group members gathered around, welcoming me with the Peruvian *beso* and telling me how glad they were that I was back.

I had brought the photos of the Ojai ritual with me. They were still in the print-shop envelope, stuffed inside my down vest, the place I always carried anything of value when in Peru. In my excite-ment, I had forgotten to show them to Antonio. In fact, in all our talking, I had not even mentioned the photos to him.

The blankets were placed over the doors and windows and everyone sat down. I was nervous, tense, and still unsure how I felt about all this. I questioned this phenomenon and at the same time was hoping that I had done my job well. I felt somewhere in between Ralph Nader and Little Bo Peep.

Ricardo intoned his prayer and Señor Pampahuallya and Señor Sollacasa immediately materialized from the ceiling with tremendous force and a rush of wings.

"Daughter Elizabeth," said Señor Pampahuallya. "You are to be congratulated. You have done well. We are proud of you. I want to introduce you to the Mamita Wakaypata, central square of Cuzco."

Suddenly a rush of wind came up from the earth in front of the altar, followed by a loud thud on the altar table. A very high-pitched female voice spoke. "Mamita Wakaypata, main square, Cuzco," she said, as if reporting for duty.

"She only speaks Quechua," Antonio whispered to me.

As she spoke he translated her words. "Four hundred *apu*s are happy with the ceremony you performed, daughter. You made possible communication between *apu*s that have not spoken in many years." I felt my face flush, I was proud and embarrassed. It was such a validation of my experience. "You brought twenty-five North American *apu*s with you. They are attending a conference on the holy mountain, Ausangate."

"Please . . ." I said, my voice trembling with the effort of speech, "I would like to talk to the North American *apu*s. Can you tell them to come to the *mesa*?" I was certain that if I could hear North American *apu*s speak in English, it would give me a clearer understanding of them.

"They will come to speak with you in a few days. They have waited a long time for this day. They send you their greetings and say they are sad to see you crying in your room." I started. No one knew I had been crying. In fact, I always made sure no one could even hear me when, at times, I'd hidden in my room to cry by myself. How could she know?

Everyone was still for a moment, and then another loud explosion came from the ceiling, and Señor Potosí of Bolivia announced his arrival. *"Ave María Purísima,"* intoned the group, greeting the Bolivian mountain deity.

"Daughter Elizabeth," he spoke to me. "We are glad to have you back. But we must get to work."

Antonio translated for me, then explained in a whisper, "They are going to do the kidney transplant." There was a lot of rustling as the sick woman was brought before the altar. They told her to lie down on her stomach, on the altar.

"Daughter Elizabeth," Señor Potosí addressed me again, "your prayers are strong. Take one of the powers and pray for the healing of this woman." Someone shoved a large quartz crystal into my hand and I closed my eyes and began to pray with all my heart. I felt a lovely warm feeling come into me, as was usual when I performed healings. I became filled with feelings of love, and began to extend that love out toward the woman.

Suddenly the Mamita Wakaypata spoke. "Daughter Elizabeth, don't smile when you pray, look serious!" She commanded. Only then did I even realize that an ear-to-ear smile split my face.

I immediately stopped smiling and became more serious. A number of thoughts and feelings ran through me in microseconds. "Oh, no. I've done the wrong thing, and somehow I've offended these beings. But why shouldn't I smile? It's a perfectly natural thing to do when you feel good. Oh, my God, they can see my face in this pitch-black room. That means they really do exist!"

I was standing in front of the altar holding the crystal in both hands. The woman receiving the operation was stretched out on the altar table in front of me. Señor Potosí seemed to be directly across from me, facing me as he hovered over the woman. He was praying out loud and seemed to be sprinkling her with holy water. Some of the droplets landed on me.

"Remember, daughter," he told the woman, "worry kills. Know that you know nothing, and that you are well." He spoke in a very warm but firm voice. A rush of affection for this being filled me. I was growing fond of Señor Potosí. He was by far my favorite *apu.*

"Gracias, Papito, gracias," the woman moaned from her lying position. She was so humble, so vulnerable. Again, my heart went out to her.

"Daughter Elizabeth, come here." Señor Potosí addressed me again.

"He wants you to confirm the operation," Antonio translated.

"How do I do that?" I asked Antonio.

"You must go and put your hand on the wound," he told me.

I moved closer to the table feeling my way in the dark. I heard a sharp inhale of breath as my cold hand found the skin of the woman's back. I felt a large bandage on her back, at about kidney level.

"There!" exclaimed Señor Potosí as my hand touched the bandage. "Now you have witnessed one of our operations, daughter." I returned to my seat on the bench feeling that I wasn't so sure I could say I had "witnessed an operation."

The *apus* attended to the rest of the people at the *mesa*. I remembered Antonio telling me that doctors sent their terminally ill hospital patients to the *apus* when they could do no more for them. He said that in many instances people recovered. I wanted to try to follow the case of the woman with the kidney transplant.

The *mesa* was nearly over. When most of the *apus* had saluted and left the table and only Señor Pampahuallya, Señor Sollacasa, and Señor Potosí remained. Señor Pampahuallya called me back over to the table.

"Daughter Elizabeth," he said, startling me out of my thoughts.

"Sí, Papito," I responded, thoroughly trained by now.

"Did you take pictures of the ritual as we instructed you?" he asked knowingly.

"Yes, *Papito*. I have them here," I replied.

"Approach," he instructed me. I took the photos out of their special hiding place and stumbled closer to the table, toward the voice.

"Give them to me," he ordered. I held the photographs out in the air in front of me. I heard small footsteps approach me from across the table, stopping at the edge. I gasped as the photos were plucked from my hand. There had been a sudden movement, as if a small hand had darted out to grab them from me. I could hear Señor Pampahuallya rapidly flipping through the photos, a sound like tiny hands making rapid and precise movements.

He and the other *apus* were commenting to one another in Quechua. *"Muy bien, muy bien,"* they said. "What were you saying in the photo when you have your hands open toward the little mountain?" he asked. Suddenly I could see the photo in my mind, and I could more or less remember what I had said.

"I was praying for the little mountain to forgive the big one, *Papito,*" I answered.

"Very good, very good, daughter, and in the one in which you are bowing your head?"

In this way the *apus* went through five or six of the photos with me. Again, it was nothing short of miraculous to know that in total darkness these beings could see and exactly describe the scenes in each of the photos. Although a part of me still wanted to believe that these *apu* materializations were some kind of trick, the evidence was quickly mounting up against it. Still, even if they were real, I felt cautious. I was too afraid to ask why the mountain spirits had not appeared in my photos. Although clearly some of the things the *apus* did were good, I didn't know that much about them, and this was all so sudden and alien to me.

On the other hand, I loved the healing aspect of what they were doing and I believed in it. I agreed with what Señor Potosí had told the woman, that a large part of her well-being had to do with her believing she was well. I was very familiar with the idea that our thoughts and beliefs directly affect our bodies and our health. The *apu* seemed to be working with this same principle.

"Muy bien, daughter." Señor Potosí congratulated me on the photos. "Tomorrow you must come to the *mesa.* It is a very special day. It is the birthday of the Mamita Wakaypata. You must bring your viola and sing for us." I assumed he was referring to my guitar. It was

interesting how their vocabulary seemed to be limited in certain areas.

"*Sí, Papito,*" I replied obediently. The *apus* bid us good-bye and departed, with a great flapping of wings.

When we were outside, Ricardo approached me and said, "Elizabeth, how many *apus* would you like to come to the *mesa* tomorrow?"

"I don't know," I said, suddenly shy. "How about thirty," I told him, joking.

"Okay, thirty *apus* will come to the *mesa* tomorrow, but only if you promise to bring your 'viola,'" Ricardo joked back, pointedly making fun of the *apus*.

That night, back in my room, I mused on the recent events. Nothing was black-and-white anymore and there were no simple answers to the questions that ran through my mind like wild horses. This new life I was leading was exciting, but I also found there were drawbacks to my increased sensitivity as well. A few things that had happened back in the States were still plaguing me. For example, after touching the belly of a newly pregnant friend, I knew that she would lose the baby . . . and that the next would be perfectly healthy. What was I to do with such information? Certainly I couldn't say anything to her, I could only try to be near her when she had the miscarriage.

Another precognition happened one day when I was running on the beach. Suddenly the wind grew cold and all the color went out of the world. I was seeing everything in black-and-white. When I looked down, the only color in the world was red. I was running in blood . . . blood up to my ankles. I looked out at the ocean and saw slaughtered bodies and heard the words "many innocent people will die." I knelt down on the ground right there and prayed, weeping and crying out, begging God not to let this happen—not to let what I was seeing happen.

Why? I wondered. Why was I seeing these things if I could do nothing to stop them? A month later I saw the exact same scene on the evening news, the bodies . . . the blood. The reporter was in China saying that at Tiananmen Square many innocent people had died in the student uprising. There were aspects of developing this sensitivity, which I had so longed for, that were absolutely torturous.

Now the *mamita* of the main square of Cuzco was telling me not to smile while I prayed! The *apus'* "astral operation" had seemed quite bogus to me. And there were other things about the *apus* that, quite honestly, gave me the creeps. At the same time the phenomenon was absolutely fascinating. I was walking in a gray and cloudy world where there were no clear or easy answers.

The next day Antonio called for me, so that we could walk together to the *mesa*. "Today," Antonio said, as we walked along the now familiar railroad tracks, "is the Mamita Wakaypata's birthday. She will be two hundred eighty-seven angel years old." He never could explain to me what angel years were in relation to human years. He said there would be a big celebration at the *mesa;* everyone would be there, including the whole "group" and many others who would come to pay their respects to the Mamita Wakaypata. "She is the most powerful of all the *santa tierras* of Cuzco," Antonio told me. He said the *apus* had explained to the group about the birth of an angel, but that no one had really understood how or why they were born. He said it was one of the things the group hoped to study once they were able to get funding and set up a study center.

The group thought I could help them with this. They wanted me to make connections in the States with someone who had money, to donate to this cause. I had actually made a contact. A private individual who was interested in alternative healing. I had only to write a proposal for the project.

I recalled a vision I had had within a week of my first visit to Cuzco. I had seen a white rainbow bridge connecting Cuzco and California, and that many people would be coming to Peru for spiritual initiation. I had felt that somehow I would be instrumental in making it happen. At the same time I was beginning to feel as though this "group" were some secret society that I was slowly being initiated into. I didn't like all the secrecy and I confessed my feelings to Antonio.

"In a way you are right, Elizabeth. Think of it—the Andean people have been very closed about their teachings, and the path has been a closely guarded secret for hundreds of years. You, a gringa, being invited into it . . . well, it is an historical event." His comment made me feel two different things at the same time: on one hand I felt special, privileged, chosen, and this struck me as dangerous. Yet I also felt as though I were under tremendous pressure to do or be something important.

Antonio and I had been sitting on a bench chatting outside the *mesa* for some time, waiting to go in, when a ruckus broke out in the courtyard. We heard angry voices. Raul, one of the group members, was speaking angrily with a young boy of about seven years old. In the rush of Spanish and Quechua voices I couldn't make out what was happening. Antonio had no time to explain before we were all hurried into the ceremonial room.

The *apus* materialized with less force today than on the previous day. The strength with which they materialized seemed to vary—depending on what? I wasn't sure. I was also wondering about the fantastic hunger I had experienced after the ceremony of the day before. "That's because *los papitos* suck a tremendous amount of force from us, in order to materialize." Antonio had explained.

"Why don't they have their own force?" I had asked Antonio, but he didn't know the answer. We resolved to ask them these questions ourselves.

When Ricardo opened the *mesa*, Señor Pampahuallya, Señor Sollacasa, and Señor Potosí materialized rapidly, one right after the other. Again, I felt a heartwarming sensation as Señor Potosí came to the table. I seemed to be developing a crush on him. It was so lovely to think that I was present at a gathering of angels. I felt special, honored to be there and to be allowed to participate in their ceremonies.

Señor Potosí spoke to the little boy, asking him to approach the table. The boy walked up to the altar table, and suddenly I heard the singing and snap of a leather whip as it seemed to be raised in the arm of the *apu* and to fall again and again on the boy. It took me a few moments to realize that this so-called angel was whipping the child, and he seemed to have a very strong arm. I was so shocked that I could not even protest. The beating was nearly over before I had really registered what was happening. What was this? Some archaic Inka custom?

"What the hell is going on?" I whispered furiously to Antonio. I was afraid to interrupt the ceremony, but this definitely struck me as *wrong.*

"The child is Ricardo's son. I'll explain to you later." Emotional conflict erupted inside me. I was here to learn and witness customs that were different from my own, but the whipping of a child was not even remotely spiritual. The explanation was that the child had stolen candy from the pocket of one of the adults at the *mesa*. Still, this explanation didn't sit well with me. I knew that culturally the Indians thought nothing of spousal abuse; they called it *amor serrano*, or "mountain-style love." But I wasn't sure about the extent of what I would term child abuse.

After the beating, the *apus* returned to business as usual, performing the various healings and answering questions for the people who had come for help. I remained shocked by the whipping. I began to question what exactly had occurred; certainly they hadn't done any real physical damage to the child? Was this punishment meant to humiliate the boy? Was there an important lesson in it? Beating a child is not acceptable in the States; in fact, parents can be put in jail for it. I debated the issue in my mind, but no matter how I thought about it, I knew the beating was wrong. Violence does not teach anything but violence.

The *mesa* ended, the doors were flung open, and the next thing that happened was enough to put any other thoughts out of my mind.

During the *mesa*, a number of women had gathered outside. Now they came filing in with plates of food covered in foil. They put six or seven of the steaming dishes down on the altar, along with a tall stack of plates and silverware. The aroma of the freshly cooked food filled the ceremonial room. Next they added more beer to the line of beverages along the back edge of the altar table.

Serving spoons were carefully set down next to the dishes. I was more than surprised when Ricardo instructed his helpers to put the blankets back over the doors and the windows. By now more than fifty people had squeezed into the tiny room. Many crowded the benches, while others stood or squatted on the ground.

Ricardo stood in front of the altar. "Thirty *apus*, right, Elizabeth?" he said, smiling at me. I nodded shyly, embarrassed that he had singled me out of the crowd. When Ricardo had finished his preparations, everyone moved back from the altar. He took his customary seat at the right-hand side of the altar and the lightbulb was unscrewed. Ricardo intoned his prayer and the group joined in with "Jesus" at the end of every sentence.

The *apus* materialized with tremendous force for this second session of the day. "Señor Pampahuallya de Abancay Prima, *buenos días.*"

"Señor Sollacasa, *muy buenos días.*"

"Señor Potosí de Bolivia, at your service."

"Good morning to you, Mamita Wakaypata, Plaza de Armas, Cuzco."

Ricardo rattled off a list of *apus* that were invited to the birthday party, and Señor Potosí called their names, ringing the bell with each one.

"Señor Huaskaran, Señor Ruma Ruma, Señor Qorichaska, Señor Saqsaywaman, Señor Volcán Misti, Apu Huayna Ausangate, Mamita Chachapollas . . ." The list went on and on.

As he continued to call and ring the bell, one by one, the *apus* began to arrive. The male deities came winging down from the ceiling and the female deities came up out of the earth. Each one landed with a tremendous thud and introduced himself before congratulating Mamita Wakaypata on her birthday.

When all the *apus* had arrived, the group members saluted them, and congratulated Mamita Wakaypata on her birthday, thanking her for her help during the past year. Although I had lost track of the names, I knew that at the very least, thirty *apus* had now gathered on the table.

"Serve yourselves," said Ricardo. I heard bottles of beer being popped open in the darkness and poured onto the ground.

"*Salud!*" said the *apus*, one after another.

"*Salud!*" the people answered.

"*Señores,* why don't you eat?" Antonio offered. And with that we heard the sound of the foil being removed from the plates and the clatter of utensils, as food was being served in total darkness.

"*Papitos,*" I began, unable to remain silent. I was bursting with questions to ask them about this curious "birthday party" and anxious to speak to the new *apus* that I had never met before, especially Apu Volcán Misti.

"Shhhhh!" Antonio shushed me. "They are eating!" The room grew silent except for the clinking of plates and silverware in the darkness, and the muffled sounds of chewing.

From where I was standing, very close to the altar, I was sure I could hear or feel the movement of any person near the altar table. But as far as my keen hearing and kinesthetic sense could perceive, not one human being had changed position since the lights went out. The sounds of clinking silverware came from every part of the altar.

"Daughter Elizabeth," came the voice of the Mamita Wakaypata, "serve yourself."

"She is offering you the first plate of food," Antonio told me, "go to the altar and hold out your hand." I did as he instructed, noticing how much noise I made as I stumbled up toward the altar in the darkness. I reached out into the blackness. Immediately a warm plate of food was gracefully placed into my outstretched hand.

"*Gracias, Mamita, gracias,*" I mumbled as I stepped back from the altar.

Plates of food were then handed around to everyone in the utter darkness. After everyone had received their plates and began eating, bottles of beer left the altar table in the same mysterious manner and were passed around the room. Finally, cookies and candies were thrown from all sides of the altar, accompanied by a good deal of laughter from the *apus*.

"Daughter Elizabeth, your viola," said Mamita Wakaypata. "You didn't think we had forgotten, did you?" she said, absolutely reading my mind.

"No, Mamita," I lied, my hopes of escaping now dashed. I sighed and began to unzip my guitar case. Again, I noticed how much noise my movement produced in this tiny room.

"We have heard you singing in your room," she said, and began to hum a lilting tune, imitating me. "Sing for us now."

I brought out my guitar and racked my brain for a song, any song. The one she was humming reminded me of an old Elton John tune and I sang it into the darkness to the mountain range angels.

"The words I have to say may well be simple but they're true. If you don't give your love, there's nothing more that we can do. . . ."

They were a perfect audience, *apus* and humans alike. They listened in silence, and when I finished, they gave me a hearty applause. Mamita Wakaypata spoke to me again and Antonio translated, "She says you have a lot of love inside you and that they are going to look for a husband for you."

"Thank you, Mamita. *Gracias*," I said, quite embarrassed by her last comment. When the "party" was over, the *apus* and *santa tierras* saluted us with their names, and one by one exited the altar table as they had come.

As soon as the doors were opened and light streamed in, I looked immediately down at my plate of food, which I had carefully placed in a corner before picking up my guitar. The plate was perfectly arranged with a *cui*, a fried guinea pig, which is the local delicacy; a lovely salad; and potatoes, all expertly served. My eyes moved to the altar table, where I saw the large serving dishes, their tinfoil covers neatly folded back, and several other plates of food all elegantly served. The *apus'* food was still on their plates, because, as Antonio explained, these mountain spirits consumed only the essence of the food. Not a drop of the food was spilled anywhere. The place was spotless except for some cookies and candies that had been thrown to us by the *apus*, that were still lying on the ground.

5

Pilgrimages of Initiation

AFTER THE "BIRTHDAY PARTY" MY CONFUSION ONLY continued to grow. There were now too many proofs for me to doubt the existence of the *apus*. But were they really angels? A week later, during one of the *mesas*, Señor Sollacasa had asked me how my throat was feeling. His voice was still frightening to me and I wondered why this "angel" had said earlier in the day that men should smoke and drink. At least that's what I thought he had said. Damn this language barrier! I had decided to put my judgments on hold and gather more information. At the time Señor Sollacasa asked me about my throat it was fine. But the next morning, I could barely croak out *"Buenos días."* For the first time in ages, I stayed home, sick in bed from a terrible sore throat and a cold.

That afternoon, a few members of the group came to my house to visit me. They came filing into my room, hats in hands, bringing me oranges and wishes for me to get better. They were very sweet and said they were sorry that I was sick. Antonio told me that a North American *apu* had come to the table that morning and it was the *apu* that had informed them I was sick. In fact, the *apu* warned them to take better care of me and then insisted they come visit me. *Damn!* I thought. *The one day the North American* apu *comes to the table, I'm home sick in bed!* The group suggested I come to the *mesa*, that one of the *apus'* "cranial injections" would fix me right up.

The next morning I went to the *mesa*. After the *apus* had materialized, they directed me to approach the altar. I felt Señor Potosí's hand, a tiny hand like that of a small child, touching the top of the head, and then the prick of the needle as he injected a substance into my scalp. Some of the liquid ran down the back of my neck.

After the *mesa* was over, I left the room and went outside with Antonio's brother. I felt fire moving through my body, and then I got extremely nauseous. When the nausea subsided, I again felt waves of energy circulating through my body. The waves were moving in a counterclockwise direction from the periphery of my body, in toward my heart. All at once, I felt pressure and then a piercing sensation, as if a small dagger had entered my heart. I was overcome with a need to cry, but I couldn't because Miguel was right by my side. He seemed to sense my emotional vulnerability and very lovingly put his arm around me. I couldn't hold back any longer. I sat down on a clump of grass and, right in front of the whole neighborhood, burst into tears. I cried hard for more than twenty minutes without knowing where the emotion was coming from. Miguel was wonderfully sweet, he just smiled at me and held my hand. Then, suddenly, I was fine. Within a half hour of receiving the injection, my cold and my sore throat were eighty percent improved. It seemed the *apus* had developed a cure for the common cold!

I had been doubting the *apus* because of the whipping of that small boy and the fact that they needed to absorb human energy in order to materialize. They were beginning to seem less and less like angels all the time. Then, after the cranial injection, for a while, all my doubts simply vanished. Although they were not like the angels I had imagined, it was hard for me to believe they were trying to trick me because neither they nor Ricardo had ever expressed a desire to gain anything from me.

During the *mesas,* the *apus* would often repeat what they had told me at our very first meeting, that I had "strong sight" and needed to learn how to use it. They taught me to practice "looking" at things with my eyes closed. But when I closed my eyes to look at the mountain peaks around Cuzco, I saw huge birds of light, standing tall with folded wings, shining brilliantly. Were these the same beings that I repeatedly encountered at Ricardo's *mesa?*

"Elizabeth," Antonio asked me the next morning, "don't you realize what an extraordinary event this is? You are being given a rare opportunity."

"Antonio, does Ricardo charge you money?" I asked abruptly.

"Huh?" Antonio looked puzzled.

"I mean, do you and the rest of the group pay him for what he is teaching you?"

"No," Antonio said, "we pay for our healings with the angels, just like anyone else."

My doubts were back in full force. "How much?" I continued, determined to find the chink in the armor.

"The same as anyone, one thousand *intis.*"

I calculated rapidly, "That's about two dollars. Okay, so it can't be the money. Then what's his angle? Why is Ricardo giving you all this teaching free?" I asked point-blank.

"Because *los papitos* have said that our group is to receive the power to call them. When we do this, then Ricardo can rest for a year or two. You see, it's not easy working with the angels. If they say 'Get up at four in the morning and do a healing for the man across town,' Ricardo has to go. He has been working with them for twenty-two years, and he is tired," Antonio explained. This comment stimulated my compassion and I admired Ricardo's dedication.

"That reminds me," Antonio told me, "*los papitos* say we need to build our group unity. The power to call has never been given to a group before. It has always been handed down from master to disciple, after the disciple has served the master for at least three years. As I was trying to tell you, this is a unique situation. The *apus* have determined that, in order for the whole group to be worthy, we must go on several pilgrimages. The first one will be up the river Saphy."

"Great . . . when?" I asked excitedly. No one loved a good hike better than I, and I liked the notion of building group unity; it felt spiritually correct.

"Tomorrow," Antonio replied. "We will come to your house at nine o'clock in the morning."

A SMALL ROCK LANDED WITH A THUD AGAINST THE WOODEN shutters of my window. I struggled out from under my alpaca skin blanket. It was the only thing that kept me warm during the freezing Cuzco nights in a house that had no heat of any kind. Under the alpaca skin, I could go from zero to toasty in about ten seconds.

I opened the shutters and looked out.

"*Buenos días*, Elizabeth," said Antonio, waving up at me.

"What time is it?" I asked, rubbing the sleep out of my eyes.

"Time to go," he told me.

"I'm not even awake yet, give me a few minutes."

"Of course. We will wait for you here."

I scrambled for my wristwatch. It was only eight. I had never known Peruvians to be early for anything. Something must be up. I flew downstairs to the bathroom and splashed my face with cold water. On my way through the courtyard and toward the front door, Panchita, the housekeeper, waved toward the kitchen. "And your breakfast?" she scolded me in a motherly fashion.

"But, Panchita, my friends are waiting at the front door."

She shook her dark brown head. "They can wait a few more minutes. Sit down, your tea is ready."

Peruvians were the most patient people I had ever met. Here, there was no pressure of time as there was in our culture. Nothing was on time here, so they didn't expect it, in fact they thought nothing of waiting an hour or two for a friend. Still, I gulped down my tea and bread with homemade jam, and headed for the door.

Outside I found Maria, Felipe, Raul, and Antonio. "*Hola*," I said, doing the *beso* with my group members.

"Elizabeth, you remember the stone plate you saw the first time we met?" Raul asked.

"How could I forget it?" I replied.

"*Los papitos* say that it should remain with you for a while," he said, lifting a heavy burlap sack. He had brought it with him. So that's what all the fuss was about.

"Oh, my," I said, flattered. "Yes, I'd love to." I held out my hands to receive it.

"It weighs eight kilos. Let me help you," Raul said, and carried the heavy sack up to my room. When we had stowed it safely underneath the bed, he began walking toward the door. I, however, couldn't resist, so I pulled it out from under the bed, yanking back the burlap to look at the plate.

"Raul, what do the *apus* say about this plate?" I asked.

He turned only briefly to look at me, and replied casually, "They say that it is a bridge to the cosmos," and strode out the door.

Careful not to make physical contact, I passed my hand a few inches above the plate, feeling the warm surge of energy that rose up from its center. I turned the plate over and ran my hand over the back. Nothing. The energy only flowed in one direction. Up.

We met the rest of the group and headed along the right side of the riverbed. The part of the river closest to Cuzco was more like a garbage dump than anything else. I wanted to hold my nose as we walked past piles of assorted refuse near the water's edge. Once past the main garbage area, we came upon small families; men in ragged warm-up suits, women with their long black braids, wearing tall stovepipe hats; children with sooty faces and bare feet; all engaged in various activities along the river's edge. Some cooked over little fires, while others washed clothes, but all were smiling and laughing, slipping out of their native Quechua only to say *"Buenos días"* to us as we passed. I knew that, except for me, every member of our group spoke Quechua; but because they were university professors and had adopted Western-style dress, rather than the traditional indigenous clothing, they were addressed in Spanish.

As we walked, Raul explained, "The Saphy is one of the four

sacred rivers that flow into Cuzco. In Inka times the river was completely enclosed by stonework and honored by sacred images that were placed in niches at key points all along its length."

We could see ruins of Inka walls on either side of us, and a force still emanated from the river. As I picked my way among the river stones, I felt as though I had slipped into a light trance. The sensation coming from the river was delightful, and it was not hard to understand why the Inkas had considered it sacred.

We walked on for about forty minutes until we reached a place where it became difficult to advance. The air had been growing steadily thicker and heavier, until it became almost impossible to lift my feet and put them down. Instinctively, I wanted to turn around.

I had felt a similar sensation a year before, while working with Cyntha and the coastal shamans in Trujillo, a city on the northern coast of Peru. Cyntha had taken us to see Chan Chan, the place where the famous Don Eduardo Calderón had been initiated into his shamanic career. He was a sculptor who had been working on the restoration of Chan Chan when he was opened up to the spirit world.

Chan Chan was the largest intact ruin in South America. We had approached the front gate to visit this enormous complex of the pre-Inka culture of Chimu, but as we neared the gate, my feet became heavier and heavier. I felt as if I were being repelled from the ruin. A panorama of thoughts and feelings opened before me: I sensed that a great war had been fought and that many prisoners had been taken, but not in a physical sense. With the help of my friend David, we soon realized that this ruin was an astral prison. I told Cyntha our impressions, which she translated to our esoteric guide, Eliazar.

He was a very mysterious fellow who apparently knew everything about Inka and Chimu esoteric knowledge, but he spoke very little. He squinted his eyes at me, but said nothing. When we had entered the gate, which I did with no little effort on my part, he gestured to me. "These," he said, showing me symbols etched into the walls inside the gate, "are spells of power designed by the Chimu to keep the Inka out." I shuddered. "It is thought by the *brujos* of this area that many souls are trapped here. . . . You can hear them crying at night," Eliazar continued. For me, it had been a huge relief to have some tangible explanation for what I was perceiving. I was not hyperimaginative, or crazy. I was just sensitive.

Here on the Saphy River, the feeling was similar but much less intense, as if we had reached a subtle energetic barrier. Antonio pointed to an outcropping of rock above the river gorge, topped with Inka stonework. "This is a watchtower, or a place of the Inka guard. No one can pass here without asking permission." The entire group stopped and bent their heads in prayer. I, too, silently asked the local *santa tierra* for permission to pass.

As we prayed, I noticed a shift in energy, the feeling of a breath being released. The group moved forward and suddenly the air was light, happy and welcoming again; we were free to pass. I marveled at the power of asking permission. This was something I hadn't experienced at Chan Chan. These psychic barriers were really energetic doors, and these doors had keys called prayers.

As we continued we passed through several of these psychic "gates." Each time I could sense them more clearly. Then, in confirmation of my perception, the group would stop and begin to pray. Permission would be given and we continued on. I realized slowly that we were walking in a sacred way, entering a different kind of time and space. I'm sure I could have walked up this river, barging through these subtle energy gates, not even noticing them.

Because we had entered the river in this way, we entered a different reality, one in which we were in harmony with the landscape, by acknowledging the energetic shifts in the environment and responding to them. During this experience, I was learning to pay attention with another part of myself, a more direct energetic perception.

After two hours of hiking the riverbed, we arrived at a beautiful Inka wall standing beneath a waterfall. "Be warned," Raul said eerily, "the female water spirit of this area is known to come and steal sleeping men's hearts." It sounded like male paranoia to me. "She particularly likes music," he continued. "I know two musicians, friends of mine, who came up here on a picnic once. They fell asleep with their guitars next to the river. One told me that when he awoke, the water spirit was plucking the strings of his guitar."

I stared at the water, thinking about the water spirit. The place didn't feel scary to me at all. On the contrary, it was relaxing. Cool green willow branches filtered sparkling sunlight down onto the surface of the water. I began gazing into the water, seeing the reflections of the trees, sky, and sunlight and at the same time looking through to the stones at the bottom. I sat there musing when suddenly I heard a silvery female voice: "Soon will come the time when once again man speaks to merman."

"What?" I asked Antonio, feeling embarrassed that the group had been telling me things and I wasn't listening. "Who was talking about the mermen?"

"No one has spoken," Antonio replied. "But perhaps the water spirit has spoken to you. What did she say?"

"Uhh . . ." I stuttered, rather surprised at this idea. "She said that humans and merpeople would be able to communicate again sometime soon." Several heads in the circle nodded in agreement. "Yes, that is what the *apus* have told us. But it seems you have a special receptivity to them." On the hike back I pondered the idea that instead of being too sensitive or overly imaginative, I could have a "special receptivity." I liked that idea.

The outing had been lovely, but the next day we were back to work at the *mesa*. The *apus* arrived with force and began to do their healings. There was a man who was suffering from possession by an angry jungle spirit. He was disheveled in appearance, and his wife confessed that he would often rip off his clothes in the middle of the night and run outside naked, screaming.

Ricardo said it would be necessary to call Señor Salkantay to the table. I knew that Salkantay was a 22,000-foot snow peak, visible on the road to Machu Pikchu. Salkantay, in Quechua, means the "Indomitable One."

The woman who received the kidney transplant had disappeared and had not returned to the *mesa*. People who had seen her in town said that she was walking around as if there were nothing at all wrong with her, despite the fact that the doctors at the hospital had told her she was going to die.

I learned by now that Ricardo worked with three primary *apus:* Señor Pampahuallya, Señor Sollacasa, and Señor Potosí. When all three had materialized, Señor Potosí spoke. "*Buenos días,* daughter Elizabeth."

"*Ave María Purísima,*" I replied, saluting the *apu.*

"We are glad that you are working with the group. Today, I want you to do something special. I want you to call the Mamita Wakaypata, Plaza de Armas, Cuzco."

"*Me?*" I asked, horrified. "But how—what—what do I do?"

"Don't worry. Your little power is on the table, that will help you. Just pray." Earlier I had left a small rutilated smoky quartz, about the size of my pinky finger, on the altar table. Our hostess in Ojai had given it to me.

"*Sí, Papito,*" I answered.

Although it was pitch black, I closed my eyes to concentrate. "Mamita Wakaypata, Plaza de Armas, Cuzco," I said, trying to focus all my thoughts and feelings into a beam of energy. We waited. Nothing happened. I screwed up my courage and prayed again, this time out loud.

A soft boom was heard and suddenly the earth at my feet had wings. There was a thud on the table and a high-pitched female voice said, "Mamita Wakaypata, Plaza de Armas, Cuzco." A small round of applause came from the human beings in the room.

"*Muy bien,* Elizabeth. Well done, daughter," the *apus* congratulated me.

"Daughter Elizabeth," the Mamita Wakaypata addressed me.

"Yes, pretty Mother," I replied as I had heard the other women do.

"I want you to meet someone special . . . the *santa tierra* of your neighborhood . . . *la mamita de las niwas.*" I knew that *niwa* was the Quechua word for a light bamboolike reed that the Indian children used to make their kites. It was a lovely name.

Again there were wings from the earth and a very high female voice said, "Good morning, everyone, good morning, Elizabeth. I am the *mamita de las niwas* of the place you call Sapantiana." That was an Inka ruin just under my window at the señora's house. I had been told it meant "seat of meditation." Excitedly, I realized she was *my santa tierra!*

"You can call on my help anytime you need me," she offered.

"Gracias, Mamita," I said.

The *apus* then went about their business taking care of Ricardo's patients. It seemed they could only remain materialized for about half an hour at a time. Then each one saluted by name and they left as they had come. Normally, there would be three or four of these sessions every day, except for Sunday. That was the day the *apus*, and Ricardo, rested.

When the lights came on again, Ricardo reached across the table and motioned to me. I walked over to him. "Your power," he said, handing me what was left of my rutilated quartz crystal. It had snapped in half. "The force of your prayer broke the crystal," Ricardo told me.

"I'm sorry," I said, believing I had done something terrible.

Ricardo laughed. "You don't have to be sorry for having strong prayers."

While I sat outside in the courtyard, waiting for the next *mesa*, I pondered all my new experiences. Most of my North American life I had been teased, laughed at, and disparaged for daydreaming and for having an imaginative, intuitive, and sensitive nature. But here in Cuzco, daydreaming, intuition, and receptivity were encouraged and considered to be "special abilities." The female side of my nature was admired and I was actually appreciated for sensitivities that came naturally to me. With this encouragement, my sensitivity was opening more and more. Peruvians had different values and this seemed to make things possible here that were not possible in the States.

We were called back into the *mesa*. When Señor Salkantay came to the table, he was even larger than Señor Potosí. The room was as pitch black as usual; but for a moment, I thought I saw him, a figure holding a small staff of light adorned with two curling snakes.

Señor Salkantay worked for a long time with the possessed man, saying special prayers of great intensity in Quechua and sprinkling him with holy water. Some of the drops sprayed me. I saw the small light staff rise and descend several times before the ceremony ended.

When the lights returned, there was a wriggling burlap bag on the altar table. To my horror, Ricardo informed me that the evil spirit had been taken out of the man and placed into a guinea pig. The animal would now be left in the bag to die!

Before leaving, Salkantay spoke to me. "Elizabeth, you were born to work with the *apus*. You were born for us." His words moved me deeply, but they also touched on a fear that I carried, the fear of not finding and accomplishing my life's purpose. Throughout my life, I had been searching, but not knowing if I was really accomplishing this purpose, until I came to California to study psychology; then I felt that I was on track—until a sense of destiny had drawn me here. During the first three months I was in Cuzco, I had prayed every day to serve my highest purpose. Certainly, in meeting the *apus*, my deepest dreams and highest long-standing hopes were being activated: to learn about the spirit world and to be able to work and live in harmony with nature. And to help in a process of change . . . of birth . . . the birth of a new kind of world. Had I at last found my longed-for spiritual calling?

THERE WAS LITTLE ACTIVITY WITH THE GROUP OVER THE next month, as Ricardo had been sent away by the *apus* to work in a town near Bolivia. After weeks with no news, Raul had finally received a letter from Ricardo, with instructions from the *apus*, saying that the group must go on another pilgrimage, this time to the Mama Simona.

"Which one is Mama Simona?" I asked Antonio, as we gazed out at the tall peaks that surrounded the city.

He turned around and pointed behind us. "You see that tall green peak?"

"The one that looks like a pyramid?" I said, shaking my head in disbelief.

"That's right," he replied as we both looked up, shading our eyes against the setting sun.

"But Antonio, I thought all mountain peaks were *male*."

"Yes. That is usually the case. Mama Simona is the exception. She is the only one of the twelve sacred *apus* in the Cuzco Valley that is female." This was startling.

"Antonio, do you remember when I first told you about my vision of the *apus* . . . you remember . . . at the IPNAC?"

"Yes, of course," he said, smiling.

"I saw three: Ausangate, Saqsaywaman, and . . . her," I said, pointing to the green peak. "She was one of the three mountains that I turned to automatically and I knew she was female. I *saw* her." My eyes were moist with emotion.

"Elizabeth, does that surprise you? Really? " His eyes smiled into mine. I had received confirmation after confirmation and still I did not believe. "You North Americans are very skeptical. You put your faith in the strangest things and believe in them, but what is right before you—your own experience—you don't believe.

"What is this thing a North American once told me about . . . how do you call it? The estock marrket?" he asked, his accent making the words sound strange indeed. "This is something that you cannot see or touch, yet you get very excited about this. Many of you spend days thinking and worrying about it, even praying to it. But what you don't appreciate is that it is your collective belief in it that gives it power.

"Here in the Andes we have a different collective belief. It is about the power of nature. For us Pachamama is very important. We spend our time caring for her, thinking about her, praying to her. She is our mother and we know that all good comes from her. We receive from her, so we must give back to her. This is *ayni*, the law of reciprocity. In your culture, you think that what you need comes from this 'estock marrket' and you pray to it. But it can never be your mother, give you food and clothing to wear, and nurture your soul with her beauty. That is Pachamama, the spirit of the earth. That is what we pray to," Antonio concluded.

Early the next morning, we went by car to the western edge of the city. Eight members of the group were able to get away from other obligations, among them Maria, Felipe, Raul, Miguel, Judith, Americo, and, of course, Antonio. Although these university professors were poor by North American standards, they had an internal richness that defied any economic status. We talked and laughed and engaged in profound philosophical exchanges, and they were never stuffy or boring like many of the North American professors I had known.

With these fine companions, I began the hike up the ravine of a steep trickling creek, which, we had been told, we were to keep always to our left. There was no trail and we had to climb over fences and cross private property. Apparently this posed no problem, as the landowners only smiled and waved as we passed by. We carried backpacks filled with provisions for lunch, and Miguel had brought a *despacho,* a traditional offering to the earth, as a gift to the Mama Simona.

The green pyramid had been clearly visible as we approached by car, but now as we climbed toward the mountain, I lost sight of her. Raul said it was a short hike, only a few hours or so, but nonetheless, I prayed to Mama Simona, asking for the strength to climb her. I was the only person to wear hiking boots. Everyone else was in street shoes, worn out loafers, or old tennis shoes.

We hiked for four hours without stopping, the Peruvians talking and laughing and strolling along at a killing pace. I lagged behind, at times desperate for air. "They say that we mountain people have a heart and lungs that are half again larger than you lowland people," Raul told me. "Now I see what they mean," he teased.

After a few more hours of hiking, we crested a ridge that at last offered a view of the high peak herself. Mama Simona, in all her glory, stood majestically before us. I sat down, breathless, and struggled to pull my camera out of my pack. The group looked at me in surprise. "I'm just taking a picture," I said innocently before trying to snap the shutter at the mountain peak. I snapped, but nothing happened. I tried again, still nothing. I shook the camera. "It's broken, or maybe the battery is dead," I rationalized. The group regarded me with a mixture of pity and suppressed mirth.

"Why don't you just put it away, Elizabeth," Antonio suggested. "If the *apus* don't want their pictures taken there is really nothing you can do," he told me, as if I were a stubborn child. Like a stubborn child, I refused to believe what he was saying. I took the batteries out and put them back in and still the camera did not work.

We ate lunch in silence. Then we took up our furious pace once again. A couple of times I lagged behind on purpose, pulled my camera out, and when I thought no one was looking, I tried again to snap the shutter. Nothing. It seemed my camera had died.

Soon we entered a valley that was much greener than the dry and stony landscape we had been traversing all day. "This is called the Valley of Dinosaurs," Raul told me. "Look. Can you see the animals in the rocks?" He pointed to a large rock outcropping. I started in amazement. "It is a *sapo*," he said. "What you call 'toad.'" Antonio's eyes bulged and his tongue flicked out as he imitated the reptile's posture, causing us all to laugh.

People began to point out the animal shapes: dogs, lions, pumas, elephants, huge insects. They were everywhere, as if the Medusa herself had passed through this valley and, gazing at these giants of their species, turned them to stone. The animal "sculptures" were very obvious; it took no stretch of the imagination to see them.

"How did they get here?" I asked, certain that they could not possibly have occurred naturally.

"There are only a few places that they can be found in the entire Cuzco Valley. No one knows why there is such a concentration of them here," Raul told me. "Perhaps because we are getting close to the Mama Simona."

As we passed through the valley and climbed out, we came to another vista point. "There it is," Antonio whispered, "the altar." I looked up and saw the pyramidal peak of the green mountain. She was covered in low brush, and just near the top where the brush ended, there was a huge rectangular stone.

"There? That one?" I asked, pointing and straining my eyes.

"Yes. That is her," Raul told me with quiet reverence.

Then suddenly he shouted with the joy of a conquering hero and ran at top speed up the mountain toward the altar. This elicited a veritable stampede from the group as everyone raced to be the first one to reach the altar stone. I joined in the fun, but after five minutes my unaccustomed lungs were complaining bitterly. I slowed and merely watched the procession up the mountain. Raul arrived first, with Antonio, Miguel, Maria, and Felipe close behind. Judith and Americo took up the rear. By the time I reached the stone, the entire group had had a good rest.

"We must make an offering," Antonio pronounced. Miguel reached into his bag and pulled out a white paper bundle, handing it to Antonio. I had seen *despachos* many times on the altar table at Ricardo's *mesa*, but I had never seen how they were made. I watched, fascinated, as Antonio emptied his coca leaf pouch and began picking out the thirty-six coca leaves that would make up the twelve *k'intus*, twelve groups of three leaves each. Each *k'intu* was offered to one of the twelve mountains surrounding Cuzco Valley, each a sacred *apu*.

The enormous altar stone was slightly tilted, as if it had been jarred from its original position by an earthquake. We sat on the south side of the stone, at the very peak of the mountain. The stone itself had clearly been worked. Although it was not the delicate Inka stonework of the Qorikancha, it appeared to have been fashioned into an altar by human hands.

Antonio unfolded the paper and separated numerous tiny packages of the curious items that made up the *despacho* kit: seeds, starfish arms, bits of wool, candies, tiny lead figures, magnetic rocks, lama fat, sugar, and colored strings. The shell and the hardwood cross would be used as the center of the *despacho*. He filled the shell with llama fat, placing that in the center of the *despacho* paper, and then placed the cross at the center of the shell. I was puzzled about the significance of the items. The *k'intus* were "glued" together with more llama fat and each *k'intu* was held up in the direction of the mountain spirit being invoked.

As Antonio faced in the direction of an *apu*, the entire group joined in as he prayed in Quechua, calling on the power of the mountain, and offering the *k'intu* in respect and appreciation for all the mountain deities generously gave to us. Finally he blew on the *k'intu* three times. After each mountain spirit was invoked, its *k'intu* was placed in a circular fashion around the center shell. Then each of the seeds, plants, and rocks were placed as well, as gifts to various nature spirits. The tiny lead figures, representing body parts or personal wishes, were placed in the *despacho* by group members asking for help or healing. Finally, the candies were placed in the *despacho* to appease the trickster spirits, so that they would not try and twist the prayer as it went to heaven.

When the *despacho* was complete Antonio wrapped it in the paper, folding it in a traditional diamond pattern, and tied the packet with red-and-white-colored string. Next, prayers to the *santa tierras* of each group member's street were written on the outside of the package.

While Antonio, Miguel, and Raul were busy preparing the *despacho*, the others went in search of little sticks and built a small but hearty bonfire on top of the altar. They sang and chanted in Quechua over the *despacho*, and Antonio handed the bundle to me to place on the fire. As we prepared to burn the *despacho*, we looked up to see two large condors circling overhead. "They have come to see how well we have done," Raul said. The condors cast immense shadows on us as they passed overhead, hovering until we had placed the *despacho* on the fire.

"Let's go," Raul commanded.

"Where?" I asked, naively.

"We have given the *apus* an offering. It is like a meal for them. We must leave, so they can come to eat it," Antonio explained patiently to me. The group moved to the other side of the rock, out of sight of the ceremonial fire and the burning *despacho*.

"If it burns completely, our offering has been accepted," Raul told me.

"And if it doesn't?" I asked, worried.

"Our offering was not made with enough spiritual energy, and we must try again," he said. After fifteen minutes or so, we went to look at the remains of the fire. Our *despacho* had been completely consumed.

BY LATE AFTERNOON WE WERE MAKING OUR WAY BACK DOWN the mountain when we saw a woman in the distance, driving a herd of llamas. She was coming closer. The woman, the only other person we had seen for hours, was driving her herd up the same zigzag trail that we were taking down the mountain. Maria went ahead to greet her and they became engaged in a lively conversation. As we hiked nearer, I could see her llamas, eight in all, and one with beautiful multicolored patches on his legs that resembled colorful stockings. I decided to call him Socks.

Something about the old woman caught my attention. The way she was moving about and talking in a loud voice made me wonder if she was drunk. She wore a red shawl around her shoulders and the typical multipetticoated skirts of the Quechuan women. But instead of the stovepipe hat, she wore one that was richly embroidered, and perfectly flat on top, as if she had an upside-down bowl on her head.

Maria and the woman spoke animatedly in Quechua as our group approached. One by one, we passed by the woman and her llamas, shaking her hand, and greeting her on our way down the mountain. Although I felt a little afraid of her because of her odd behavior, a strange happiness filled me as I approached her. And when I took her hand it was the softest thing I had ever felt, and sticky too, as if it hadn't been washed in a while.

"*Buenos días*," I said.

"*Buenos días, Mama linda,*" she said, and began rattling away at me in Quechua. I noticed she did not look me in the eye, and that increased my suspicions that she was drunk. But I shook her hand warmly, then quickly moved on down the trail. "Socks" passed me by, and again I marveled at his jaunty colors. All of her llamas were beautiful—perhaps the most beautiful I had ever seen. The woman wanted to talk and kept Maria a long while after we all had passed. I felt she would have kept me too if I had understood her.

After a while Maria caught up with us. "What an interesting woman. She didn't want to stop talking!"

"But she wouldn't even speak to me," said Raul, a bit disgruntled.

"Hmm . . . that's true," Maria mused. "She didn't speak to any of the men."

"What did she say she was doing?" Raul asked.

"She said she had come from where she lived, way up on the mountain." The group stopped and came together to listen to Maria. "She asked for food and I gave her some oranges. She said she was going to a funeral," Maria continued.

"But she was not wearing the black mourning cape—she was wearing red!" Antonio shouted in excitement.

Raul dropped down to his knees. "*Madre Santísima,*" he prayed out loud, crossing himself. "We have just been deeply honored."

"Antonio, what does this mean?" I asked, feeling shaky.

But it was Raul who looked at me with tears in his eyes. "That was no old woman. That was the Mama Simona herself!"

The whole group now fell to their knees, looking back in the direction the woman had gone. They prayed emphatically and crossed themselves, and some cried softly.

Antonio explained, "It is known that the *apus* may materialize in human form at very special times. In all the old stories and myths about this, the *apus* always say, 'I live way up on the top of the mountain,' in a place where there are no houses. They often appear poor or drunk to test the compassion of the initiates in question."

"*Us!*" I shouted.

"That's right," he continued. "The initiates must have their wits about them, recognize the inconsistencies in the story, and call the *apu* by name. It is said that if you do this, you may then ask the *apu* for a gift."

"I guess we didn't have our wits about us," I said dejectedly.

"You had better change your attitude, Elizabeth . . . it was an honor just to have her present herself. Besides, we didn't do that badly. Thank God for Maria," Raul said, rising and giving her a bear hug. "At least you saved us from appearing as total fools by giving her the brush-off. I am so embarrassed. I thought she was drunk."

"No matter, we are still learning," Felipe said, humbly.

"Had we understood what was happening we could have asked her for the *mesa*," Miguel chimed in.

"But apparently we are not yet prepared!" Antonio countered.

"It's wonderful to know how close we are coming," Maria said, with a gleeful look in her eye. She had saved the group by her sensitive interaction with this supernatural being, and she was rightfully proud.

A FEW DAYS LATER, RICARDO RETURNED FROM BOLIVIA. HE called us together almost immediately, to have a special meeting with the *apus*. The group arranged to meet at Antonio's house, as Ricardo's regular meeting place was not available. I arrived early to help prepare the room. We moved tables and chairs to convert the living room into a *mesa*. Ricardo arrived and greeted us warmly. "*Los papitos* say you have done well on your pilgrimage."

"We hope so," Antonio replied.

Quickly Ricardo made the final preparations on the altar table and the room was made dark. After repeating the prayer and the low whistle, the first two *apus* arrived with a soft boom and a rustle of wings; but oddly enough, this time they came from a framed picture on the wall, instead of from the ceiling.

Señor Pampahuallya announced himself, and, shortly thereafter, Señor Sollacasa wished us all a good morning. "The group is improving," Señor Pampahuallya said. Antonio translated that the *apus* felt that we would soon be able to try calling them without Ricardo. But still, we needed more unity. Suddenly the arrival of another *apu* was heard, and a high-pitched but strong female voice greeted us.

"Mama Simona, at your service," said the female deity. I was amazed. The Mama Simona herself had arrived! *"Grupo,"* she said, "you came to visit me at my house."

"Sí, Mama linda," Antonio replied, full of respect.

"Indeed, you shook hands with me, but you did not know me." The group members gasped and Antonio muttered "I knew it" under his breath.

"Remember those eight llamas that you saw?" she continued.

"Sí, Mama linda," Raul answered.

"Eight of you, *el grupo*, and eight of us. And the one with the colored socks, the one Elizabeth liked so well, that was a North American *apu*." My mouth dropped open in surprise. But somehow it made sense, that llama was so different from any I had ever seen before. "The two condors you saw overhead—they were Señor Potosí and Señor Rio de Janeiro." After a few more moments of shocked silence on the part of the group, she continued, "The group may now attempt by themselves to call us. You must make the attempt tonight at nine o'clock at Elizabeth's house."

"Why my house, please?" I asked.

"Because you still don't fully believe in us, daughter."

That night the full group, thirteen members in all, gathered in the courtyard of the señora's house. We met at eight o'clock so we could prepare my room and ourselves. I had, on instinct, brought a white tunic from the States, because I felt I would undergo some sort of initiation ceremony, and as this seemed like the perfect opportunity, I put it on underneath my jacket. When we had all gathered in my room, the same room in which I had had my first vision of the *apus* more than six months before, we sealed it for light and carefully, following Ricardo's instruction, set up the altar.

By eight-thirty everyone except Antonio had arrived. We sat in a circle on the cold wooden floor; the tiny electric hot plate, our only source of heat, didn't even make a dent in the cold night air of Cuzco.

A few minutes before nine Raul said, "We must begin."

"But Antonio's not here," I protested.

"We must be on time. Antonio is too late," pronounced Raul. Heartbroken, I closed the door and locked it myself. We turned out the lights, leaving only a single candle illuminating the space. The experience reminded me of the slumber parties we used to have when I was young; we would sit around and tell stories by candlelight, trying to spook each other.

We had agreed that Raul would call first, then Felipe, and finally Miguel. Raul began with the prayer of the "opening of Jesus Christ" through which the *apus* could materialize. We supported him with the Our Father, and repeated together "Jesus" at the end of each prayer. We waited. Nothing happened. Raul tried for over twenty minutes, repeating the prayer, sometimes well, sometimes badly; he forgot a few words, or added some.

Felipe tried next. He repeated the prayer with more heart and focus. I felt good while he called, but he could not remember the words of the prayer half as well as Raul. Still, nothing happened. Next, it was Miguel's turn. He certainly had the intensity of feeling that Ricardo told us was required. After ten minutes or so the room suddenly filled with the smell of roses and flower water, a curious smell that always accompanied the materialization of the *apus* at Ricardo's *mesa.* The group took heart, but there was nothing more.

After nearly two hours of intense concentration, we were exhausted. "Well, I suppose we are not yet prepared," Felipe said sensibly. We exchanged *besos* and I let them out. I was sure Antonio's absence had something to do with our failure, and I said as much to Raul.

"Antonio is not reliable," Raul said coldly. He did not do the *beso* with me but walked out upset, almost angry.

The next day Maria and Felipe came to the house to speak with me. "We feel there is something you should know about Raul," Maria said, as we settled comfortably into some tea and bread in the upstairs living room. "Raul is a very good person, but he has had trouble in the past."

"What kind of trouble?" I asked, feeling the plot about to thicken. Felipe and Maria exchanged glances. He nodded for her to go ahead.

"A few years ago Raul worked with another teacher."

"An Andean priest?" I asked.

"No, someone who claimed he was a spiritual teacher. He was a very powerful person. Now Raul openly admits that they were working with black magic. One of his best friends died because of it."

"Wow." I put my head down, thinking that this was exactly the kind of thing I wanted nothing to do with. I visualized Raul in my mind and his face took on a diabolical appearance. I shuddered.

"His life changed after that," Maria continued. "He became much more devoted to God, a devout Catholic. But sometimes I think he is still after power."

Over the next few weeks animosities grew up suddenly and without explanation between members of the group. This infighting did not sit well with me especially since I had made a contact to fund our research. I had been in touch with a foundation in the States that was interested in funding research in alternative healing. They had asked for a proposal delineating how much money was necessary for the group's project and how the money would be used. One night I stayed awake until dawn writing and rewriting the proposal. At eight in the morning Antonio knocked at my door. An emergency meeting of the group had been called. I dressed rapidly and Antonio took me to the meeting.

I entered the door of an unknown house where Raul, Maria, Felipe, Judith, Americo, Miguel, and Liliana were already assembled. No *besos* were exchanged and anger thundered through the silent room.

"What's wrong?" I looked at them out of a shallow fog of sleeplessness. "I have the proposal here . . ." I began, holding the research proposal out in front of me, almost as if it were a defense.

"That's enough of your talk," Raul said savagely. "We know that you are betraying us."

"What?" I replied, aghast, the intensity of his emotion bringing me more fully alert. Raul scowled at me.

"You refused to buy chairs for our meeting room," Judith said, glaring at me.

"You didn't invite us to work with the cosmic plate. In fact, you have kept us from working with it these last weeks," Maria joined in.

"You gave it to me!" I declared. "What's wrong with all of you, anyway?" I demanded indignantly. Clearly they all felt that I had become their mutual enemy.

"Why are you saying these things?" Antonio asked on my behalf.

"Quiet, you!" Raul glared at him. "We know you are in it with her."

"In what, Raul? What are you all talking about?" I looked at them, hopelessly bewildered.

"You were so clever. You pretended to be our friend. Well, we have found out about you. It's because of people like you that the Andean Path has been closed for so long. You are selling Andean secrets to the CIA and getting paid well for it!" Raul spat. The idea was so paranoid and ludicrous that I almost laughed.

"You can't really believe this!" I looked at them, incredulous. Their faces were iron gates, their mouths slits of impassable anger. They did believe it.

I did not know how to defend myself. I was exhausted and the idea that I had just been up all night working on their behalf, only to be treated like this, was worse than horrible. I was so hurt that I became engulfed in self-pity, and I, who never cried in front of anyone, began to weep huge wet tears. I felt certain that my tears would be proof of my innocence. But to my shock and surprise, my tears had no effect on them whatsoever. They regarded me unflinching, unmoved. I felt even more powerless.

I made a supreme effort to hold back my tears, as my hurt

turned into burning anger. "You people are a bunch of paranoid maniacs!" I shouted, losing all control. "For your information I have been up all night typing this proposal to get *you* funding for *your* project and this is how you treat me?" I was on a roll. "Do you seriously think that I would be here, without family or friends, leaving behind a job at which I could make eighty dollars an hour, to sit around in a dark room with a bunch of nincompoops? Tell me, how much money did I get from the CIA? I hope it was enough to cover me for having to put up with this bullshit!" I threw the proposal on the floor and stormed out of the room. I noticed, with some satisfaction, that my Spanish was much improved.

The next day I received an official apology from the group, but the damage had been done. A schism had developed. Antonio, his father, brother, brother's girlfriend, and I were on one side, Raul, Maria, Felipe, Judith, Americo, and their relatives on the other.

6

The Cosmic Plate

OVER THE NEXT SIX WEEKS, THINGS WENT FROM BAD TO worse. Maria and Felipe's son, Enrique, became ill; and they blamed me, claiming I had worked some kind of black magic on the boy. This indictment was particularly painful because I had always felt a special fondness for Enrique, and the mere idea that I could hurt him intentionally was devastating. Throughout this ordeal the origins of the group's strange suspicions about me remained a mystery.

I grew angry with everyone, including the *apus*. It seemed to me as if these "angels" were pitting the two factions of the group against one another. They told us that we had to build more group unity, but then they held private *mesas* with each party. This undermining behavior was classic to a dysfunctional family, but could I judge this situation by my North American psychological standards? Perhaps they didn't apply to a shamanic experience. What were the rules for dealing with *apus* from the invisible world? Who was creating all the problems, the *apus* or us?

I knew from reading books that many shamanic initiations were "tests," such as resolving difficult conflicts or performing acts of tremendous courage, even sorting out confusing situations. Often, in order to succeed, the initiates had to develop the ability to stand their ground and fight. In the stories I had read, initiates were tested by their teachers; at times they were even put into life-threatening situations to see if they could overcome fear and develop spiritual strength. This was the question I now asked myself: Was I being tested by Ricardo and the *apus* in their attempt to teach me? Or was I being used as a pawn in their unfathomable game?

I hated fighting and conflict in any form, and had spent most of my life trying to avoid it. But I also despised feeling as though I were being intimidated or manipulated. On several occasions Ricardo had asked me to go and disrupt the *mesa* of one of his other students who had "betrayed" him. He told me all kinds of stories about this student's evil doings. But it wasn't until the *apus* got into the act that I really felt pushed.

At one of Ricardo's *mesas*, Señor Potosí petitioned me to perform this same task. "Do you love angels, Elizabeth?" he had asked me. When I said that I did indeed love angels, he commanded, "Then you will do this for us." When Señor Potosí asked me initially, I agreed; but I felt manipulated and at the same time guilty because I didn't want to do what they asked. I had not come to Peru to do battle with Ricardo's other apprentices. I had come to learn about healing. With all of this confusion I even began to doubt Ricardo's intentions. The whole situation was becoming more and more like some strange spiritual *Peyton Place*.

I recalled advice from my mother's friend, a powerful clairvoyant. "Remember," she had told me emphatically, "higher beings *never* make you feel bad or guilty." But I *did* feel bad *and* guilty. I was ready to give up the whole thing and go home. But so much of my life's dream was tied up with being here in Peru, and following what I thought was my destiny. I couldn't just run away.

In the midst of all this, Antonio took me to a *mesa* that made it clear the situation was out of control. The *mesa* was well under way with the usual cast of *apus* including my personal *santa tierra*, the Mamita de las Niwas, when the Mama Simona suddenly spoke to me: "Daughter Elizabeth, you must travel," she said. "You must take the plate and go to Argentina!" The *apus* wanted me to sell the cosmic plate for them, and they even had a buyer and a price in mind: I was to sell the plate to Señor Martinez—the man who had initiated my friend Carlos with the staff of power—for a sum of sixty thousand dollars. With this money the group could then purchase the *mesa* from Ricardo, and we would at long last be given the power to call the *apus*.

My mind leapt back to that day in California, just a few months ago, when I had walked into Reb's library and pulled the book about the Holy Grail off the shelf. Could this stone dish, this unusual artifact that I had had under my bed during the past few months, have something to do with the Holy Grail? And could bringing this plate to an encounter with the keeper of the basalt staff have something to do with the prophecy Carlos had told me about so many months ago? A thrill of destiny ran through me. If condors could materialize in this small room, then nothing was impossible But *was* this *apu* phenomenon real? That was the question.

Something in me snapped. I had to find out if there was really anything there on the table. Remembering that *apus* could see in the dark, I got up suddenly and pretended to trip and stumble forward, lunging my hand out along the altar table in a false effort to steady myself. Immediately my hand encountered something warm and firm and fleshy, like the foot of a chicken, only much larger. Something that felt alive. "Don't touch my foot!" the Mamita de las Niwas squealed. So there *was* something physical there. I had just touched an *apu*.

"Oh, excuse me," I stuttered. Embarrassed but satisfied, I sat back down and agreed to what the Mama Simona had proposed to me. I agreed because, as far as I was concerned, I was taking the cosmic plate to a long-awaited appointment. I would go to Argentina to meet Martinez, keeper of the staff of power, and reunite these two ancient power objects. I would fulfill the prophecy Carlos had told me about so many months before. It was a mission that suited me. Besides, it would take me away from the maddening power struggles of the group and the *apus*, and give me a chance to think.

MY TRAIN TRIP TO BUENOS AIRES LASTED SIX DAYS AND WAS physically exhausting. Once there, I continued to find myself confused. Martinez, when I finally succeeded in finding him, turned out to be a tall, dignified, silver-haired man of about seventy-five. I told him a little of my story and that I knew the plate had to encounter the staff but I wasn't sure how to make it happen. Then, to my amazement, Martinez himself suggested we make a plan to meet one week later with the cosmic plate, the staff, and a few of Martinez's handpicked students.

The next week I arrived promptly at the appointed hour. Martinez introduced me to the four of his students who would assist with the session. I discovered that Martinez was an esoteric teacher who routinely initiated his students into a hermetic society with the staff of power. That staff, the same one Carlos had been initiated with, was laid out on the table when I arrived. It was beautiful, just as Carlos had described it: about two feet long and made of a jet black stone called basaltic rock.

Although it was midafternoon, Martinez began the session by closing the shades, leaving the room in a kind of twilight. He and his students closed their eyes as Martinez began to tap on the wooden arm of his chair in a rhythmic, drumlike fashion, intended to induce a trance, I assumed. The atmosphere in the room became thick and heavy, as if the air had become filled with smoke. I found it strange that there was no opening prayer, no thanks, no invocation of the divine. We just jumped right into it.

After a while, Martinez began to speak in a strange, rasping voice. "I see seven sorcerers in the mountains . . . in Peru they are giving you the—" He gurgled something unintelligible, and then almost shouted, "The cosmic plate!" He gestured toward the plate. "Yes, the cosmic plate is an old friend of the sacred staff."

When Martinez slumped back down in his chair and became quiet, there was another gargling sound, this time from the other side of the room. One of his students began to react. She growled and writhed, and then suddenly she stood before me shouting "Parsifal . . . Parsifal . . . Parsifal."

Parsifal was a historical figure. He had been the bearer of the Holy Grail! Why was she calling me by this name? Then, in low tones, she began to plead with me, "Sing to the staff . . . sing the colors of the staff. Sing Parsifal, sing." Her voice grew louder as she commanded me over and over again. It seemed the woman was completely mad.

Despite my mental reaction, uncannily, sound welled up in my throat, waiting to be poured out. I began tentatively to release the sound, to "speak" to the staff. I let myself go another notch and the sound came out in long pure tones, like frequencies. I had never made such sounds in all my life. I could see colors with the frequencies of sound and it seemed the two power objects were being woven together by a brilliantly colored web of sound. I continued to emit the sound and slowly the sounds formed themselves into words. "From the darkness . . . from the darkness . . . there will come the light." I made words as the sounds became intelligible to me, and as soon as the sounds became words, the song was over.

My consciousness faded for a time, and when I opened my eyes I found I had slid off the couch and was sitting on the floor, my chest level with the table. The tip of the staff was actually touching my chest. All at once I felt a burning sensation, as if the staff was penetrating into my body, piercing my heart and moving completely through me. I knew it was an energetic phenomenon, but it felt as if the staff were actually forging an opening. It was frightening and wonderful all at the same time: the most delicious piercing, like sex, but on a spiritual and emotional level.

Not until that moment did I realize something that had been obvious from the beginning. The two artifacts were male and female power objects. The piercing, penetrating power of the staff was strongly male, while the receptive, holding quality of the plate was female. It occurred to me that the keeper of the staff could become overly male and would need the balance of the feminine side. Perhaps, then, what I needed was the laser focus of the staff.

At the moment the session was over, there was a tremendous clap of thunder. Outside a torrential rain began to pour. Nature herself was making a statement about our work.

Señor Martinez opened the shades, smiling. He seemed quite pleased with the session. I had to make a decision on the spot. In our first meeting, Martinez had told me that he could not purchase the plate. Like most spiritual teachers he did not have a dime to spare. Although my instructions were to sell it, I did not want to, and yet I was afraid to disobey the *apus.* I wanted to do right action, the morally and spiritually correct thing.

"Let it remain with you for now," I told Martinez as I gave the plate into his hands. "You and your students will be able to use it."

A FEW DAYS LATER I WAS GROWING RESTLESS. THE DECISION to leave the plate with Martinez no longer sat well with me. Certainly I did not want the plate to fall into the wrong hands—and as I inquired further into his character, I was told that Martinez was considered a fanatic, motivated by power. I made a weak excuse and got the plate back.

Over the next several weeks I wandered all over Buenos Aires talking to spiritual teachers, clairvoyants, and anyone else who could give me more information about the cosmic plate or the *apus.* No one had ever heard of either, until one day when I was told about a spiritual teacher who was said to be very powerful. He held consultations once a month, and synchronicity secured me an appointment with him. I arrived, cosmic plate in hand, and had to wait for nine hours in a long line of people.

When I entered his office and unwrapped the plate, telling him a little of my story, he stopped me with a wave of his hand. He pulled a coin out of his pocket and tossed it into the plate. The coin disappeared. Now, instead of the inside of the stone dish, I saw a hundred shooting stars. He reached his hand into the stars and retrieved the coin. "Wha—how—?" I stuttered.

"This coin is made from the same material as the Holy Grail," he stated flatly. I felt hypnotized and wondered if this man could be a master hypnotist.

"But the plate . . . the *apus* told me to sell it," I told him.

"Sacred objects cannot be sold," he said in the same tone. I felt a wave of relief and joy, as the confirmation of his words resonated deep inside my body.

"Please, I need your help. You know the *apus?*"

"I know them," he stated in the same monotone.

"The *apus* told me I was born for them."

"No," he said authoritatively, "you were born for yourself." I sat stunned by his simple words, so plainly stated. These words began to undo a knot of energy in my belly. Somehow his words were freeing me. The consultation had lasted no more than fifteen minutes, but it was clear that I had received what I had come for. I thanked him and left.

On the way home I began to realize that, without knowing it, I had connected the wonderful and delightful mystical experiences of the past months with the creatures in the dark. When the *apus* told me that I was born for them and destined to work for them, I began to believe that my newly awakened spiritual life and abilities were due to them. I realized now that I had unconsciously linked events, making the *apus* responsible for my visionary experiences, and for my power. I felt indebted. But more than indebted, I had begun to feel enslaved!

This was definitely not right. "Even if they *were* the forces of nature, I should not feel enslaved to the *apus*. I should work together with them," my reasoning mind told me. But I couldn't, because I was afraid of them. Something about all this had gotten off the trolley somewhere and needed to be righted, and soon! I was not yet ready to return to Peru and face Ricardo and the group. There was more to this puzzle than I could fathom and I needed to stay in Argentina until I attained some degree of clarity.

After more weeks of searching and not finding any clear answers I woke up one morning full of despair. Part of me wanted to throw all of this hocus pocus away, head back to North America, and become normal again. Maybe I could get a job as a janitor scrubbing toilets somewhere, or just be a plain old psychologist, helping regular people in mundane ways. Things here had gotten too complicated, filled with intrigue and out of proportion.

I wanted to go back to my smaller self, my naive self, the one that had never had any visions, had never felt a spiritual calling, the one that had never seen the invisible world manifest before her eyes, never experienced the impossible. Maybe then the impossible would leave me alone. I felt as if a host of beings and people and energies were pulling at me, bidding for my attention, asking for all kinds of things and promising all kinds of things. I just wanted some inner peace and quiet.

I began to walk without any intention or direction, walking just to walk, to feel my body moving and to divert my attention from the tension of my inner struggles. Shortly I found myself standing right in front of the cathedral of San Isidro. Unconsciously I had sought out the comfort of this church, although I was sure it wasn't the church that made this place comfortable. For me it was a power spot, and I wondered if it hadn't been built over some indigenous sacred site, like so many other churches. I had been here several times before and the place had a wonderful feeling to it.

The rain stopped momentarily, and the deep amber and golden light of sunset began to filter through the clouds. The curtain of green foliage that hung before the cathedral was washed in gold, and in that moment a dozen weeping willows became holy. I could have stayed there forever, looking at those trees. They soothed my aching soul.

Quickly the sky clouded over again, and as night began to fall, the rain picked up, this time with force. I was worried now, afraid I was going to get soaked to the skin. Certain that the cathedral was locked, I hadn't even bothered to approach the door. I knew it closed at five o'clock, and it was already five-thirty. Now that it was raining harder, it seemed at least worthwhile trying the door.

I walked up to the enormous door and pushed it. Solid as a rock. It occurred to me to try turning the handle. The door glided open easily and I stepped inside. Except for a janitor cleaning wax from the floor at the far end of the cathedral, I had the place to myself. I approached the altar and took a seat in a pew about halfway up to the front. Although I didn't consider myself Catholic, I crossed myself, perhaps for the benefit of the janitor, and sat down. I bowed my head and began to pray.

As I prayed, a tremendous peace and warmth began to expand inside my chest, and my entire body relaxed as the storm of feelings within me subsided. After a few minutes of prayer I sensed a presence that made me look up, toward the altar.

There, on the left side of the altar, a figure is floating six feet off the ground. She is of a rare and refined beauty and is over seven feet tall. Clothed in ivory-colored satin, on her dress delicate plant forms make a pattern of exquisite beauty. Her body is sensuous and extremely refined. Huge brown eyes that show no whites dominate her facial features and long antennae extend from her head. She is at once like a plant, an insect, and a most exquisite fairy. She is a female nature spirit, the embodiment of the beauty and delicate grace of nature. The queen of this land. A sensation emanates from her of the most refined love and beauty I have ever beheld. My attention moves to the right-hand side of the altar, and there, equally tall and stunning, also floating off the ground, is another figure. She is wearing a blue robe with a white hood and mantle. Her face is radiant, her hands open, extended in a gesture of supplication. Around her head twelve stars are shining and blinking, circulating in a clockwise direction. She is beautiful. She is the Virgin Mary. The Cosmic Mother. She is the emanation of divine female energy. I stare transfixed, my heart drinking in their love, their beauty, their most pure and highest essence, their feminine power. I do not move. I cannot. All at once my attention is drawn to the altar between the two figures. I realize that I am seeing a vision and my eyes are open, wide open. Before me and in the very center of the altar, a large golden chalice materializes in slow motion to the sound of a single bell. And then, holy choirs of angels, sacred song, and the bell; and over and over and over and over again she appears, the Holy Grail reappears reappears reappears reappears on a hundred . . . a thousand . . . no . . . on every single altar in every single church in the world. She returns. Singing. She returns.

Unable to bear the intensity of the vision any longer, tears streaming down my face, I looked down at my body, now trembling with the impact of what I had just experienced. I heard the swish of robes, and out of the corner of my eye I saw the priest who had just come in. He was standing in front of the altar. I looked up. *They are still there, and so is the chalice, right in the very center of the altar, shining. He cannot see them, but they are right there.* The female figures remained unmoving, emanating. They did not see me because this was not a personal vision. I was simply a witness to a much larger event.

I told no one about this vision, but it is forever burned into my mind. To this day I can still see the female figures when I close my eyes. Initially it was so powerful that my conscious mind could barely retain it. I couldn't help but wonder if the meeting of the staff and the cosmic plate had anything to do with this. Over the next few days, my thoughts turned continually to the vision, but I did not know how to interpret it. Words were unable to contain its transforming power. I could only jot a brief note in my journal, as a point of reference, tethering this numinous experience to something in the concrete world.

But all too soon other worries claimed my attention. I was reviewing the efforts of my research. Many of the spiritual teachers I had seen were suggesting that perhaps the *apus* were elementals, less evolved as opposed to higher beings. Or perhaps they were "lower astral beings," the lost or punished souls of dead people that had gotten stuck on the lower level of the astral plane. I had heard that to pierce through to the higher spiritual plane, one had to travel through the lower astral realm, a world of deception, guile, illusion.

Something about that description seemed to fit—but not completely.

I didn't really believe in the New Age division between the "light beings" and the "dark beings." It seemed too facile a formulation in a complex and mysterious world. I was more prone to thinking like a Jungian, working toward the integration of the difficult, unconscious, or "shadow" aspects of my human nature. Like Jung, I had believed that evil was nothing more than projected aspects of one's own shadow. If one could integrate the shadow, then one had access to the life force of the unconscious. But was this true? Jung was the only one of the old psychological theorists I had read who talked about allying with the unconscious, the unknown or mysterious aspect of our humanity, and honoring it, rather than treating it as an enemy, or trying to "amputate" it. The Jungian view was a more "shamanic" psychology. In traditional Judeo-Christian thought, the "lower drives" like sex and aggression were all lumped into the category of evil. This was not a very satisfying answer to a critical mind and heart.

Before I had come to Peru I hadn't believed in evil. Now I wasn't so sure. Still, I couldn't just write off Ricardo's *apus* as evil. I had learned a lot from them. They, too, were a part of the great creation. I felt I had to know how to deal with them. However, I certainly had my doubts as to whether or not they were looking out for *my* best interests. The *apus* seemed to have their own agenda and because I was no longer doing their bidding I became frightened of what might be in store for me.

AFTER MONTHS IN BUENOS AIRES, I KNEW THAT I WAS AT last ready to make my decision. I felt settled enough into my new perspective that acknowledged the spirit world as a reality, yet maintained a discerning eye on its "phenomena." It was now clear that my time in Argentina had come to an end. I knew that I had to go back to Cuzco and give the *apus* their cosmic plate. After all, it wasn't mine, and besides, this was the move that felt the most freeing when I imagined doing it. Although I was dreading it, clearly it was time to return.

I bought a bus ticket from Buenos Aires to northern Chile. The long trip through the desert gave me time to ponder what had happened to me, and imagine what was yet to come. I tried to control my fear. I was just beginning to understand how I generated my own states of mind, particularly fear and guilt; and it was very difficult to distinguish between a projected fear or fantasy and a true intuition. The psychic opening I had experienced first in Peru, then in San Francisco, and all my visions since then had taught me that not everything I sensed was my own projected fantasy. However, I also knew that not everything I perceived psychically was fact. It was difficult to discriminate between real intuition and a projected fantasy.

Now, as I ruminated about my inevitable meeting with the *apus*, I couldn't trust what I was feeling. Was my foreboding and dread based in a clear psychic perception of the future, or was it an emotional state I had generated out of my own fears?

I was walking a line between the fantastic and the real. How did thought and matter interact to create what we perceive as reality? Certainly this was the question that had fascinated and yet eluded me for months. Before my experience with the *apu* materializations, the division between thoughts and material reality was marked by a clear and concrete boundary. But here in South America, the lines between the material and spiritual worlds were not so sharply drawn.

During my investigations in Argentina I had learned that in the *spiritista* tradition practiced in Brazil, spirits used human ectoplasm, or bioenergetic force, in order to materialize. Could this explain the phenomenon of the *apus*? Or was Ricardo actually a very powerful psychic who could gather and project human ectoplasm in any form he pleased? Thinking psychologically, I considered the possibility that the *apus* could be materialized projections of Ricardo's subpersonalities. Whatever the explanation, I knew that thoughts and beliefs did have the power to act on the material world, and now I needed to be careful with my own.

It took me eight days on the bus to get back to Cuzco. Eight days of dread. When I finally did arrive, I was delighted, much to my own surprise, to be back in that beautiful city. Above and beyond all my troubles, there was something so wonderful, so joyous about Cuzco that for a while I forgot my sense of impending doom and spent a few fun days with friends. I even began to wonder if I could simply drop off the plate at Raul's house and be done with it. But that was not to be.

A few nights after my return, on my way home from the disco, I was walking down one of my favorite streets, Calle Loretto. This street was almost completely intact from Inka times, with perfect Inka walls running along both sides. It still showed the niches where golden idols were said to have been kept. I was reminded of the greatness of the Inka civilization, and filled with the certainty that there had to be more to the spirituality of this advanced culture than what I had experienced so far.

As if in response to my thoughts, a figure appeared in one of the niches. It was a man with a fringed headdress. His skin was dark, his body large and powerful, and he had a regal bearing. This impressive figure radiated power, but his power was not frightening, it was controlled power. "Remember," he said, addressing me as a colleague, "it was the Inka who commanded the *apus*, not the *apus* who commanded the Inka." The figure instantly dissolved.

"Of course!" I nearly yelled out loud with the impact of the sudden realization. Instinctively, it had bothered me from the very beginning that Ricardo's *apus* told everyone what to do. But now, I understood my discomfort on all levels, psychologically, esoterically, and in my gut. You simply cannot let children run the zoo.

As a therapist I had observed this family pattern frequently. If the children in a family are given too much power the results are disastrous, because the parents' power is weakened and the family system collapses. Similarly, if the children are ignored or mistreated, the family as a whole suffers when the child fails, or acts out in school. I postulated that undoubtedly this pattern must hold true for our own unconscious impulses as well. If we are directed by our lower impulses, chaos results; but if those same impulses are repressed, we lose our life force. Perhaps the trick was to make sure one's life force was guided and channeled by a firm, directing consciousness. Of course these children are not bad or evil—they are simply in a role that is inappropriate.

Therefore the forces of nature, the *apus*, could not be in charge, as Ricardo's *apus* seemed to be. The evolved human consciousness— the Inka—was meant to direct and guide these forces of nature. Historically we had once been dominated by nature, at the mercy of its overwhelming power. Then, Western society tried to dominate or repress nature in response to that experience of helplessness. In my culture, this had created a society of lifeless people, afraid of their bodies and their own spontaneous impulses. But neither extreme worked. What was really needed was a strong, guiding hand that allowed the power of the unconscious to be used and channeled constructively. For Ricardo, clearly, things had somehow gotten out of hand. He was being "eaten" by his own *apus*.

The next morning, exactly four days after my arrival in Cuzco, Ricardo himself came to my house, surrounded by a small entourage of people that I did not recognize. I saw his car from my window and I almost asked Panchita to tell him I wasn't home. But, at the last minute, I changed my mind. Something inside me stood up. I had to go and face Ricardo. The moment had arrived.

"Elizabeth," Ricardo called up to me from the courtyard. I had come out of my room and was standing on the balcony, looking down at him. I did not go down, and I certainly was not going to invite him up. "*Los papitos* want to speak with you," he said. He was not smiling, nor did he look angry, as I had expected he would.

"Yes, Ricardo," I told him in a firm, careful tone. "I will speak with them tomorrow. What time is the *mesa*?"

"At eleven in the morning," he answered.

"Very well. Until tomorrow then."

"Until tomorrow," he said, bending his head to get through the door that led back out onto the street.

That night, I saw Antonio for the first time. "Strange things have been happening since you left, Elizabeth," he told me. He did not look like himself. "I have hardly been to the *mesa* since you went to Argentina. Things that I did not like began happening more and more."

I nodded in assent. "These *apus* are not higher beings. You must not let yourself be commanded by them," I told him. "Antonio, last night I saw an Inka," I said, pointing to my forehead to indicate it was a vision. "He told me that it was the Inkas that commanded the *apus*—not the other way around."

"That's right," Antonio said, his eyes sparkling as if he were waking out of a deep sleep. "I have also been thinking that Ricardo is powerful, but his power has become distorted."

"Precisely," I affirmed. "Antonio, come with me tomorrow to the *mesa*. I have something in mind and I want you to be there."

"I wouldn't miss it for the world," Antonio said smiling.

The next morning Antonio, Miguel, and his girlfriend, Elena, arrived at my house around ten-thirty. It would be a lie to say that I was not terrified. I wasn't exactly sure why, but I knew that I had to confront the *apus* and speak directly to them. My surety of purpose gave me confidence. And because my Spanish had improved enormously over the past five months, I knew at least that language would no longer be a barrier.

We all drove together in a truck for nearly an hour outside the city, to the house where the *mesa* would be held. As always, Ricardo and his students had to go through a long process of clearing out the living room to make space and then sealing the doors and windows for light. During all this time I had the leisure to get completely nervous, and then to relax completely. By the time they were finally ready, I was ready too.

"Daughter Elizabeth, why didn't you complete your mission?" Señor Pampahuallya demanded upon materializing.

"Because as you know, Señor Pampahuallya, sacred objects cannot be sold," I replied, my voice shaking with anger, truth, and just a little fear. It was amazing how different I felt now. I was much more sure of myself.

"That's correct," he answered, to my complete surprise.

"And now, *Papito,* if you don't mind, I have some questions for you." I was shaking, unsure how the *apus* or the humans in the room were going to respond to this turn of events.

The angry voice of one of Ricardo's students could be heard in reply. "You don't have to answer her stupid questions, *Papa lindo.*"

"We will answer," replied Señor Pampahuallya.

"Are you beings of light?" I began my inquiry realizing that six months ago, I had been too cowed by the *apus* even to formulate these questions.

"No, we are dark," Pampahuallya answered me directly.

"Are you from the third dimension or another dimension?"

"We are from this dimension," he answered again.

There was silence, so I continued. "Why are you here? What is your mission or purpose?"

"We are here to help people who cannot go to the regular doctor."

"Why do you suck people's energy?" I asked.

"To eat, to feed ourselves," he replied.

"Why can't you take energy directly from God?" I pursued.

"No. That is not permitted," he answered in a neutral, factual voice.

"And to work with us you must suffer," added Señor Sollacasa, in a particularly vicious tone.

"Well, I guess I don't work for you anymore," I said triumphantly. "I have come to give you back your cosmic plate. Thank you very much. Good-bye."

"*Ciao,*" said Señor Sollacasa.

"*Ciao,*" said Señor Pampahuallya, as they dissolved into the ceiling with a beating of wings.

When the lights came on, I went right up to Ricardo and shook his hand. He showed me no anger, no visible response of any kind. He simply returned my handshake politely. The other students refused to shake my hand, so I waved good-bye and nearly ran for the door with Antonio, Miguel, and Miguel's girlfriend, Elena, following right on my heels. We headed for Elena's house, just a few blocks away. I was skipping and jumping high into the air, whooping from sheer joy and relief.

"Whoof, I'm glad that's over. Now we know what that was all about. Did you hear that? 'To work with us, you must suffer,'" I said, imitating the voice of Señor Sollacasa. "How creepy." I laughed. "Well, that makes everything very clear to me."

"Yes, to me also," Antonio said, looking a little sad.

"Disappointing, isn't it?" I said.

"Yes, very," replied Antonio. "I suppose you'll be going home now," he said, looking forlorn.

"Yes, that's right. But don't worry, Antonio. I love Cuzco. I'm sure I'll be back."

I HAD NO IDEA THAT IT WOULD BE MORE THAN TWO YEARS before I would return to Cuzco. But my reentry into the United States was not so easy. The fact was that I was desolate. I couldn't reconcile myself with normal North American life. The people in the States seemed so lifeless, so colorless, so bored. Even the most expensive organic food in the grocery stores tasted like plastic to me, after the rich, vibrant vegetables and fruits from the Sacred Valley of the Inkas. Worst of all, everywhere I went, Pachamama was covered over. Her power was pushed down by cement and buildings and roads and houses. In contrast to Cuzco, here I could not feel the life force emanating from the earth. My therapist called it a bad case of "culture shock." I called it a serious case of cultural schizophrenia.

On my trip back to San Francisco, as we were flying into Miami, I felt as if a large psychic helmet was being lowered down over my head, blocking my higher awareness. Perhaps this was a good thing. Perhaps I had become too open.

During my layover in a Texas airport, I watched the crowds of people walking up and down the long airport corridors. There was something wrong with their bodies, but the "wrong" was so familiar that, at first, I couldn't figure it out. Then I saw it! My mind flashed on an image of a group of Cuzqueños and the way they stood on the earth with such natural grace. It was as if there were an invisible line of energy that connected their bodies to the ground. These people looked as if they belonged to the land they were standing on, and there was an obvious, natural relationship between their bodies and Pachamama, a love relationship.

These airport bodies, on the other hand, looked disconnected. There were no lines of energy going through them and into the earth, no relationship whatsoever between the bodies and the earth they were standing on. It appeared as if they could have been picked up and put down anywhere on the planet, or any other planet for that matter, without severing any ties. In that moment, I realized the value of what I was leaving behind and I was overcome with grief.

7

Kurak Akulleq:
Fourth-Level Priest

OVER THE NEXT TWO YEARS I WORKED AS A FAMILY
therapist. On my days off, I sat in my house, sheltered under
my alpaca skin blanket, and tried to understand what had happened
to me in Peru. A new world had opened up to me. A world that had
no place in the United States. I had returned to the unfinished business of my psychotherapy license, and because I now spoke Spanish,
I was able to get internships with Latino families. This helped ease
the pain of my culture shock, but part of me was still in that other
world.

I dreamed of Cuzco almost every night. In fact, I felt as if I were
actually going there, drawn by some unseen force to return. It was
very hard for me to focus my attention in the North American continent.

To get some practical understanding of the left-brain kind, I
began to read books about the Inkas and to learn a little about ar-
chaeology. At first, I tried living in San Francisco, but the concrete
was too much for me. After a few months I moved to Mill Valley

with a wonderful group of psychotherapists. I finished my training in family therapy, but my heart wasn't in my work. I had been opened to an entirely different layer of reality, and it kept haunting me.

One evening, after finishing up with my clients at the counseling center in the Mission District of San Francisco, I noticed a warm feeling begin to spread throughout my body. I looked up and saw a large golden sphere hovering above my desk. It was a lovely presence and I invited it to approach. The presence spoke to me, encouraging me that everything was going to be all right. It seemed to be telling me that everything that had happened in Peru had happened for a reason that I could not yet understand, and that I needed to keep writing, working on the book, something I had been driven to do from the day I had returned to the States. Writing was my only salvation, the only way I could integrate the very disparate worlds that I had lived in before and after Peru. After a while, the golden presence receded and my resolve to write became stronger than ever.

I wondered if I was going crazy. Talking to golden spheres seemed less unusual in Peru, but here in the States it was downright strange. I got up from my desk and walked a straight line. I tied and untied my shoes and then reread my client notes. My notes were very coherent. Although I had just had an "otherworldly" experience, I seemed to be functioning just fine in the "regular world." As I drove home I began to wonder if it wasn't me but rather my ideas about what it meant to be human that were crazy. Perhaps visionary experience was a normal and healthy part of human development. Perhaps what I was experiencing was "evolutionary stress." Whatever it was, it was anything but comfortable.

However, my extreme discomfort continued until I moved back into nature, to a place where I could hear the voice of Pachamama again. That was when I knew. In February 1992, I moved out to a house in the San Geronimo Valley of West Marin, where the sounds of nature were still louder than the din of the city. It was then that I realized it was time to return to Cuzco. Synchronistically several women from the women's group I had been leading for the past year began nagging me to take them to Peru.

The next thing I knew, I had called a travel agency and made plane reservations for Cuzco, for the end of June. I telephoned Señora Clemencia in Cuzco, and asked if I could come and stay for a few weeks. She and her husband were delighted to hear from me and she very warmly assured me that my room was there waiting for me, and that she was still working on her *pensión* project, so there were plenty of extra rooms for friends.

In early June 1992 our little band flew down to Cuzco. We hiked the Inka trail and did tourist things. It was wonderful to see my Peruvian friends again and experience the gorgeous landscape of Cuzco once more. The ache in my heart began to disappear.

We were nearing the end of our two-week stay when, as I was walking toward the main square, my eyes fell on a poster that read "First World Congress on Andean Mysticism." The dates showed that the conference would take place in three days, and we were scheduled to leave in two! I ran to the nearest phone and quickly called my office in California to see if I could arrange to stay for an extra week. Fortuitously there was no problem. I easily changed my plane reservation, and two days later said good-bye to my traveling companions.

I was so excited about the conference that I could hardly wait for it to begin. Perhaps, at last, I would get some answers to my many many questions. I attended the first day, notebook and tape recorder in hand. My high enthusiasm quickly turned to dismay as I listened to speaker after speaker engage in lifeless academic bantering about the Inkas and their mythology. The *apus* were mentioned, but only as myth and legend. No one spoke about anything like the experiences I had had. I walked out of the first day of the conference deeply dejected.

"You look disappointed," said a deep voice with an English accent. I looked up into the sparkling blue eyes that belonged to the voice.

"Peter! How are you?" I replied, happy to see an old friend, as we exchanged the traditional Peruvian *beso*. Although we had only met at the end of my two-year stay in Cuzco, Peter Frost had worked in Cuzco as a guide for adventure travelers for more than twenty years.

"I'm fine, but this is rather a boring conference. It's too bad the person who knows the most about all this isn't here," he replied.

"Please. Tell me who that is. It's very important, you see, that I find someone who knows about the *apus*."

He smiled at me. "*Apus*, eh? Well, that would be Juan, Juan Nuñez del Prado," he told me, scribbling down a phone number on a piece of paper. "Here. Call him. If he can't answer your questions, nobody can."

"But Peter, tell me more about him. Who is this Juan?"

"He is an anthropologist, a *mestizo*. He teaches here, at the university. In fact, his father, Oscar Nuñez del Prado, was a very well-known anthropologist. He discovered a group of Indians who claim to be direct descendants of the Inkas," he told me.

"Really. How fascinating. But Peter, an academic?" I asked, wrinkling my nose at the idea. Peter and I had had long discussions about the rigid thinking of the academic world.

"Oh, no. He's not like that. Don't worry. Juan has worked with the Indians for years. Then Indians themselves initiated him as an Andean priest. In fact, he apprenticed for more than ten years with the most famous Indian healer of the Cuzco Valley, Don Benito Qoriwaman. Juan was chosen by Don Benito to carry on the teaching of the tradition." This sounded quite promising.

"Thank you so much, Peter," I said, hugging him while clutching the phone number tightly in my hand as if it were some kind of li-patriciane. I ran home and headed straight for the telephone. I dialed the number half expecting that no one would answer.

"'Allo," I heard a man's voice on the other end.

"Juan Nuñez del Prado, por favor," I asked in my best Spanish accent.

"Sí, this is Juan." I was so stunned I didn't know what to say. I hadn't imagined I would reach him so easily.

"Juan, I—I'm sorry to bother you," I stuttered.

"It is no bother. How can I help you?" he answered kindly.

"You don't know me, my name is Elizabeth. I am a friend of Peter Frost. He gave me your name . . . you see . . . er . . . I've had an experience with the *apus*. Peter said you would be able to help me."

"Yes. What sort of experience?" he asked.

"I'm sorry . . . I know you must be a busy person . . . but I would feel much better if we could talk in person," I said, sure he could somehow see my face turning red over the phone.

"Yes, it is better to speak of these things in person," he agreed. "Can you meet me in the main square at six o'clock?"

"I would be delighted," I answered, relieved by the ease of the conversation.

I had just enough time to have dinner and run down the street called Pumakurku, "Puma's Shoulder," to the main square. I arrived out of breath a few minutes after six.

There, sitting on the agreed-upon park bench, was a man with a salt-and-pepper beard, wearing blue jeans, a tan jacket, and a little white felt hat that made him look like a mushroom.

"Juan?" I asked.

"*Sí*, Elizabeth, it's me," he said, reaching out his hand to shake mine. I sat down on the bench with him, feeling a bit wary. He didn't seem anything like Ricardo, but still I was uncomfortable. He had something I desperately needed—knowledge—and that put me at a disadvantage.

Juan appeared to be in his late forties. His dark eyes twinkled when he smiled, yet his look was direct, and strong. The knots in my stomach began to loosen slightly. "Well, you see, a few years ago I lived here," I began haltingly.

"Here in Cuzco?" he asked, surprised.

"Yes . . . I . . . well . . . I worked with an Andean priest."

He seemed to sense my tension. He looked at me with very big, very serious eyes. "Really?" he said. "Me too." And then he burst out laughing as if that were the funniest thing in the world. His laughter was contagious and soon I was laughing too, mostly at my own seriousness. In only a few moments Juan had masterfully and quite disarmingly given me a way out of one of my biggest stumbling blocks, my own self-importance.

I began to tell Juan everything, including my first encounter with the egg diagnosis, my vision of the *apus* alone in my apartment, the *mesas* with Ricardo and the *apus,* and my confusion about the group and their strange behavior toward me. As I talked with Juan, he listened closely, and took me very seriously. It was clear from his expression that he was neither surprised nor amazed, rather that he understood exactly what I was talking about. I grew infinitely more comfortable. I must have, because after a while I realized that I had spoken uninterrupted for over twenty minutes to someone I had just met, on a subject I rarely discussed even with close friends. Finally I clammed up again.

Juan looked at me hard. Then he said in a very serious tone, "You have had a very strong contact with the path. This is wonderful! However, I think your first experience, your vision of the mountain spirits . . . that was the most important."

"But . . . but . . . what about Ricardo and the creatures that materialized in the dark! Do you know about that? Have you ever experienced that?" I protested.

Juan appeared completely unperturbed. "That is not so important. To understand who is your master, you must look at what happens around him. Everything you have described about Ricardo tells me that he is very powerful, yes, but he has not attained the fourth level. He is not a *kurak akulleq.*"

"A what?" I asked.

"Ricardo is an *altomisayoq.* As you know, that means 'high priest' in Quechua. But there are many varieties of high priest. The things you have described about him, the fighting and conflict, the fear and the punishments of his *apus* . . . these things all belong to the third level. A *kurak akulleq* is a priest of the fourth level," he patiently explained.

"The third level . . . the fourth level? What are they, what do they mean?" I asked, curious and relieved that I had finally found someone who not only knew what I was talking about but also could add clarity to my confusion.

"In the Andean Path there are many powerful high priests and, let me tell you, there are very few people, even natives of Cuzco, who manage to have the experiences that you have had! I do not know Ricardo personally, but I have heard many stories of initiates who began their training with teachers like him. You see, I had the good fortune to begin my apprenticeship in this path with the best. There are very few fourth-level priests left. Don Benito Qoriwaman, my master, was one of them. Don Benito was an incredible healer. Everyone knew him. In fact, I am told that one of your American actresses, Shirley MacLaine, has written of him in one of her books." Juan spoke of Don Benito with such love and tenderness that small tears grew in the corners of his eyes.

I wanted to shout for joy and cry at the same time. I knew it, I knew it, I knew it! Deep inside, I had always been certain there was something far beyond what I had learned from Ricardo. I began to get very excited. Then I checked myself. "But, Juan, the *apus*? If those things in the dark, if those are the *apus*, then I don't like *apus*," I said very firmly.

"Yes," Juan said, showing extreme patience with his new student, "at the third level, the *apus* are seen as punishing. But do not confuse the master with the path. Ricardo's *apus* can only appear as his level permits. The transition from the third to the fourth level is very important. At the third level, the initiate encounters the invisible world and the forces there are experienced as frightening, indeed terrifying. You must learn to wrestle with them; you must learn to fight and conquer—your own fear. If not, you remain forever at the mercy of it, like Ricardo.

"The fourth level is a completely different state of mind, you become free, the *apus* become your friends, and you learn to work in harmony with the invisible world. My *apus* are sweet, charming. According to the prophecies, the transition from the third to the fourth level is the most important occurrence of this time!" he concluded.

I took a deep breath. What he said made sense, he was providing a context for my experience. My relief was unbounded.

"Prophecies?" I asked, but Juan brushed my question aside.

"Who is your *itu apu*?" he asked me.

"What is *itu apu*?" I asked.

"Your 'guiding star,' or as you North Americans say, your 'spirit

guide.' Here in the Andes we have a physical teacher, like Don Benito, and a 'guiding star' in the energy world. For a traditional Peruvian initiate his or her guiding spirit is the mountain spirit nearest to
where the initiate was born. As a *paqo*, or initiate on the path, your
progress is guided by the *apu* you were born under, or the one you see
in a vision. As you progress along the path, your 'spirit guide'
changes with your level.

"When I found Don Benito, I worked through the first three
levels very quickly, in less than a year. I thought I would take the
fourth-level initiation right away, but I was wrong. I was not ready.
For the fourth-level initiation, I had to wait ten more years!"

With his words, my hopes were dashed. I wanted so badly to
learn more, but who was I? Only a bare beginner.

"The highest of the third-level priests generally come under the
guidance of Apu Ausangate. When you first arrived here, you had a
vision of Apu Ausangate, which means you began at the highest
rung of the third level, and you have a right to be taught by a priest
of that level," Juan told me.

"Like, say . . . Ricardo?" I asked. Juan nodded his reply.

"Who is the guiding star for the fourth-level priests?" I asked,
always wanting to be precocious.

"Andean initiates begin by talking to small rivers, little streams,
low hills. As they progress through the first, second, and third levels
they come into empathic resonance with larger and more powerful
aspects of Pachamama, the spirit of Mother Earth. At the highest
point of the third level, the Andean priest can speak directly with
the tallest mountains, like Ausangate, and the ocean herself, Mama
Qocha. At the fourth level, the initiate has direct contact with spiritual beings that inhabit the *hanaq pacha*."

"What is *hanaq pacha*?" I asked.

"That is the superior world, similar to the Christian idea of
'heaven.' To understand the Inkas, you must first know that they
viewed their reality as a plethora of diverse types of living energies.
This reality is divided into three planes of existence that are distin-
guished by the quality of energies you find there. The "underworld"

is a plane of dense or heavier energies. The "middle world" or plane of material consciousness—the world of our daily life—contains both refined and heavy energies. Therefore, 'heaven,' as you call it, is a realm of very refined energies," he explained, "and it is inhabited by highly refined spiritual beings. Fourth-level priests have a vision of these beings, for example visions of certain Inkas who live in the upper world, the Buddha or even Jesus Christ."

I let out an involuntary shriek, jumping right off the park bench as he finished his sentence. Juan looked at me, startled. "Elizabeth, are you all right? Have I said something frightening?" he asked.

"No . . . no . . . Juan. I'm sorry," I said, settling back on my perch. My heart was pounding in my chest. "Juan, I have to tell you something." He nodded for me to go on, and I related a story from my very first trip to Peru.

The scene rushed back into my mind. "The first time I was in Peru, I had come here to Cuzco, with my best friend, Cyntha Gonzalez. One afternoon, we went out shopping in the market, where we bought masks from the jungle, and a few statues made of black serpentine stone. Cyntha had warned me to be careful picking the masks because, she told me, they often had spirits attached to them. The coastal shamans in Trujillo had taught her all about this.

"You know, Lizcita," she had said one day as we were discussing her studies, "I learned a lot from the coastal shamans, but the one thing I didn't like is that they would yell and scream to exorcise the molesting spirit that was bothering their client, but they never helped that spirit. This molesting spirit would just jump out of one body and into another. I think you have to help these spirits to move on." Little did we know, we would have an opportunity that very night.

I was careful with the masks, but I just picked up the statues in a hurry, at the last minute. It wasn't until we got back to our hotel that I realized there was something eerie about one of the statues, the puma statue. Before we went to sleep, I put it down on the nightstand between our two beds.

At around two o'clock in the morning, I was startled awake

from a bad dream by the sound of little feet running around our room. I had heard it first in my dream, an angry, agitated sound. When I woke up and sat up in bed, the sound continued.

"Cyntha," I whispered.

"Yes, Lizcita, I hear it too," she responded, just as wide awake as I was. "The puma," she said. Being a practical person, Cyntha reached over and turned on the light. The sound stopped. "Molesting spirits," she said to me. I nodded.

"What do we do?" I asked.

"Pray," Cyntha said simply. "We know this little spirit wouldn't have gotten to us unless it needed our help. Pray for its release," Cyntha told me. We began to pray, and as we did so, I sensed what I could only describe as a curtain of light descend and begin to envelop the room. When I felt afraid, I noticed that the curtain of light would retreat. I got control of my fear, and the curtain descended again, this time completely enveloping Cyntha, me, and the entire room.

It seemed the molesting spirit had attached itself to the puma statue and hitchhiked into our room. Then it had thrown a sort of tantrum to attract our attention. But why?

When the curtain of light was full and bright, I "saw" something shadowlike step onto the curtain and disappear. After about fifteen minutes, we let out simultaneous sighs. The atmosphere of the room, which only a few minutes before had been filled with fear and dread, was now positively charged with a warm, life-giving energy.

"Mission accomplished," Cyntha said laughing. We shook hands for a job well done and, feeling calm and happy, turned out the lights. I was just ready to fall asleep again when I felt another presence above my bed, only this time it was a tremendously warm, loving, vibrating presence. My body grew warm from head to toe and my heart felt so full that it began to hurt, as if it were going to break open.

Jesus, hands outstretched in a gesture of blessing, is looking down on me. Spontaneously I raise my hands under the covers. I open them, mirroring the gesture, receiving it. My body grows warm and I feel my molecules vibrat-

ing faster. I hear his deep sweet voice. "As you have helped this younger brother, so I will help you. As you have opened your heart and given without fear, I will open my heart and give to you. This is that great chain of love that links all existence.

"Until that moment, I had considered myself a Buddhist," I told Juan, laughing. "Christianity gave me the creeps, and I wasn't even interested in Jesus. I never read the Bible—I—"

He waved his hand, cutting me off. "This is excellent," he said, his eyes sparkling at me. "This tells me something very important. You have already had a touch with the fourth level! I think perhaps you may be nearly ready to receive the fourth-level initiation," Juan said, studying my face. "But first you will have to cut your ties with Ricardo."

"What?" I blurted out, not sure which of his statements had been the more shocking. "What do you mean 'cut my ties' with Ricardo? It's been more than two years since I've even seen him."

Juan looked at me forcefully and replied, "That is true. But isn't it also true that you have been feeling unable to move forward in your life? In fact, isn't that why you came back here?" he asked, absolutely reading me like a book.

"Yes," I said, hanging my head, ashamed of my exposed vulnerability.

"That is because Ricardo still has some of your energy. Attaining the fourth level has to do with developing the astral body. When you were in the States did you dream often of Cuzco?" Juan asked.

"Yes," I said, surprised again by his knowledge.

"That's because Ricardo has trapped a part of your bubble," Juan explained.

"My 'bubble'?" I asked.

"Yes, the field of living energy that surrounds your physical body. The Andean masters call that a 'bubble,'" he told me.

"But, Juan, how do I get it back?"

Juan looked at me and said simply, "We must go to see him."

Well, the last thing on earth I wanted to do was to go and visit

Ricardo. Coincidentally, just a few days before my meeting with Juan, I had run into Maria, one of the professors from Ricardo's group, on the street. She forthrightly apologized for having thought badly of me and for all the conflict and trouble I had had with the group. Her son Eduardo, she told me, was fine. The conversation with Maria had been a relief and a closing of that old chapter. Maria said she still saw Ricardo on occasion, and mentioned that he was now holding his *mesas* on Pardo Street, a small side street off the Avenue of the Sun. I had not had the slightest intention of going anywhere near the place. But now I found it curious that, like it or not, I *did* know where to find him.

With more prompting from Juan, I told him that Ricardo worked in the mornings. So we made a plan to go at noon the next day, in order to arrive near the end of the *mesa*. The next morning a few minutes before noon, Juan picked me up at the main square in his little yellow Volkswagen. I had narrowed the location of Ricardo's *mesa* to within two blocks. As usual in Cuzco, there was no exact address. I was more than half hoping we wouldn't be able to find the house and that I would be off the hook. But no such luck. As we drove past the houses I could feel Juan psychically sniffing the air.

"That's the house," he said, pointing to a brown garage door.

"But you don't know Ricardo. How can you be so sure?" I asked, hoping it wasn't so.

"I am sure. When you've worked in this path as long as I have, you know," he said in a tone that left no room for doubt.

Still hoping against hope, I got out of the car and went up to the door. There was a man standing next to a small entryway alongside the garage door. "Excuse me," I said politely, "does Ricardo work here . . . does he hold his *mesas* here?" Juan had parked the car and now walked over to join me on the sidewalk.

The man looked at me very hard, scrutinizing me, then he looked at Juan. Finally he nodded and gestured for us to go in. "Be careful of the dog," he said, in a serious tone.

We walked down the short cement alleyway and turned left into a small waiting room which was occupied only by a large German shepherd—who turned out to be very friendly. My tension escalated as I entered the waiting room, and then sheer panic took over. I wanted to run out of the room. "If they offer us anything to drink, don't take it," Juan said in an authoritative, fatherly voice. I nodded, feeling very small. We sat down in the two available faded and frayed armchairs.

The *mesa* was going on in full force in the room adjoining ours. My knuckles went dead white as I gripped the arm of the chair. I could hear the flapping wings as the *apus* materialized next door. It was all I could do to keep myself from bolting out of the room. I wanted no part of whatever was going on in there. Juan, however, appeared completely undisturbed. He could just as easily have been sitting at home in his living room. He nonchalantly flicked a spot of dust from his jacket and settled in. Then he regarded me compassionately. "Open your *qosqo*," he told me.

"My what?"

He looked surprised, "Your spiritual stomach. Didn't Ricardo teach you this . . . how to open your spiritual stomach and eat heavy energy?" I shook my head. "Feel the energy next door," Juan continued in a low voice. "It is very strong, but very heavy."

I couldn't help but feel the "heavy energy," but for me, just being there was horrifying and it was literally impossible for me to open anything at all. Fear and a sense of imminent danger had slammed all my doors shut. Then I did something I had never done before in my life; I called on Jesus to protect me. "Dear Jesus," I said under my breath, "please help me. Sweet Lord Jesus, protect me from harm." Slowly I began to feel a warm glow around me, which began to permeate the white frost of fear that had by now encrusted all my internal organs. For a moment I could breath again. It was the only thing that had any power against my fear. Slowly I began to unthaw.

After a few minutes, the doors opened and people began to come out of the ceremonial room. "Is that the last *mesa* of the day?" Juan asked the crowd of people, with complete nonchalance, and without even rising from his chair.

"Yes," a man told us before hurrying out the door clutching a small bag of herbs, doubtless a recipe given to him by the *apus*. The familiar smell of flower water exited with him, raising the hair on the back of my neck.

"Juan, do we have to?" I asked, getting up. I struggled to contain my panic.

"Wait . . ." he said sternly, holding up his hand for me to stop, practically sitting me back down in my chair with the force of his gesture. As Juan looked at me, I felt my panic begin to ebb. I wondered if he was eating *my* heavy energy. I sat back down again, suddenly more calm.

A large crowd of people came walking out, but no Ricardo. In one last moment of wild hope I thought we had mistakenly come to the wrong *mesa*. Then I heard his voice from the inner room. I stood up, drawn and repelled at the same time. Juan joined me on my feet and we walked together toward the door and into the inner chamber. As we crossed the threshold, Ricardo was shaking hands with his last client. He looked up and let out a characteristic low chuckle when he saw me.

"Elizabeth, it's been a long time," he said, extending a hand toward me. As I looked at him now, I saw him in an entirely different light. He did not look at all powerful. He looked vulnerable, like a little boy. I lost my fear and began to feel compassionate, even affectionate, toward him. I even started to think that I must have been crazy ever to imagine that he could harm me. I felt all my sympathy go toward him, until Juan's voice shook me awake.

"So, you work with the *apus*," Juan said in an unusually crisp tone.

"Yes," Ricardo said looking at me, his eyebrows making a question mark.

"Oh, I'm sorry, this is Juan, a friend of mine," I blurted out, introducing the two. They shook hands. At the sound of Juan's voice my wariness of Ricardo had returned.

"Tell me . . . who are your teachers?" Juan spoke in a friendly manner, but I had the uncanny sensation that he was lashing his tail, sizing up Ricardo.

"Don Henrique Malchez from Ayacucho . . . Don Arturo . . ." Ricardo rattled off a list of names, none of whom Juan recognized.

"Have you ever been to Q'eros?" Juan asked in the same friendly tone.

"Yes. In fact I've worked in Q'eros," Ricardo said, smiling.

"With whom?" Juan asked.

"Alone. I work with only the biggest and most important *apus*," Ricardo stated, somehow managing not to sound grandiose, "as Elizabeth will tell you." That seemed to be the answer Juan was waiting for.

Suddenly, Juan seemed to grow about two feet taller. He fixed a frightening gaze on Ricardo and said, "Is that right? Well, *now she is working with me*." His words were not loud, but each one seemed to carry a tremendous force. I wanted to rub my eyes. It seemed as if Juan had just grabbed Ricardo by both arms and locked him in a full nelson. Physically neither man had moved a muscle.

Ricardo exhaled. I had a vague sensation of something around me letting go. Ricardo suddenly seemed far away. He no longer looked vulnerable, nor was he angry. He looked like a balloon that had had all the air let out of it. Juan spoke to Ricardo now in a normal tone. "I have been to Q'eros, Ricardo. Don Benito Qoriwaman and Don Andres Espinoza were my masters. If you would ever like to go to Q'eros, I will take you there."

"Yes, thank you," Ricardo said, first shaking my hand and then Juan's.

"*Adiós*," Juan said, saluting Ricardo.

"*Adiós*," he responded.

We got into Juan's yellow Volkswagen and drove back to the main square in silence. I couldn't explain how, but I felt distinctly different. Juan stopped the car and we sat another moment in silence. "Very good, very good," he muttered to himself, seeming exceedingly pleased. "So, Elizabeth, what do you think?" he asked, looking at me pointedly.

"I'm not sure. What exactly happened in there?" I asked him cautiously.

"What did you see?" he asked, handing it back to me.

"Well, it seemed like there was some kind of fight, almost like you and Ricardo were arm wrestling or something, but you never even touched each other," I said, feeling stupid about my answer.

"Yes. Very good, Elizabeth," Juan said encouragingly. "You see, in my tradition, when two *paqos* meet it's natural to have a challenge, as we just did. But rather than physical strength, the challenge is to see whose bubble is stronger. When he said he had worked alone in Q'eros I knew that he could not have my level. No one works alone in Q'eros. It means he has never encountered a teacher from Q'eros. Then it's just as if he's never been there. The only remaining fourth-level priests come from Q'eros."

"What's Q'eros?" I asked, feeling stupid again.

Juan laughed. "Actually it is a nation of Andean Indians who live at about fifteen thousand feet altitude. They are direct descendants of the Inkas." That must be the place Peter Frost had mentioned! He stared at my confused expression. "Let's just call it the Oxford of the Andean priests," he told me.

"They taught you . . . this?" I said carefully.

"Correct. The priests of Q'eros and Don Benito Qoriwaman."

"So this 'fight' you had with Ricardo was . . . energetic?"

"Precisely," Juan said.

"And you . . . won?" I tried the word on to see if it fit.

"In a way. But not the way you Westerners think of winning," Juan explained. "You see, in my tradition when there is a challenge between two initiates and one shows they have a higher level, the 'winner' is obligated to teach the other how they won. That is the meaning of competition for us, and that is why I offered to take him to Q'eros. I bested Ricardo, now I must offer to teach him what I know and how I learned it."

"That is a very interesting view of competition," I said, liking Juan's teachings of the Andean philosophy more and more. "Juan, really, I don't know how to thank you," I said, reaching out to give him a hug.

"Ah, but I do know how," he told me. "Now you are ready to receive the fourth level. The best way for me to advance along my path is to teach. I must teach all that I know. It is the law of *ayni*. What you can do now for me, and for your own learning, is to return to Cuzco with a group of twelve North American initiates. If you do this, I will give you and your group the ten-day initiation of *hatun karpay*. That is the 'great initiation' that my master, Don Benito, gave to me five years ago." I was honored by the invitation.

"One more thing, Elizabeth," he said, gazing at me. "My guiding star is telling me that you must write down all of your experiences with the Andean Path, to share with others." I was heartened to hear him say this.

"Really, Juan? To tell you the truth I have been writing. You think it's okay? I mean . . . you wouldn't mind if I wrote about all this?"

He looked at me full of emotion, and said, "Do you know why I would like it, Elizabeth?"

"No. Why?" I asked.

"Because it would give honor to my master, Don Benito."

I was moved by Juan's deep devotion to his teacher and I knew Don Benito must have been very special. "But Juan, if it took you ten years before you were ready to receive the fourth-level initiation, then why are you willing to give this initiation now to people that have never even been here?" I asked.

"There are several reasons. First of all, these levels are universal and can be achieved through any kind of spiritual work, not only through the Andean Path. Many of you North Americans have most likely already advanced through the first three levels. Secondly, contained within the structure of the *hatun karpay* initiation are all of the previous levels. But the even more compelling reason is that, according to the Andean prophecies, the world is passing through a very critical moment."

"Yes, please tell me more about these prophecies, Juan. I feel this may have to do with why I was so drawn to Peru in the first place!" I told him, feeling my pulse quicken.

"I have been researching these prophecies for the past twelve years. This next nineteen-year period, 1993 to 2012, marks a very important time of transformation. It is a time we in the Andean tradition call the *taripay pacha*. Don Benito and my other Andean masters have taught me that we must work for what can be the coming of a golden age of human abundance. *Taripay pacha* literally means the 'age of meeting ourselves again.' This is a time when human beings must really begin to work together.

"August first of 1993 marked the end of the *pachakuti*—a 'cosmic transmutation'—and the beginning of the first phase of the *taripay pacha*. This initial phase is supposed to last from 1993 until the emergence of the fifth level of consciousness, a group of healer/priests with extraordinary powers. At the time when they appear, we will have entered the second phase of the *taripay pacha*. The second phase will last until the manifestation—or the return—of the *sapa* Inka, a sixth-level priest. This is the level of consciousness of the Inka rulers of old. A person with the Inka level of consciousness must be an extraordinary political and spiritual leader, who will be able to re-create and surpass the empire of the ancient Inkas. The full-blown form of the *taripay pacha* will begin when the sixth-level priests emerge, which could be around 2012 or so. The dates are uncertain because this is only an opportunity, a possibility. We—humanity—must do the work.

"This time period from 1993 to 2012 represents what your people in developmental psychology would call a 'critical period' in the development of human collective consciousness. These nineteen years mark the time when a significant percentage of humanity can and must pass from the third to the fourth level. We must be able to leave fear behind and learn to share our cultural gifts and achievements, and enter into a friendly relationship with the invisible world and the forces of nature. It is up to the people of the earth, us, to maximize this critical period in order to bring in the *taripay pacha*," Juan said emphatically.

"Yes, I see," I told him numbly, feeling completely overwhelmed. I looked down at the rusted dent on the door of Juan's little yellow VW bug and at the worn front tire. As Juan spoke, it seemed the entire car had entered into an exalted state. I half expected to see us floating a few feet above the cobblestoned street.

"You see, Elizabeth, we are simply laying the groundwork, or preparing the conditions through collective spiritual work, for the emergence of the next steps in human evolution," he told me simply.

"Juan, I don't—I'm not—I—"

"Elizabeth." He stopped me with a gesture as he read my thoughts. "Why do you think we are sitting here now? Do you think it is for nothing that you were given the vision of the mountain spirit?"

"But Juan . . . it all sounds so . . . so . . . big," I said, feeling very small and very vulnerable.

"Each person must do their part. Nothing more. But nothing less. Let the energy world guide you. Do only what your heart tells you is right," Juan said.

I hugged Juan again and opened the car door in a daze, thanking him for his offer and letting him know I would think about it.

I RETURNED TO THE STATES, AND OVER THE NEXT SIX months I began to feel "normal" again. Curiously, I had been unable even to contemplate the prophecy Juan had told me about. But I *had* wondered if regaining my equilibrium had anything to do with recovering the part of my bubble that had been trapped by Ricardo. In fact, I was so sure there must be a connection that I telephoned Juan to thank him.

"I am glad for you, Elizabeth," he said, his voice crackling over the long-distance connection, "and I think you are now feeling more autonomous." "Autonomous!" That was exactly the word. Juan reminded me again of his offer, and I thanked him without making any promises, and we said good-bye. The truth was, that after my previous experience, I was afraid of doing any more spiritual work in Cuzco. The idea of being a tourist didn't bother me, but something about being involved in esoteric work in Cuzco still had me scared silly.

A few weeks later, I heard that a new discovery had been made in northern Peru—a tomb with more gold in it than King Tut's tomb had been unearthed in a place called Sipan—and a museum in Los Angeles was exhibiting the treasures. I went down to have a look. After a grand total of about thirty minutes inside the exhibit I got the creeps so bad that I had to leave. There was something tremendously frightening to me about the Chimu culture and it seemed connected to my fear of returning to Peru. I thought back to the unnerving experience that I had had with Cyntha and my friend David in the enormous ruin of Chan Chan.

We had all three been overwhelmed by the call for help from the entrapped souls there. That place was the perfect example of psychic powers having been used for an evil purpose. It was an astral prison. The idea of somehow locking up or torturing someone's soul was even worse to me than physical torture.

On the plane back from Los Angeles I realized that I was being haunted by fear. Just as Juan had described, fear had gotten ahold of me and was controlling me—the challenge of the third level. This aroused the fighter in me and by the time I got back to my home in West Marin, I had come to a decision. I was going to investigate this fear. Sooner than I had expected, the opportunity presented itself.

A few days later, during one of my morning meditations, my skin began to crawl and the hair on my arms stood straight up as an image appeared in my mind's eye. I found myself staring into the face of the most horrific creature I had ever seen. On sight the image produced an abysmal feeling of dread. Its facial features were large and thick. The creature had charcoal-gray skin that covered its hairless poll. Its eyes were glaring yellow. A putrid ocher light bathed its head and shoulders, and its torso was covered in a thick gray leather armor. Around its neck was a collar of huge iron spikes. A sadistic expression moved across the twisted features of the creature's face as it spoke to me in a tone that broadcast imminent danger.

"I am intelligent, organized evil," it said in a dark scratchy growl. The air about the creature was stiff with threat. It looked like an image from the Sipan exhibit. Large drops of water rolled down my sides, as I began to sweat with terror. What had I called up? I knew this was an image in my mind, yet I was certain that somewhere, sometime, this creature had also had a manifested existence. This creature and what it said most definitely embodied my deepest fear.

In the past, I generally believed that evil was really more a matter of misunderstanding and that basically people did not want to do evil to each other, but had only learned by bad example. This was something entirely different. This was a creature that consciously and intentionally perpetrated acts of cruelty and violence and gained energy by harming others.

I tried to protect myself. I imagined pushing the creature away or putting a barrier between me and it. Nothing worked. Then all at once I realized that I wouldn't be able to see it at all unless there was some part of *me* that corresponded to *it*. Suddenly memories came flooding through me of times when I had intentionally done things to hurt others, from small, silly things to larger, more important events in my life, which now made me blush with embarrassment.

I recalled what Juan had told me, that the Andean masters said that the world was made up of different kinds of living energies, some heavy and some more refined. At Ricardo's *mesa*, Juan had told me that the energy there was very strong but very heavy, and that I should open my *qosqo*, my spiritual stomach, and eat it. At the time the idea seemed crazy. At this moment it seemed my only viable option. This creature, imagined or otherwise, was not going anywhere. Particularly now that it had shown me that it was some aspect of me. Once I surrendered to this fact, a feeling something like grace overcame me. My perspective shifted. Instead of being afraid, I became filled with compassion for this miserable creature. And without another thought, I opened my arms to the creature and pulled it into me, into my *qosqo*. I embraced it. And with it I embraced that part of my own darkness. Completely. Tenderly. Like a mother.

The creature got a rather perturbed and then suddenly delighted expression on its face. And it began to break apart. The force of its dissolving energetic structure literally sent shock waves through my body. I rocked involuntarily back and forth on my meditation cushion with the release of energy.

Within a few weeks of this liberating experience, I knew it was time to gather my group. I was ready for the fourth level.

PART II

Hatun Karpay:
The Great Initiation

8

Inka Seed

"WE BEGIN HERE," JUAN ANNOUNCED TO OUR GROUP, still bleary-eyed from the previous day's twenty hours of air travel. The pained expressions told me that nearly everyone was suffering from some form of altitude sickness.

"Here?" I asked Juan, puzzled. At nearly eleven thousand feet altitude, we were standing on the main square in front of the central cathedral of Cuzco, shivering in the chill morning air of an Andean spring. The Catholic cathedral, made from huge blocks of sand-colored stone, had first been built by the Spanish in the mid-1500s, but had been razed several times over the centuries by earthquakes, while the antiseismic Inka stonework underneath remained intact. The sky behind the cathedral was a rich and brilliant blue, with tufts of snow white clouds hovering around the thrusting peaks that surrounded the city of Cuzco. We stood gulping the pure, thin air into our oxygen-deprived lungs.

It had been more than a year since I had last seen Juan, and in that year I had managed to do what he had asked. I had gathered or, more accurately, a group had coalesced almost of its own accord, around the idea of going down to Peru to experience the initiation Juan had told me about. The group members, a mix of colleagues and friends, knew next to nothing about this Peruvian spiritual tradition, just a few garbled explanations and stories I had told them from my own adventures. Yet each person had come with a deep reverence for the earth and a hearty respect for the process of spiritual initiation. Curiously, all of them had in their various unique ways expressed feeling a mysterious soul-level urgency to participate in this trip, as if something far beyond their own personal agendas were at work here. I, too, was at a loss to explain any of it; I knew only that some deeply instinctual prompting had led me to the spot where I was now standing. I, like that fateful amphibian who first stepped out onto shore, now stood at my own water's edge.

"I had to wait more than ten years to receive this initiation," Juan told his captive audience. "But even *I* was shocked when my master, Don Benito, took me *here* to begin the first day of the great initiation, the *hatun karpay*."

"Who's Don Benito, Juan?" Nina, a tall, slender strawberry-blond massage therapist asked.

"Don Benito," Juan began, and again I noticed the water come to his eyes, "*was* one of the most powerful and well-respected healers in the entire Cuzco Valley. He was a little Indian, about this tall," Juan told us, holding his hand up to mark less than five feet in height. "And he was an amazing man."

"The first time I met Don Benito I was a hard-core anthropologist, very committed to the rational approach. I had a grant from the Ford Foundation to study the religious beliefs of the Andean Indians and I was sent to Don Benito, an Andean priest, as one of my primary informants. At that time I didn't speak Quechua very well, and I brought with me one of my students who spoke fluent Spanish and Quechua. We went to Don Benito's village, bringing with us the little pack of coca leaves and small bottle of liquor that are the traditional gifts one must offer to an Andean priest. And Don Benito invited us into his humble house.

"We sat down at a little table and he brought out three tiny cups to offer us some of the liquor we had brought. This little Indian man was very poor, but a very refined gentleman! We each drank one little cup of liquor and he and I began to talk with the help of the translator. Don Benito then invited us to another cup of liquor and he began to talk directly to me, using a mix of Spanish and Quechua. This encouraged me, and so I responded in the same way, mixing both languages. Don Benito invited us to a third cup of liquor and soon I noticed that he was talking directly to me, but not in Spanish, or Quechua, or Chinese, or any other language I could recognize. The strange thing was that not only could I understand everything he was saying, but I could see in clear pictures all that he was telling me about. Somehow I was even able to respond back to him in that same language! More strange still was that at the time, all of this seemed perfectly normal. We talked like this for the better part of two hours before Don Benito gave an end to the interview. When we stood up to go out of his house, I found that my translator, a man known for his tremendous capacity for alcohol, was totally drunk. And not only that, he had not understood one word of our conversation!

"Over the next month I had something like a nervous breakdown. All my previous rationalist approach to things could not begin to explain this experience. Finally I gave in and became Don Benito's disciple. I worked with him for ten years," Juan said, wiping away a tear that had strayed down his cheek and into his bushy beard.

Juan's story had captured not only our complete attention but also our hearts. The authenticity of his tale and his delightful description of Don Benito had won us over. Clearly, what we were about to learn was the real thing! So complete was the spell of Juan's tale that we had almost forgotten that we were standing on Cuzco's main square.

I knew from my studies that the Spanish cathedral before us was built on the site of the ancient Temple of Wiraqocha; but what I didn't know was what Juan told us next. "For Andean priests, and certainly for Don Benito, this site remains a key part of the sacred geography of the Andean area. This temple is an energetic opening to the superior world, the world of refined energies." The group turned in unison to cast an eye on the cathedral that stood behind our tight circle. I had heard before that cathedrals and churches in many parts of the United States had also been built on land considered sacred by the indigenous peoples.

"Juan, what do you mean by a 'world of refined energies'?" Sam, a tall and handsome computer programmer from Florida, queried. Sam was a hard-core scientist who had recently discovered that his great-grandfather was full-blood Lakota.

"You see, the Andean priests have never been trained to think like us. They are not focused on buildings, cars, houses, roads, or even symbols. They are much more concerned with energy. My masters do not inhabit a world made up only of solid objects. For us," he said, referring to Andean priests, "the world is made up of infinite varieties of living energies, collectively called *kausay.*"

"But certainly they don't deny that the material world exists?" protested Sam, a little perplexed.

"Not at all," Juan responded gently. "We all experience the world of material consciousness, including the Andean priests, but for them it is not the only world and it certainly is not the primary world. Every material object also has a spirit or energetic aspect. The mountains, the trees, rocks, plants, rivers, even buildings and cities, possess an energetic consciousness. All creatures, from the tiniest protozoa to human beings, elephants, and whales, all possess this same energetic consciousness, a "bubble" of living energy that surrounds and interpenetrates the material body. To enter the world of the Andean mystical priest you must learn to communicate and interact directly with this world of living energies and with the energy bubbles of other people, beings, and places."

There were coughs and sighs as people shifted uneasily back and forth on their feet. While these ideas were not completely new to most of us, they certainly did challenge the reality we had all grown up believing, the reality that delineated our world and made it secure, known. Certainly, for years, theories of modern physics, including quantum mechanics and Einstein's theory of relativity, had been paving the way for these ideas to enter the Western mind. But that didn't make them any less personally challenging. Intellectually grasping an idea is very different from experiencing the living reality.

In Peru I had had my own direct experiences of the malleability of the material world when I had witnessed the *apu* materializations, and while they were fascinating, they had also been downright terrifying. I knew what it was like to have my beliefs shaken down to their roots. But I wondered how the others in the group, who had never had such personal experiences, would relate to these ideas.

Juan continued to explain the fundamental energetic principles of Andean mysticism. "First you must understand that for Andean priests, within the world of living energies no positive or negative energies exist. There are only gradations of more subtle and refined living energies, and energies that are more dense or heavy. The various types and gradations of these diverse living energies make up the basic order of Andean cosmology," he explained.

"The Andean cosmos is divided into three planes of existence, each with its own distinct energetic qualities. The first plane is the superior world, *hanaq pacha*, or what native North Americans call the 'upper world.' This plane is extremely spiritual and inhabited by the most refined energies, including various spiritual beings such as Jesus, the Virgin Mary, various Inkas, and a host of local saints. The second plane, *kay pacha*, is the realm of humanity and the world of material consciousness, and it consists of a mix of both refined and heavy energies. It is also known as the 'middle world,' or the world of our everyday existence. Invisible and mystical beings such the *apus* also dwell on this plane alongside humanity. The final plane, *ukhu pacha*, is the interior world, or the 'lower world.' As conceived of by Andean priests, the interior world is the plane that resides within the earth, and within each individual. Although occupied largely by heavy energies, the interior world is not a type of hell. Rather it is a place where spirits begin to learn the sacred art of reciprocity, *ayni*."

Juan informed us that our first ritual would connect us to the refined energies of the superior world, and it would begin by experiencing the traditional Catholic mass. "For the Inkas, sacred objects were considered gateways to the refined energies of the superior world. When the Spanish came, the Inkas understood their worship of the icon of Jesus and the Virgin Mary as a way to absorb refined masculine and refined feminine energies by connecting to the energy bubbles of these highly spiritual beings." Juan told us we would participate in the Catholic mass, but worship Inka style, before these icons. If we wished we could take communion.

Several people in the group expressed concern about the use of Catholicism to achieve what we were led to believe would be a uniquely Andean experience. Juan dismissed these worries by explaining that the Andean system is extremely flexible and adaptive. "Most importantly it is inclusive," he informed us. "It has a structure—yes, but there are no rigid rules or dogmas and only one law, *ayni.* You must understand that the Inka empire had more than twelve million inhabitants composed of over one hundred ethnic groups that spoke more than twenty different languages. They were a study in what today you would call 'diversity.' Part of why they were so successful is because the Inkas allowed each group its religious identity, bound together by one unifying deity, the Sun. The Inkas believed in sharing and integrating new knowledge, including spiritual knowledge. My master, Don Benito himself, was a devout Catholic. We are a very devoted people and for us no form of worship can be wrong. In fact, you will see today that the Andean tradition is designed for initiates of diverse religious traditions to exchange their knowledge via the greatest human common denominator, the *kausay pacha*—the energy universe. Do not be fooled by religions' outer forms. But nothing is obligatory here. If you feel like it, take communion, if not, don't."

Puzzled and foggy-brained now from a combination of sleep deprivation, altitude, and this influx of new ideas, yet determined to, as Juan said, "try them on," we entered the main doors of the cathedral. We followed Juan toward a small altar near the back of the church, where the twenty or so Peruvians who were attending morning mass sat on scarred wooden pews, their hats in their hands. As we approached, the priest asked his small congregation to participate with more fervor. Just as we were sitting down, they began to sing. But not even their singing could penetrate this dismal, dank atmosphere.

By now it was about nine in the morning, and inside the cathedral the air was freezing cold. The thick walls and high-vaulted ceilings made for a dark and ominous interior and the enormous, imposing solid silver altar in front of us created anything but a cozy atmosphere. The only relief from the bone-chilling dreariness came from the strong rays of the Inka sun that filtered in through a stained glass window above us, casting a magnificent shaft of colored light across the pews to our left. It was a perfect metaphor for our initiation; nature shone a ray of hope into this dark, man-made world. The cathedral itself only conjured images of the Spanish conquest and the heartless massacre of Indian peoples. I sat in my pew, shivering from two kinds of cold.

I looked up at the eight-foot-tall, jet-black crucifix suspended above the altar before me. Christ's face was large, with a mournful and very vulnerable human-looking expression. On his head was an overly large crown of thorns.

Juan's words were moving through me, loosening up the fixed ideas I carried about Catholicism and Catholic iconography, ideas that had never before been challenged—at least not like this. I concentrated on the image of the crucifix, trying to imagine it as a doorway to refined masculine energy from the superior world. Just the thought of taking in refined energy from above felt good, cleansing, and grounding, as if I were actually bringing a cleaner air into the cathedral. I concentrated, and slowly I felt my consciousness shift as I turned my attention from the two-dimensional symbol to the energetic presence of the Black Christ.

A strong and warm radiance, penetrating like the sun, swept through me, literally warming my body—a sharp contrast from the oppressive cold of the church. I tried to pull in more and more of this refined masculine energy. As I did so, it came rushing in.

Time that I could not measure passed, and I sensed peripherally that the group had finished and was ready to move on, but I was still deep in trance. A profound sense of peace filled me and a knowledge that spiritually I had at last come home. From somewhere far away, it occurred to me that I had to get up, to go with the group, but my thoughts did not translate into movement. My body did not respond.

"Stay until the flux of energy has finished," Juan whispered to me, somehow able to perceive what I was experiencing.

Long minutes passed before I opened my eyes to see the Peruvians lined up in front of the altar, waiting to take Communion, and, to my complete surprise, every member of my group had joined in the line. We were viscerally experiencing the juxtaposition of rituals that Juan had just been telling us about. Incomprehensibly I, too, felt no contradiction, no friction or problem in practicing these two seemingly disparate spiritual traditions that had existed side by side for the past five hundred years.

Without speaking, we walked en masse to the enormous painting of the Virgin Mary, which was just inside the front door of the cathedral. When we first entered the church, I had seen many Peruvians kneel for long moments, heads bowed, praying to the Virgin. Now, as we took our places before the icon, I registered an uncanny sensation, as if the Holy Mother of love and forgiveness truly inhabited this area. I wondered if this was because, as Juan had told us, the location itself had a special power.

I kneeled, trying to pray, but I was distracted by my own thoughts about what I was doing, about the icon, my ideas about the Virgin. After a few minutes my thoughts calmed. Again I focused my intention, trying to perceive the energetic emanation from the icon. There was a rush, an influx of a very refined but enveloping energy that was distinctly different from the sensation I had experienced in front of the Black Christ. I became wrapped in a mantle of gentle, magnetic love force. And as I stood there, somehow I was able to perceive the most expanded feeling of compassion and forgiveness I had ever experienced. Involuntary tears welled up in me as I accepted this gift of divine feminine energy. Again it seemed that hours had passed, yet it was only several minutes before we rose to leave.

Juan gestured to the left of the icon, toward a sandy-colored ovoid stone about a meter high sitting unobtrusively in the corner of the church. Even if I had known about the egg beforehand, I would never have noticed it if Juan hadn't pointed it out. "In the sixteenth century," Juan said, addressing the group in a hushed voice, "Juan de Santa Cruz Pachacuti drew a diagram of the main altar of the Inkas, showing the pantheon of Inka gods. In the upper center of the diagram there is an egg that the Inkas called Wiraqocha. The egg that is represented in that drawing is here now, in the cathedral." Juan pointed again to the egg-shaped stone.

Several of us drew in audible breaths of surprise to find an original Inkan artifact sitting so unceremoniously before us. "It is the third icon, the one with which we shall complete this ritual." It seemed strange to talk after such an unexpectedly moving experience in front of the Virgin Mary icon. But at the same time, somehow the explanations were reassuring, giving my mind something to latch onto.

"This large stone egg, like the Black Christ, is a *khuya*. *Khuya* literally means "passionate love," but in its mystical interpretation it refers to the love energy infused into an object, usually a rock, and given to the student by his master. This love-gift transmits the power of the master to the student. This stone egg is the *khuya* of Wiraqocha from the superior world. It is the love-gift to the people of the material world, from Wiraqocha, the metaphysical God of the Inkas, and the great master of the superior world. The egg's full name means 'the great unifier of all things,' and certainly here it has served that purpose." We regarded this third icon with awe. There it was, a simple egg-shaped stone, which looked as if it were now being used as a door stop.

"Since the conquest of the Inkas," Juan explained, "this cathedral continues to be used as a temple of initiation by Andean priests, meaning that over the last five hundred years, Catholic and Andean priests have been carrying out their rituals under the same roof.

"Last year, in December, a friend of mine, Abran Valencia, published a book describing the Inka tradition. After the book came out, the Catholic priests tried to stop the practice by removing the egg from the cathedral. At the time the archbishop was out of town, but when he returned, he received many visits from many people in rapid succession, and a few days later the egg was returned to its rightful place." Audible exhales of relief were heard from the group as Juan paused a moment in his story. How sad, I thought, that we humans were so threatened, so frightened by our differences.

"The function of the egg is to serve as a 'heavy-energy eater,'" Juan told us as we all stared at the stone. "Another important concept in the Andean tradition regarding the maintenance of the energetic economy not only of oneself, but of one's environment, is that it is always better to receive refined energy first, then release our heavy energy. In the first part of this ritual, we received refined masculine energy from the superior world through the crucifix, and refined feminine energy through the icon of the Virgin Mary, now we are prepared to release our *hoocha*, or heavy energy. We can do this by giving all our heavy energy to the stone egg.

"Quechua has many words to describe energy, like *hoocha* and *sami*, as I have already told you. In Quechua the word designating the field of living energy surrounding the human body is called *kausay poq'po*, literally meaning 'energy bubble.'"

That was it! I thought excitedly—that was what I had felt in front of the icons—as if I were like a bubble that was being filled up!

Astonishingly, Juan spoke my thoughts aloud. "We begin by filling our bubbles with refined energy," he informed us, "because if we were to release our *hoocha* first, we could collapse and be left drained and without energy. So, first we fill our bubbles with refined energy and then release our heavy energy to the egg. You must not be afraid to give your heavy energy to the egg. It likes to eat your *hoocha*, you see," he told us, smiling.

This part seemed rather hard. Receiving refined energy was easy, but releasing heavy energy? Somehow, it felt like littering. It took a lot of coaxing from Juan for us to believe that it was all right to put our heavy energy into the egg. "Remember, *heavy* energy is not *bad*. Besides, what is heavy energy to you could be refined energy to someone else. You people really believe in original sin, don't you? Besides, the egg was made for this purpose. It wants to eat your heavy energy."

Reassured, one by one, we went up to the stone egg, kneeling before it, much as we had done with the icons. But this time we prayed to the egg to take our heavy energy. Feeling like the shepherd (or should I say llama-herd?) of the group, I waited until everyone was finished, and then with great reverence for this last remaining icon of the Inka culture, I knelt before the egg. Immediately I felt a natural outflowing of energy, as if the egg were magnetically sucking something out of me. I formed an intention, making my heavy energy into an offering to the egg. Embarrassed at being the focus of the group, I remained only a few minutes, then stood up and began walking back, toward the rest of the group. But as I did so, I felt the tremendous sucking power of the egg draw me back. It wasn't finished with me yet. Juan sent me back with a wave of his hand, laughing and commenting to the group, "Oh, you see, she has lots and lots of heavy energy."

The group sat, mute with the power of the ceremony, outside the cathedral awaiting the truck that would take us to the next ritual site. After a long silence a few comments were exchanged attesting to the group's fascination with this philosophy that seemed to be an ancient practice based in the most modern theories of quantum physics.

As we drove the twenty-minute bus ride behind Saqsaywaman, toward the ruin of Q'enko, tongues loosened further and several comments were made about the uncanny and tangible sensations of energy people had experienced. The practice of the rituals involved conceiving of ourselves in a completely new and unfamiliar way. No longer were we just physical bodies but rather we were "energy bubbles" exchanging heavy and refined energies with sacred places and objects. It was an appealing concept, and the most astonishing thing was that it was really quite easy. This was what had struck people most, that what at first had sounded so foreign, mysterious, and complicated in theory was actually quite simple, natural, and easy in practice. Using Juan's energy terminology, it even became easy to talk about.

AFTER PARKING OUR BUS JUST ABOVE THE RUIN OF Q'ENKO we walked across the road and climbed over a barbed-wire fence. We passed a small eucalyptus grove and entered an area of grassy hillside that contained several large gray boulders about twice as tall as a man and set into the hillside. In between two of the boulders and about half as high was a flat, blackened stone that made a shelf or a ledge between the boulders. The surface of the stone and the rock behind it looked as if it were used continually for ritual burning. "This ritual site is called Illia Pata, which means 'Platform of Light,'" Juan told us. "You can see that this site is still in constant use," Juan stated, gesturing toward the fresh ashes on the stone. "My master, Don Benito, taught me that this site is considered to be the equivalent of the Qorikancha, the ancient central temple of the Inkas in Cuzco, just off the Avenida del Sol. It is thought that the Andean priests retreated to this site when the Qorikancha was taken over by the Spanish. This is a very ancient site and may even have been the Inka's primary temple, used to make offerings before the Qorikancha was built."

I wondered if the "platform of light" referred to the flat altar stone. Sure enough, Juan walked up to it and put his hand on the stone, saying, "The rock of this stone altar is called 'growing rock' because it is considered to be alive. The force of Pachamama is concentrated in it. The feminine part of the ritual we will do with the rock. The masculine part of the ritual we will do with the *apus*."

I started. This was going to be my first encounter with the *apus* since my last visit to Ricardo's *mesa*. But it was hard to feel afraid now, because the context was so vastly different. First of all, I was not in a darkened room, and second, the *apus* were presented as only part of the living system of nature rather than the oracles and authority figures; and besides, I was with a group of people whom I trusted implicitly. Not to mention, of course, our excellent guide.

JUAN CONTINUED HIS EXPLANATION, "THE *APUS* ARE—GENERALLY speaking—masculine energies of nature, or deities that inhabit the highest mountain peaks. Here at this site, we are going to work with the high level of the material world, and with the masculine power of the *apus* and the feminine power of Pachamama." Juan's smiling eyes grew suddenly serious as he said, "In working with *kay pacha*—the world of the material consciousness—we must learn to interchange personal power, whereas in working with the superior world, we receive power. Through the ritual of the *apus* and working with this altar stone you will learn to exchange personal power through your spiritual stomach, your *qosqo*. Therefore the first thing you must learn is how to use your *qosqo*," he said, patting his stomach in the solar plexus area, just a few inches above his waistline.

Juan took a small, brightly colored bundle out of a white canvas bag and placed it on top of the altar stone before he went on. "Don Benito explained it to me like this: You have a stomach to eat and digest food, but your energy body or bubble, your *poq'po*, has a spiritual stomach to eat and digest energy. *Qosqo* is the Quechua name for the city of Cuzco, meaning 'navel of the earth,' that is one reason why this is such a powerful place, it is the *qosqo* of Pachamama, the belly of our planet. In the Andean tradition, humans are an integral part of nature—in fact, our bodies are made in the image of Pachamama. So you see, it is of central importance to learn how to command this center, because through it," he said, tapping his belly and looking pointedly at Nina, "you will learn to sense energy, to eat heavy energy, to draw power from the forces of nature, and to connect to the ritual sites."

Juan paused for a moment, letting the importance of his last words sink in. "The purpose in learning to use your *qosqo* is that you become very good at eating heavy energy. Once you can do this you will be comfortable in any situation, because you will never have to defend yourself against 'negative energies,' you only have to eat them. The more heavy energy there is, the more of a meal you can have, and the more powerful you can become; but you have to be able and willing to digest heavy energy, you must let it pass through you. We Westerners are so stuck in the idea of good and bad—negative and positive—we have the most trouble with this concept. You must learn to do *ayni*, energy exchange. You must not be afraid to be in the exchange, to give and receive *all* the energies."

Juan then told us to place a hand in front of our *qosqo* until we could sense the energy—then try moving our hand first closer, and then farther away. As I placed my hand over my *qosqo* I immediately sensed a warmth and tingling in my belly. This increased and decreased as I moved my hand closer and farther away. Suddenly a number of belly-oriented metaphors came to mind—"gut reaction," and "I can't stomach it"—and I wondered if they actually referred more to the perceptive power of the *qosqo*, rather than to the physical stomach itself. "Use your *qosqo* like the diaphragm of a camera. Open it, close it, and try to feel energy with it," Juan directed us.

Picking up the bundle, he walked over to the group and then explained to us that this was his *mesa*, a small ritual pack he always carried, filled with the *khuyas*, or stones blessed by all of his masters. An itching curiosity made me want to open the pack and look inside. Juan walked back to the stone altar, and, praying softly aloud, he placed his *mesa* on the rock and stood over it, this time praying for several minutes. Then he picked up the *mesa* and carefully carried it to where I was standing. Moving my hand aside he placed his *mesa* firmly against my *qosqo*, continuing to pray out loud.

"Give all your heavy energy to my *mesa*," he whispered to me. Just as in the cathedral, I felt an outflow of energy from my *qosqo*. Abruptly Juan released the *mesa* from where it had almost seemed attached, and carried it to the rock altar. For a moment I thought I saw a little string suspended between my *qosqo* and the altar stone. I blinked and it was gone.

He performed the same action with each of us. Several more

times I saw the strings. When he was finished, a moment of non-ordinary vision showed me what looked like a spider web, all twelve *qosqos* attached by tiny strings of light to the main altar stone. I looked again at the altar stone and saw a layer of blue-white light that now covered it and extended about six inches above the rock. Juan regarded me curiously, cocking his head to one side. "Now you know why it is called the platform of light," he said, in a tone pitched so that only I could hear him.

WE WALKED DOWN A SHORT EMBANKMENT, JUST BELOW THE Illia Pata, to a flat area that had several carved Inka stone seats, and we all sat down in the hot sun. We were going to make a *despacho* invoking the power of the wind. Juan unfolded one of the white paper packages that he had bought in the central market on our way out of town. He took out the shell and the lead crucifix. He then passed around the shell, symbol of the feminine, and the crucifix, symbol of the masculine, telling us to place our highest prayers into the objects. When he retrieved them, he placed first the shell in the center of the *despacho*, then placed the cross on top of it. We each chose three perfect coca leaves and began "arming the *despacho*" by forming *k'intus*, clusters of three leaves. Juan told us to blow on the leaves three times, offering our energy to the *apus* as we invoked each *apu* of the surrounding mountains by name, and placed the coca leaves in a specific order around the central objects.

The completed *despacho* was a beautiful work of art. The twelve *k'intus* placed in star fashion around the central shell made a lovely nature mandala. Juan asked us to call silently on the power of the wind, using it to expand our awareness—and therefore our bubbles—out to touch each one of the *apus* we had just invoked. I closed my eyes to concentrate and rather than sensing anything frightening I found that by connecting with the mountain spirits in this way, I received a psychic impression of delight from the *apus*. In fact, they seemed downright pleased by what we were doing; and I thought of Juan telling me that his *apus* were "sweet and charming." This was miles away from my experience with Ricardo, and I sensed it was the beginning of the healing of my relationship with the *apus*.

When I opened my eyes I sat watching our mandala, surprised by the fact that, while it was not a windy day, the light breezes that were stirring the bushes around us did not disturb even one of the groupings of delicate coca leaves in our *despacho*.

Next Juan folded the *despacho* paper over the leaves and shell, making it into a neat little package, which he tied with a silver string and placed inside his *mesa* bundle. Juan paused a moment, and said, "It is curious that, although this is currently the most important initiation in the Andean tradition, this is by far one of the most simple offerings."

In order to make the *despacho* to the sun we moved to another site, this time walking up above and behind the Illia Pata to another flat, open area. There was a plain flat gray stone, raised only inches above ground level, but clearly it had been worked by human hands. Juan sat down next to it, placed his *mesa* on the stone, and began to make another *despacho*. I could only assume that this too was an altar stone.

"In this *despacho*," Juan told us, "we will be drawing in and concentrating the energy from the *apus*." We began again by saying prayers into the shell and the cross and placing them in the center of the offering. Just as before, we chose groups of three perfect coca leaves to make *k'intus*, but this time, as we invoked the *apus* of the area, we drew the energy into the *despacho* by extending our leaves out to the *apu*, invoking them by name and drawing the coca leaves to our foreheads and down into our hearts, concentrating the energy rather than expanding it.

As we made this *despacho*, I realized that we were creating a microcosm of the balance between human, earth, and cosmos within the offering itself. The cross and the shell represented the cosmic masculine and feminine energies, our prayers represented the human factor, and the coca leaves, the forces of nature. The focus, prayer, and attention to detail involved in making a *despacho* was really quite impressive. When we were finished we tied the offering with a golden thread and Juan placed it in his bundle.

NEXT, JUAN TOLD US, CAME THE *AYNI KARPAY*, THE RECIPRO-
cal exchange of personal power. We walked back to the Illia Pata
where Juan brought out the first *despacho*, the offering to the wind,
and motioned for us to come and stand on top of the altar stone.
One by one we crawled up on top of the Illia Pata, grabbing on to
hand- and footholds in the rock. As we got to the top, we found that
there was a space behind the boulders where we could stand.

Using his medicine bundle filled with the *khuyas* from his master,
Juan said prayers over us and then explained that each one of us
would now make an interchange of personal power with him. He
told us first to think of the highest experience we had ever had and
fill our bubbles with that experience. Next, place our hands on top
of his head, energetically transmitting the experience to him. He
would receive this energy, then place his hands on our head to transmit the power of the tradition back to each one of us. The rest of
the group had only to hold a supportive attitude while one by one
we each took our turn on the altar stone.

No one moved. I sensed nervousness in the group, so I volun-
teered to go first. I stepped up to the altar stone and stood before
Juan. I closed my eyes, trying to empty my mind, in the hope that a
memory or experience would come to me. After a moment, quite
naturally, I began to recall an experience I had had as a child, in
which I had felt an almost exploding life force course through my
body, the sheer joy of being alive. I surrendered myself to the memory, and let myself be filled with it.

Then I placed my hands over Juan's head, forming an intention
to "give" the experience to him. It felt wonderful to share this
silently with Juan. After a few moments I put my hands down, and
now a delightful sensation filled me as Juan placed his hands on top
of my head. My awareness was immediately filled with magnificent
images from nature: beautiful green valleys, silver rivers, and enormous mountain peaks passed before me as if I were a condor soaring
above it all yet in intimate relation with great Nature. I opened my

eyes and looked into the shining eyes of a child. Juan and I giggled spontaneously, and then bowed to each other, ending the ceremony.

As they worked, both Juan and the initiates appeared to have strong experiences, for as each one received, his or her body would sway back and forth like a branch in the wind. There was a tender, nurturing feeling about this *ayni karpay* ceremony. I loved the rich silence that was developing. I had never witnessed any religious ritual in which teacher and student *exchanged* energetic experience; this was an equalizing process by which the power and knowledge of both teacher *and* student were being honored.

Finally Juan ritually cleansed each one of us with the offerings we had made. "You release a lot of *hoocha* when you do this. It comes to the surface of your energy bubble and needs to be cleaned," he said, using the wind *despacho* to scrape *hoocha* from us. "The *apus* will eat the heavy energy when the *despacho* is burned," he explained.

As we completed the *ayni karpay* ceremony, Juan pointed to the feet of one of the group members and said, "Look, you're standing on the altar!" She seemed startled and slightly embarrassed as she quickly moved to step down off the altar, but Juan stopped her. "No, I am teasing you," he said, laughing. "Don't you see that you have been standing on the altar the entire time? In the Andes we must touch the sacred. The fact is, we are always standing on the altar of Pachamama, sacred Mother Earth. Can you imagine what would happen if you stood on the altar in a Catholic church?" Juan said, dissolving into such a fit of laughter that soon the rest of us were laughing too. It was a funny image. He continued chuckling to himself as he gathered sticks to prepare the fire that would burn our *despacho*, transmuting our offering into something the mountain and wind spirits could eat.

WE PILED BACK INTO THE BUS AND DROVE ANOTHER THIRTY minutes away from Cuzco and on to the next ceremonial site called Amaru Mach'ay, or "Serpent Cave." The bus stopped near a large

granite rock formation to our right, sticking up out of the flat countryside like a giant mushroom. It was about sixty feet across and
thirty feet high. We got off the bus and walked around to the opposite side of the rock and saw a perfect Inka stairway carved into the
solid rock, and leading up to a thin vertical slitlike opening in rock
face. It looked like a vagina. We climbed the stairs and approached
the slit. It was the entrance to a cave.

On the right- and left-hand side of the entrance were two barely
discernible pumas, symbols of *kay pacha*, in bas-relief. As we entered
into this cave/temple, Juan pointed out the serpents in the walls,
also in bas-relief. "The Serpent Cave," someone whispered. We
headed toward the back of the twenty-foot-long cave, where there
was a large stone altar, and a source of light. As we approached the
altar and our eyes grew accustomed to the gloom, we could see that
directly above the altar, at the very back of the cave, was a small
opening to the sky. This cave/temple was very womblike.

Juan directed us once again to stand up on the altar. Then he
gave us these simple instructions. "Review your life, and as you do it,
give your *hoocha* to the cave walls. See your mother and father come
together in loving union, and try to go back to the moment of your
conception. As you do this," he directed us, "take in as much refined
energy as possible from the superior world, and release *hoocha* from
every part of your bubble. This cave is a very powerful heavy-energy
eater. Let the stone suck the *hoocha* out of you," Juan told us.

I closed my eyes and tried to imagine my mother and father in
loving union, but it was impossible. They had been divorced since I
was eighteen years old, and in my whole life I had never seen them
exchange one loving gesture. Frustrated, I stopped trying to imagine
it. Instead, I concentrated on giving my heavy energy to the cave and
bringing in refined energy. Breathing deeply, I let my mind travel
backward in time over as much of my past as I could conjure up. My
attention stopped or seemed to get stuck at each tragic or traumatic
event from my past, until I patiently released the heavy energy from
each experience to the walls of the cave. This seemed to free me to

travel further back—as if my past were like a giant tail tethering me in the present moment—and I was smoothing out the psychic knots of energy in my past, combing my tail.

Suddenly my awareness shifted and I began to feel as if I were floating free and high above the earth. I experienced a sublime joy and boundlessness as I roamed through space. I had no body! I looked down and was attracted to a young couple who were both intelligent and good-looking. Both had very strong wills. I seemed to be communicating directly with their energy bubbles. Incredulous, I realized that they were my parents! Remembering Juan's words I visualized them coming into the cave with me and invited them to release their heavy energy. They did so with great abandon, giving their *hoocha* to Pachamama. Tears streamed down my face as I saw my parents as never before, as two souls in a state of complete purity and beauty.

Now they were able to see each other's beauty, and they spontaneously joined together in a loving embrace. Suddenly I saw an enormous fertile ovum, and cells dividing and dividing and dividing to create all life in the universe, all diverse forms. My perspective shifted again, and it was the fertile ovum in my mother's uterus that would soon be my body. I sat mute on the cold stone altar, amazed by what I had just seen and felt.

Without exception everyone in the group could attest to the powerful suctioning force we felt from the cave as we performed this ritual. Our driver, Eduardo, who had eagerly agreed to join us for the rituals, was physically yanked backward so hard by the sucking force of the rock that he almost fell off the altar. Finally Juan directed us to take in refined energy from the superior world through the top of our heads and, placing his bundle at the base of our spines, told us to release *hoocha* from our sacrums. I stumbled out of the cave, blinking in the sunlight, as if I were issuing forth anew from the womb of Pachamama.

Back in the bus and on the way to the next site, Juan explained that we had just successfully completed the Andean initiation for becoming an adult. As we released the *hoocha*—the spiritual impurities of our mother and father—from the moment of our conception, we were transferring our "energetic umbilical cords," and therefore our psychological and energetic dependence, from our biological mother to Pachamama, Mother Earth. We were now plugged into Pachamama as the source of life, making all humanity our brothers and sisters since we share one mother, the earth. My mind could not get this, but my bubble was humming with renewed energy.

FOR THE LAST PART OF THE RITUAL WE DROVE FOR HALF AN hour to the lake where the last Inka, Huaskar, was born. It was about six in the afternoon and the sun was just beginning to set. The sky was alight with beautiful rich golds and deep pinks as we arrived at a dark blue lake surrounded by tall green and golden reeds. We descended from the bus and walked past an old whitewashed house where there were two magnificent handmade reed boats that had just come in off the lake. The setting was magical.

We passed a large rambling whitewashed country house, the only structure on the lake, and descended from our bus. Past the tall reeds that surrounded the southern edge of the lake, we arrived at the spot where we were to perform our final ritual of the day. There in the reeds and bushes by the water's edge was yet another Inka stone seat carved into the rock. It looked inviting, so I sat down on the carved stone. The rest of the group found seats and listened for instructions, but I was distracted. In fact, I was spooked from the moment we had arrived; I felt that something was going to happen here.

"How much do you know about Inka history?" Juan began. Everyone looked blank. Some shook their heads. "Huaskar and Atahualpa were half brothers, the sons of the Inka Manco Capac, who divided the empire in two. Atahualpa ruled in what is now Quito, Ecuador, and Huaskar ruled here in Cuzco. Atahualpa was not satisfied with only half an empire and wanted to take Cuzco as well. So the Inka brothers were actually in the middle of a civil war when the Spanish, led by Pizarro, arrived.

"Atahualpa was at that moment in jail in Cuzco, so Pizarro, who was a very clever man, got a message to Atahualpa saying that Huaskar was planning to kill him. From jail, Atahualpa ordered his followers to kill Huaskar, which they did. Then with the two Inka rulers out of the way, Pizarro took over. The Inkas say that because Atahualpa and Huaskar did not perform *ayni*—meaning that they inherited an empire but did not give an empire back to their children—they both went to live in *ukhu pacha*, the interior world. There, they must teach *ayni* to the beings of the interior world. But it is said that the Inka are waiting for the day when they will once again return to this world, to *kay pacha*. On this lake, the place where Huaskar Inka was born into *kay pacha*, we will invoke his presence," Juan pronounced.

The air was still, unnaturally still, as we took in his words. Before Juan had finished speaking there was already a strong sensation of a presence. The energy of the lake was so strong that I began to get chills. "Don't be afraid," said Juan, laughing at me. "This is nothing dangerous. You are not going to go unconscious. Rather we are going to practice what is called 'incorporation.' In the Andean tradition this does not mean that you are taken over by the spirit. It simply means that you invoke the spirit of Huaskar to enter you, making an energetic addition to your bubble of the Inka's power." That seemed like a friendly concept, however I had been literally trembling for the last several minutes. Without knowing it, that was exactly what I had been feeling afraid of. I had an odd premonition that something—perhaps the spirit of Huaskar—was going to come into me. "I promise it's not going to hurt," said Juan, winking at me.

Juan instructed us to draw in vital energy from the lake, then Juan took his *mesa* and began to call the spirit of Huaskar. "*Hampui. Hampui.* Come, Huaskar Inka," he called softly. Suddenly a clump of tall reeds to my right began to sway violently and I felt an enormous presence in the water all around us. A voice sounded deep within me, and each word he spoke shook me down to my roots.

"I was not able to finish my work. I was taken from *kay pacha* before it was complete," the voice said. The presence was a deep, fierce, and booming *love*. I felt compelled to speak his words aloud as he continued, "You people must go forward on the earth and carry out my work to its fruition." As I spoke the words, first to Juan, in Spanish, my heart was beating hard and my palms were sweating. Then, just as suddenly, the presence was gone. My breathing calmed and my body relaxed as I translated the words into English for the group. Juan looked at me surprised, and nodded, saying, "Yes. That is the message of Huaskar Inka."

As my heart rate returned to normal, Juan drew out of his bag the sun *despacho* that we had made at the first ritual site. "When you do this ritual, you release a lot of *hoocha*," he said, gesturing to me to come and stand next to him. "With the *despacho* I will clean your *hoochas*, then we will give this *despacho* to the spirit of the lake." One by one, we stood beside Juan as he carefully cleaned our heavy energy by scraping the entire periphery of our bodies with the sun *despacho*. "We have received vital energy from the lake, now we must give back," he said. He took the sun *despacho* and walked down to the water's edge. There he called out to the spirit of the lake, telling it to come and take our offering; he tied the *despacho* to a small stone and cast it into the water.

Upon his return from the lake, Juan approached me and, placing a small square stone in my hand, put his *mesa* firmly on my head and began to pray intensely. He moved the *mesa* first to my right shoulder and then to my left, all the while praying rapidly in Quechua. I felt exactly as if I were being knighted, except with a *mesa* instead of a sword. My eyes were tightly closed and I only realized he was gone when, a few minutes later, I opened them again. There in my hand was the small square stone, my first *khuya*.

I looked up to see that he was carrying out the same ceremony with each initiate, and as I watched I couldn't help but think again about the ritual of knighthood. As Juan finished with the last initiate, my eyes swept over the faces of my group members. They were soft and glowing in the amber light of sunset. I felt an intense pang of love for these people, and a deep and grateful devotion to them for agreeing to come with me here, into the unknown.

"This last ritual completes the first day of the great initiation." Juan's face shone with deep satisfaction as he spoke. "Now you have become Inka seeds, carrying with you not only the energy of the Andes, but some intellectual knowledge of its traditions as well. We receive many visitors from Tibet. Tibetan monks, and even the Dalai Lama himself, have come here. I had the good fortune to speak with one of the assistants to the Dalai Lama. He told me that the Tibetan tradition is a mountain tradition in the masculine. He said the Tibetan spiritual tradition has put out its seeds all over the world, but the seeds will come to implant themselves and grow in the rich fertile soil of the feminine center that is the Andes," Juan told us. This corroborated what I had heard many times during my years of spiritual investigation in Peru, that the Andes was the place where people would come for initiation into the feminine mysteries.

9

Wiñay: Germination

THE NEXT MORNING JUAN CAME EARLY TO PICK US UP AT
Señora Clemencia's house. In the year that I had been away, the
señora had done wonders transforming her home into a fourteen-
bed hostel that she called Apu Wasi, home of the *apus*. I was delighted to share my Peruvian home and family with the group, and
the señora took excellent care of us. Many of us hadn't slept much,
if at all, another side effect of the altitude. But I recalled one of my
graduate school teachers once saying how a little sleep deprivation
"softened the ego structures." Perhaps this was working to our benefit. Certainly no one was unhappy, just very "softened."

Wearing sunblock and broad-brimmed hats that the señor had
insisted we take for protection against the intensity of the Inka sun,
we clambered into a minivan and headed up the mountain. From my
years of living in Cuzco, I knew that we were taking the back road
into Saqsaywaman, the largest Inka ruin in the city of Cuzco. As we
rounded the last turn in the winding road, several group members
caught their breath at the site.

There before us was an expansive green field, walled on the right side by three rows of enormous Inka stone walls. These walls, so perfectly constructed that the stones, some weighing up to two tons, fit together like pieces of a puzzle, with joints so tight you couldn't pass a hair between them. No mortar was used to hold the stones together, making the flexible walls antiseismic as well. The three zigzag walls, shaped like the teeth of pinking sheers and made of mammoth charcoal-colored stones, climbed the hill to our right. It was said that the Inkas had designed the city of Cuzco in the form of a jaguar. Saqsaywaman was the head of the jaguar, and these three zigzag walls the jaguar's teeth. Along the opposite length of the field ran a low and straight stone wall with a hill of extruding rock rising up behind it. There was something about the stones themselves that set my skin tingling and freed my mind to roam in another time, another dream. This was clearly a place of power, and the stones were alive.

From up ahead, Juan, in his little white felt hat, waved us on. "Over here," he called to us. We crossed the field, hopped over the low stone wall, and climbed the small hill, following Juan, who disappeared over the top of the large hump of protuberant rock. As we reached the very top of the hill, we saw how the rock had been carved into the three-tiered seat known as the "throne of the Inka." We arrived at the "throne" just in time to see Juan's figure descending the far side of the hill to disappear behind another pile of rock. We were breathless when we finally caught up to him. Juan was standing waist deep inside a circular depression about ten feet in diameter and ringed with Inka stonework. Climbing even a little hill at this altitude was cruel work.

"This is the place of Pachakuteq, the ninth Inka ruler, and all this"—Juan's gesture took in the entire ruin—"is considered to have been built by him." As Juan spoke, the scenery slowly settled back into place for our spinning, oxygen-deprived brains. "Pachakuteq was the name given to the son of the eighth Inka, after he took power and revolutionized the Inka system. Pachakuteq literally means 'world turned upside down.'

"*Pachakuti* has another meaning. The Andean Indians don't reckon time like Westerners. They see history in terms of discrete epochs with a *pachakuti*, or 'cosmic transmutation,' in between. So Pachakuteq earned his name because, in just two generations, he and his son, Inka Yupanki, turned the little kingdom of the Inkas that only extended about twenty-five miles around the city of Cuzco into an empire stretching across most of the western continent of South America.

"In the Andes it is believed that a place holds the energy or spirit of the person it is associated with. This is the place of Pachakuteq because he lived and worked here and his living energy has permeated this spot. Yesterday we were in the birthplace of Huwaskar Inka, great-grandson of Pachakuteq, where we incorporated his spirit. Today, be aware that we are in Pachakuteq's domain, and try to absorb his spirit into your bubble."

"Juan, what are these? Some kind of baths?" one of the initiates asked, gesturing to the beautiful Inka stones that appeared to be carved into aqueducts of some kind.

"Exactly," Juan replied, smiling, "and now you are helping me to move from the history lesson to our work for the day. This is a water temple, and the first ritual we will do today is with the spirit of water. You recall that yesterday at the Illia Pata we worked with earth energy in our *qosqo* by connecting our 'spiritual stomachs' to the altar stone and to the living energy of Pachamama." Heads were bobbing up and down around the circle. Some of us still had sore *qosqos* from yesterday's workout.

"In our tradition," Juan continued, "we work with the living energy of the five elements to bring them into harmony within the body. The *qosqo* is the center through which we connect with the spirit of the earth, Pachamama. The base of the spine, or the sacrum, is the center through which we connect with the spirit of water. When we talk about the 'spirit' of an element, we are literally talking about the very refined aspect or essence of that element. Water has a physical component, but according to the Andean philosophy, it also possesses a nonphysical, subtle, or energetic aspect as well. It is this very subtle and refined aspect of the water element that we will work with now. Here, at this Water Temple, I will use my *mesa* to help you open the center at the base of your spine, and we will ask the spirit of water to enter through your base of the spine."

As was becoming usual, Juan approached me first as his guinea pig. "Put all of your heavy energy into my *mesa*," Juan instructed as he brought the colorful bundle out of its pouch and offered it up to the *hanaq pacha*, softly mouthing his prayers. Then he placed his *mesa* firmly against my sacrum and began to pray louder and more fervently. I felt a flow of energy move to the base of my spine, and then I experienced a distinct and sudden pop, as if the sacrum had been uncorked. "Good!" Juan exclaimed. "Now that your center is open you must visualize sending a root down to absorb the spirit of water into your base of the spine." As he moved to open the next initiate's sacrum with his *mesa*, I settled back against the rock wall of the water temple, focusing all my attention on my sacrum.

Since the "pop," the base of my spine had been tingling with a burning sensation and now it felt positively soothing to invite the spirit of water in. I visualized a white tubelike root descending from my sacrum into a clear pool of water. Cool, silver water slipped into me in a thin stream, filling my sacrum area, then my entire spine, with a refreshing watery sensation. As the thin stream moved up to my brain, it became a lake and finally an ocean. My awareness crashed on the ocean's surface within the towering waves, taking me back down deep inside where colorful fish swam in and out through my rib bones playing hide-and-seek.

My vision wavered as if I were beginning to see through a curtain of time into the past at this very same location.

I stand in water that covers me to my waist, inside the circular stone wall of the Water Temple. Its niches display numerous golden idols. I gaze across the water at two priests in short white tunics, who wear tall head plumes and sit inside a two-level bath. A steady stream of golden light from hanaq pacha *cascades over the head and shoulders of the elder priest as he sits and prays in the bath above. His entire body glows and the emanation extends*

from his energy bubble into the silver water that courses around him, caus-
ing it to glow golden. The initiate sits in the bath below, hands open in a ges-
ture of receiving as the shimmering water from the higher bath flows through
the stone channel and cascades over the younger priest's head.

I drew in a sharp breath, eyelids fluttering. One moment the
image was sharp and clear, the next it was gone. I opened my eyes
fully and gazed into Juan's face. He regarded me curiously, his head
was cocked to one side as if he were searching my face for an answer
to something. The other initiates all stood with their sacrums against
the stone wall, eyes closed as mine had been only moments before.
"Juan, I saw them. Priests." I whispered, not wanting to distract the
others. What was it about this place that made inner visions come so
easily?

Juan nodded, whispering back enigmatically, "Thank you. That
was the thing I was forgetting." We waited patiently until all eyes
were open once again. "These are Inka baths," Juan explained. "I
learned how they were used during an initiation way up in the high
mountains with one of my masters from Q'eros. You see that large
circle over there?" Juan pointed behind us to a huge circular depression. It was just like the one we were all standing in, but this one was
hundreds of feet across. So large, in fact, that I hadn't even noticed
it. "That is the cistern that once held the water supply for the entire
city of Cuzco. You see the niches along the wall?" Classic Inka niches
were spaced every fifteen feet or so, all around the circumference of
the circular wall. "During that initiation, I had to immerse myself in
a glacial lake that adjoined another higher lake. I didn't notice that
my master had gotten into the upper lake until I felt a flow of force
coming from his lake into mine."

"Incredible," Barbara, a nearly six-foot-tall corporate executive,
exclaimed. "Do you know, Juan, that is exactly what I saw. I closed
my eyes and I saw three priests doing a ceremony just like you described, but here, in these baths." Dear Barbara—it was because of
her insistence that I take them to Peru that the group had come together in the first place, and due to her persistence that we were all

here in Cuzco now. Several others had also seen the priests. Curioser and curioser. Individual visions were one thing, but almost everyone had seen some variation of the exact same theme. I felt relief. At least now I was not the only one seeing things.

Juan continued talking about the ritual. "Because I was his student, I had the right to receive my master's finest energy, just as you have the right to receive *sami* from me. Coupled with the natural power of the lakes themselves, this becomes a tremendously effective purification ceremony.

"Like everything in the Inka mystical tradition, the baths have two uses, one practical, for washing and cleaning, the other mystical, to cleanse energy. Don Benito taught me that the Inkas used these baths ceremonially, to initiate their priests, so I would have to confirm what you have already been 'seeing.' This ceremony was also performed to bless the water for the city of Cuzco." I thought about priests blessing the water supply of an entire city, as I tried to imagine what it would be like to live here, in Cuzco in Inka times, where every mundane act was a ritual that held sacred significance.

The group settled into seats around the edge of the stone circle to listen to Juan's comforting explanation for what had been, to some, a startling first vision. "*Huaca* is a word that is used to describe many things in the Andes, but basically it means 'sacred.' The niches were *huacas*, meaning places where golden idols were kept. But the idols had much more than a decorative effect. They were collectors of sacred energy. The priests blessed the idols, and the idols were placed over the water to permit a constant flow of refined energy into the water supply and on to the people of Cuzco. In Inka times, the 'everyday' was sacred," Juan said, voicing for the group what was in everyone's thoughts.

Suddenly I was reminded of an afternoon I spent with Cyntha at the Carmel Mission in California. It was my first Catholic mass, and during communion I saw a beam of light come down and cover the priest and then the wine and the glass. I realized that as each person came up and took communion, they were taking some of that energy away with them. Even that Catholic ritual had mystical significance very similar to the Inkas, I thought, and then turned my attention back to Juan.

"It is said the ruling Inka was so filled with sacred power that his subjects would be forced to the ground by coming in contact with the sheer energetic power of the Inkas' bubble," Juan said, as he gestured for us to begin walking back toward the van.

We drove for nearly an hour, leaving the city of Cuzco behind and headed out to the Sacred Valley of the Inkas. We were going to the town of Pisaq. I had been to the Pisaq market several times, and I had seen from a distance that the mountains were striped with Inka terraces, but I had never been up to the ruins.

We entered by the back way and drove up a dirt road as far as we could before abandoning the van to continue on foot. The Sacred Valley absolutely lived up to its name. Breathtaking brilliant green, iron red, and jagged black mountains capped with snowy peaks ringed us as we walked along a terrace that led up into the Inka ruin. Early afternoon sun warmed the rich green foliage as smoke rose from the cooking fires of the people who lived at and tended this place. Farmers, it appeared, still worked some of these ancient terraces, agricultural wonder of the Inkas, each terrace creating its own microclimate specific for growing certain types of foods.

At one point Juan left the trail and we all skittered after him through the underbrush, trying to keep up. We fought our way to the other side of a patch of dense foliage and looked up to see strange gaps or holes burrowed into the red face of the cliff wall before us. "Grave robbers" was Juan's two-word explanation. Apparently these were burial caves of the Inkas that have been discovered and then plundered. How had the Inkas made those holes and buried their dead in the sheer face of the rock cliff? But we didn't have much time to ponder—Juan had disappeared again.

"Over here," someone shouted. The foliage of another huge bush was held back to reveal a beautiful and absolutely hidden cave, directly beneath the burial mountain. Juan had entered the shallow cave overhung with fronds and was already seated at the back in meditation posture. We gathered inside the cave and sat there, sensing its power. Several people began to tremble involuntarily. "This is another place of encounter with Pachamama. Her force is here to be touched. Give out heavy energy from your whole bubble and take in the force of Pachamama through your *qosqo*," Juan instructed us.

We sat in silence. However powerful, the place was also absolutely charming. As I released my heavy energy, I felt enveloped again by a loving presence that was very earthy, as if I were sitting in the giant lap of an enormous mother. I relaxed completely and nearly fell asleep. I was nudged alert as Maryann, a tall and handsome black nurse from Oakland who was sitting next to me, began to tremble violently. I looked up to see large tears falling down her cheeks. Maryann was an intense and powerful person who worked with premature babies. In her work Maryann faced death every day. Now, as she cried like one of the babies she cared for, the group moved instinctively around her, protecting her in a cocoon of love.

After several minutes the storm of emotion subsided and when Maryann smiled up at us, laughing like a child through her tears, it was if the sun had come out again. "I . . . my ancestors come from the land, from the earth, but I never felt a power like this before in my life. She is alive, Pachamama is alive!" Maryann's voice nearly rose to a shout. She scattered her surprised companions as her large body suddenly bolted up and out of the cave. The woman needed room to dance. In a flurry of arms and legs she began her spontaneous ritual dance, jumping up and down and shouting, "Pachamama lives!" at the top of her lungs. We all joined in her enthusiasm and her dance became a group celebration with Juan, the biggest partier of all.

"We must carry this joy on with us to the next place," Juan told us after our hearty jig. Drunk with energy and breathing hard, the group, despite the altitude, was now leaping along the trail behind Juan as we headed for the next site.

Soon we passed through an Inka stone doorway and on through a narrow cavelike tunnel. As we emerged on the other side, we looked out onto the ruins of a magnificent gray stone temple about a hundred feet below us.

"So far today, we have worked first with the spirit of Water," said Juan, "and next with the spirit of Earth. Here at this temple, my master Don Benito taught me that the Inkas not only performed a ceremony to "tie the Sun to Earth" at the winter solstice, but that the priests also performed an initiation to bring the spirit of the Sun and the concentrated energy of fire into the hearts of the initiates. In the Andean system we do not use the Hindu term *chakras* to indicate the body's energy centers. Instead, we see the human energy bubble as having a series of belts or bands of energy that surround it. Each belt has a center, or an eye, in a certain spot on the body. The "eyes" are located in the *qosqo*, the base of the spine, the heart, and the throat. Each eye and its energy belt is associated with an element. Here, at this altar, I will open your heart center with my *mesa* while you try to connect your heart with fire and the spirit of the Sun. We say Father Sun, because here in the Andes we do not objectify nature, we have a personal, intimate relationship with the forces of the natural world."

One by one the initiates went up to the altar stone to make their personal relationship with Father Sun, and to have Juan's *mesa* placed on their chests. Juan held his *mesa* over their hearts and prayed, drawing out the heavy energy. Then slowly he pulled the *mesa* out, away, and up, gesturing with it toward the Sun. Again I saw tiny tendrils—like strings from a spider's web—that were drawn out from each person's heart and sent up into the Sun.

When it came to be my turn it seemed as if I had already experienced the ritual twelve times. My heart was ready to burst as Juan placed his *mesa* on my chest, and, seeing with my other vision, I witnessed a tendril of light shoot out from my heart and plant itself firmly in the center of the Sun.

I was swept outside of my body, and my ordinary awareness faded.

I move with infinite grace and precision, there is no time, no hurry. I travel on a beam of light, my destination clear. I go, without going, along a shaft of light. I am weightless. I go toward a greater brightness that I am forever part of. I go home. I arrive at this brightness and with great joy I greet Father

Sun. A door opens. I travel into the center of the Sun. I arrive at a throne of light, where a large Indian sits. He is someone I know very, very well. He embraces me and the fire of his love, radiant, pure, enters my heart, my body. I am full of goodness and strength. The Sun is shining within my heart. The Earth is turning within my heart. The planets orbit the Sun within my heart.

"Yugh!" I exclaimed, feeling as if I had just been slugged in the stomach. I opened my eyes and saw Juan holding his *mesa* over my head and looking worried. My body was sore all over and I felt as if my consciousness had just been slam-dunked through a tiny hole at warp speed.

"Are you all right?" Juan asked, his worried expression lessened slightly.

"Yugh!" I exclaimed again. It seemed to be the only word I knew.

"You went a little too far, Elizabeth. I was afraid you weren't going to come back."

"Yugh," I repeated, nodding.

AFTER A GOOD HOT PERUVIAN LUNCH AND A REST, I HAD recovered my entire vocabulary. "Juan, I saw an Indian in the Sun." He nodded, cleaning his teeth with a toothpick as we lounged below towering Andean peaks in the warm afternoon sun. We were sitting inside the courtyard of a charming restaurant in the town of Calca. A pair of miniature monkeys tied to a tree in the courtyard screeched, and several brilliantly colored parrots in a cage next to our table yabbered, imitating my speech.

"But, Juan, I remember him. It was the Indian I used to talk to all the time when I was a little girl. Only I didn't think he was an Indian, because when I got older and saw Indians on TV, they didn't look like him."

"That's because your cowboy movies don't show South American Indians," Juan replied. "The Inkas used to say that when Pachakuti Inka died, he went to live with his father, the Sun. You know that the Inkas were known as the 'children of the Sun,'" he told me, casually.

"Wow," was all I could reply, still somewhat befuddled from my encounter with the Sun. Peru seemed to hold keys not only to my growth and future, but to my past as well.

"Elizabeth, we must go or we may arrive too late to complete our last ritual," Juan said as he herded everyone away from the remainders of dessert and out toward our van.

"Where are we going now?" I asked Juan.

"Ollantaytambo," came the reply.

During the time I had lived in Cuzco I had observed that Peruvians in general, and Juan in particular, had this uncanny ability to fall asleep at the moment they entered any moving vehicle. This foiled my plans each time to ask Juan about the next ritual and get a jump on things. I began to think he was falling asleep on purpose. Then I realized what an annoying North American habit I had of always wanting to know what was coming next. Why must I know? Did I so distrust life that I couldn't just allow my experience to unfold? When I had lived in Peru, this was what I had loved most about the people: no hurry, no worry, no constant fear or preocupation with the future. I was sad to realize how I had unconsciously reverted back to this North American neurosis. Now I made a conscious effort to relax, sit back, and enjoy the ride.

We arrived at the majestic ruin of Ollantaytambo five minutes before it closed. Luckily the guard knew Juan and waved us in. Everyone in the group was struck silent by the charm of this ancient Inka village. Ollantaytambo, a wholly intact Inka town of sandy-colored stone, complete with Inka aqueducts, stone houses, and cobblestone streets, was nestled in the lush vegetation of the surrounding patchwork-quilt countryside. The net effect of the Inka architectural design and layout of the city was that it created a sense of deep peace and complete harmony with the surrounding landscape. It was utterly charming. Tourists came and, without knowing why, could barely drag themselves away.

We climbed the enormous stone stairway, forty flights up, to the unfinished Sun Temple. Six gigantic magnificently carved pinkish white stones made up the center of this temple and I assumed that this, our last ceremony of the day, would take place here. Juan walked right past the huge stones and over to the edge of the ruin, where he had to grab hard onto his little white hat to keep it from blowing away. Standing on a high ledge that looked out over the Sacred Valley, he appeared to be smack in the middle of a ninety-mile-an-hour wind. I had been to this ruin before, several times in fact, and never noticed this wind phenomenon.

"Look down there," Juan yelled to be heard over the wind, which seemed to blow only in this section of the ruin. Far below us, the Sacred Valley was laid out like an irregular patchwork quilt with a silver stripe running through it—the Urubamba—the sacred river of the Inkas. At the far end of the valley, where Juan was pointing, was a glacier between two towering mountains peaks. "That is called the 'Windgate,'" Juan told us, stepping out of the fierce current long enough to be able to converse in a normal tone. "This is the place where we will open and connect our throats to the spirit of the wind."

We lined up in a row at the edge of the ruin, but just shy of the path of this extraordinary Windgate. Juan opened his pouch and took out a small wrinkled plastic bag filled with coca leaves. He stood in front of us one by one, giving us each a handful of coca leaves and whispering his instructions. I couldn't help wondering if he was telling us all the same thing. But I knew, once we were in the Windgate, no one would be able to hear a word that was said.

When Juan came to me and opened his bag of coca leaves, the pungent green smell filled my nostrils and I had a sudden yen to chew some of the leaves. "You will come and stand in the Windgate and I will open your throat with my *mesa*. Then you must put your deepest prayers to the spirit of the wind into your coca leaves and, at the right moment, offer the leaves to the wind. Throw them up over your head and let the wind spirits take them. Then let the wind cleanse your *hoocha*." I nodded my understanding as Juan looked down on me like a proud father.

The group began the ritual and one after another, each went to stand in the cleansing blast of the Windgate, offering his or her prayers to the spirit of the wind. Against the setting sun, arms went up, and coca leaves went swirling to disappear into a vast and quickly darkening sky.

Before this moment, I had never consciously and intentionally stepped *into* a raging wind. As I watched the ceremony, it now came home to me that, conversely, I had been unconsciously trained to avoid the power of nature, to get out of the rain, away from a strong wind, to arrive armed against sun, snow, or hail, to somehow and at all cost keep nature from touching me. But to seek it out actively, participate, and even revel in it? Only my long-ago-stifled child self knew the ecstasy of getting *into* a downpour.

It was nearly dark when my turn came, and as I walked up to place myself in the tunnel of wind, I experienced a heretofore unknown rage at the unwitting social programming that took me out of participation with the natural forces, and even placed me in a defensive posture against them. I wanted to scream my fury, but instead, I focused all my intensity into a prayer to Wayra, the spirit of the wind. I prayed with all my might for the power to open my throat and tell the truth, to overcome my deep-seated fear of speaking out.

Suddenly, in the darkness and the roaring, I felt the reassuring touch of Juan's *mesa* against my throat, filling me with energy and determination. Wind howled through my flesh and blood, penetrating into my bones and scouring, scouring away the black fear that was stuck there like tar. Juan's *mesa* pulled at the rage and fear until there was nothing left but a deep and empty sadness at the terrible loss, the loss of my birthright, the loss of my intimate relationship with Pachamama. As Juan took his *mesa* from my throat, a deep and unknown grief began to issue forth from my body. First as a whimper that grew into a long wailing cry, followed by gut-wrenching sobs that I was grateful made no sound against the roaring. All this I gave to the wind to carry away.

Spontaneously, and seemingly into the space my grief had occupied, my heart filled with a prayer to Wayra. "Wind spirit, let my true voice find its way out of my heart and into the world, to travel freely as you do, and bring Pachamama's message to the world." I spoke the words into the dry green leaves, casting them high into the air, where they danced for a split second before they disappeared.

A sense of deep well-being came over me and I felt a cool sensation in my throat as gales of laughter and a voice, crackling like a dry autumn leaf, said, "Go forward, sister, and speak what you know. We are glad that you can hear us. Know that we stand with you." Wayra, the spirit of the wind, was talking to me.

Suddenly my attention was drawn to my heart, where I could feel Father Sun warmly smiling and supporting me. From my belly a long umbilical cord extended down into the earth and I felt the powerful solidity of Pachamama. A silver-cool-wet feeling in my sacrum alerted me that the spirit of water was also present. A fantastic sensate experience of being completely connected to and supported by all the elements filled my awareness, as if I were wearing a giant, natural seat belt that held me lightly in place between heaven and earth. Large tears of gratitude began to roll down my cheeks.

Elation, relief, and a moment of confusion passed through me as I wondered what it was that felt so comforting about this "natural seat belt." Slowly I understood, perhaps for the first time in my life and on a visceral level, that I belonged to this Earth. I had just discovered that it was possible—no, vital—to my sense of identity and well-being to feel like this, to feel related to and in harmony with the natural forces of Earth. My body now possessed irrevocable knowledge that it and I were a part of one vast and glorious creation. Finally, and for the first time, I knew, beyond any doubt, that I belonged here.

10

Phutuy: Flowering

THE TRAIN CHUGGED ALONG THE RAILS EVER SO SLOWLY as we, squeezed in between our luggage and each other, drew endless minute after endless minute nearer to the abode of my heart. "Machu Pikchu," the cabin boy yelled after what seemed an eternity but was really only four hours in a first-class tourist train. I had been to Machu Pikchu at least ten times before, on horseback, on foot, and on the infamous local train, sharing seats not only with the Peruvians but with Peruvian dogs, pigs, chickens, and guinea pigs. This was my first taste of the tourist train, and from the perspective of my other experiences, I was seated in the lap of luxury.

However, for my traveling companions, this was a difficult, even grueling experience. My sympathy was not stimulated in the least. I explained to them in graphic detail what it was like to have been stuck for ten hours on a broken-down third-class train, with six extra people and various and sundry animal life sharing our four-person seat, on what was supposed to be a three-hour train ride. It was when I mentioned the conditions of the bathrooms that they began to glance around cheerily and comment to one another on the beauty of the landscape as we came upon the subtropical vegetation of the lower Machu Pikchu area.

The steam brakes gasped the train to a halt and we grabbed our bags, nearly diving out the door to the pavement below. I had warned the group that we only had a few minutes to exit before the train continued on its route deeper into the jungle town of Quillabamba.

We lunched in silence after the bus took us up the innumerable switchbacks and on to the entrance gates and the tourist hotel of Machu Pikchu. Every member of our group was struck dumb by the quiet majesty of the lush green and velvet black mountains that surrounded the ancient ruin of Machu Pikchu like the warm, embracing arms of Pachamama.

The air was rich with oxygen and humidity as, after lunch, we filed one by one through the entrance, handing our tickets to the gatekeeper. We had dropped nearly two thousand feet in elevation from Cuzco, and the climate was much warmer here. Opening our qosqos to "taste" the refined energy, as Juan had instructed us, we passed into this seat of ancient power and harmony with the forces of nature. As we rounded the final turn in the path and came out upon a terrace that gave us our first full-on view of the citadel, tears welled up in the eyes of many of the group members. A memory was stirred somewhere deep in our bones, or perhaps deep in the collective unconscious, the memory of another way of life. A life in which sacred meaning was made manifest in each simple, mundane act of everyday living.

"Two days ago, in the Serpent Cave, you became children of Pachamama," Juan said. "We Andeans mean this very literally, because we believe that our bodies are made in the image of Pachamama. The qosqo of Earth is the city of Cuzco. And just like us, the city of Machu Pikchu has a qosqo, and it is right over there," Juan informed us, pointing to a large round towerlike structure made of very fine Inka stonework situated near the center of the citadel. "This tower is the site of our first ritual." We walked on another few minutes approaching the edifice, and I noticed that it was the only round building in the entire complex.

As fortune was with us, the overseer of Machu Pikchu, a very kind man, highly in favor of the ancient ways of his ancestors, appeared from behind us and, sensing the purpose of our endeavor, nodded for us to follow as he unlocked the gates that barred us from entering the inner chamber of the temple. "Quietly," he told us, and looking around to see that there were not many tourists in our immediate area, he quickly locked the gates behind us and followed us inside. Highly refined stonework surrounded another large natural stone altar that looked made to lie down on, with natural depressions for head, elbows, and buttocks.

"*Gracias, hermano,*" Juan said, regarding him deeply for a moment. "Please join us for the ritual." Much to my surprise, the overseer got out his own private pack of coca leaves, and, forming a *k'intu,* he blew on the leaves as I had often seen Juan do, and muttered a blessing to the *apus* and Pachamama in Quechua. It gave me indescribable joy to see and know that the overseer of Machu Pikchu was in fact a man steeped in his own native traditions.

Juan, too, got out his *mesa* and blew in a circle around the group, as always, offering his living energy to Pachamama. "This is the part of this temple that is connected with the sky, it is a masculine place. Open your *qosqos* and draw in the refined masculine force from this part of the temple," Juan instructed us. We sat a long while, pulling in the energy that was delicious and felt very highly concentrated. After a few minutes, as people began to open their eyes, I spoke. "Juan, this place feels different, it feels 'juicier.'"

"That is because you are sitting in the center of a powerful concentration of earth energies," he replied simply. "Look around you. Do you see how all the peaks of the mountains converge around this central tower?" We stood on our tiptoes looking over the edge of the wall to the landscape beyond to see that we were indeed surrounded by mountain peaks. Now I saw what moments before had been only a visceral sensation: the mountains themselves poured life force into this central temple. "But, Juan, how did the Inkas know this was the *qosqo*?"

"Look around you and feel with your own *qosqo*, feel with your entire bubble . . . don't you know it too?" What he said now seemed so painfully obvious, and so natural, that I could not even imagine how I had spent my entire life never noticing the feeling of a landscape, never hearing what it was so clearly proclaiming. Sure, I had always appreciated the beauty of nature, but from a distance, as if it were a painting in a museum. I had never felt this deep personal involvement with the landscape, never really understood that I was a part of it, or how much I was influenced by it. Until now, there had been an embarrassingly large hole in my education.

Next, Juan led us to a series of descending stone chambers that were connected by channels just like the Water Temple at Saqsaywaman. "These were the baths of the Inka. As you can see the water begins here and flows all the way down the side of the mountain. For this ritual we will have two people in each cubicle. Let your bubble connect with the place, then pull in energy from *hanaq pacha* through the top of your head and send it down to the persons in the bath below you."

In short order, our newly trained group of initiates had created a quite tangible cord of energy connecting each bath with the one below it. It felt as if we were all inside of one long energy snake.

Feeling this energy was exciting but I was curious to see how the water channels worked. Almost as if in response, a sudden rain began to fall. In this place, I felt no need to remove myself from the rain. We all, by silent simultaneous agreement, decided to remain in the baths and in the rain. Within minutes the channels of water filled and a small stream of water began coursing down the long chain of interlinked bathing chambers. Clearly the rain was here to stay, but we had to move on.

We climbed out of our baths and followed Juan, now hurrying through the increasing downpour. We ducked down a long stone stairway and through a narrow passage and then we were standing on top of a large stone platform with three stone seats. "This is the

Condor Temple," Juan said, looking down at what now looked like the beak and white stone collar of a condor's neck. From our vantage point, it seemed we were standing on the back of the condor, just between the wings.

"The condor represents the collective spirit of the the Andes. Here, in the Condor Temple, try to connect yourselves with the collective spirit of the Andes," Juan told us.

I closed my eyes and immediately felt the power of the condor's wings surround me. Again I was surprised, amazed that with just this simple instruction and the powerful forces that were present in the temple itself, I could move into a visionary state. In my mind's eye I saw the enormous condor approach—or was it I who approached? The distance between us closed until there was no distance. Instantly I felt the tireless strength of huge black wings, the power of cold detachment to do the job that must be done. To eat away death in order to bring forth life. I felt myself merge with that strength, that resolute manner. I heard the distant call of a condor.

"The rain is coming harder, we must go on," Juan said, snapping me back to the present time and place. As we all followed quickly after Juan's disappearing figure, Barbara sidled up next to me.

"Wow!" she puffed, trying to maintain her breath and talk at the same time as we half jogged after the group. "Elizabeth, that was incredible! There were condors everywhere. I began to move like a condor, and I even began to cry like a condor—I couldn't help myself. Then I got on his back and we flew all around the ruin, he showed me so many things. I'm sorry, I know I must have been cawing really loudly because now my throat is sore. I hope it didn't disturb you," she told me, looking a little embarrassed.

"No," I answered. Barbara had been standing right next to me on the stone platform. "Now that you mention it, I do remember hearing a condor cry, but it was very far away." What was it about this place that allowed my sense of time, space, and physical perception to alter so dramatically?

Juan stopped at a large stone house that, like all the other structures in the citadel, had no roof. I stopped, my eyes riveted to the ground in amazement. I looked up at Juan, speechless, pointing to the objects in the floor of this temple. "This is called El Templo de los Espejos Siderales—how would you say—the Temple of Cosmic Mirrors." There, built into the floor of this stone temple, were two round and deep stone dishes that looked just like the cosmic plate, the object I had carried for months in my backpack through all my adventures in Argentina. But I had no chance to ask my urgent questions.

"These two mirrors represent a *hapu*, which is the most perfect form of a *yanantin*, or 'sacred couple.' Since you are from North America, you carry with you the spirit of the eagle, the bird that represents the collective spirit of North America. You have just connected yourself with the condor spirit. At this temple you must use the energy of the *yanantin* to join the spirit of the eagle and the condor together inside you." This felt like a tall order, and the other initiates and I exchanged wide-eyed glances. Quieting my uncertainty, I nodded with semifalse self-assurance for them to go ahead.

Again I closed my eyes, and within moments I felt the condor all around me. Then, abruptly, I was outside the condor, watching the eagle approach. It was a lighter, more refined bird, built for precision and able to scan a huge field for a tiny mouse, very different from the ancient and seemingly "heavier" power of the condor. I saw the two birds come together and stop in midflight. Interlocking talons, they twirled and tumbled earthward. Under some strange airborne alchemical transmutation, the two birds merged, creating a new species that possessed the power and endurance of the condor and the lithe grace and precision of the eagle. The new bird was beautiful and powerful, a mottled light gray, gold, and dark brown, with a golden beak and talons. Again, Juan spoke, bringing me abruptly out of my visionary state.

"We must make a decision now," Juan told the group, "either to go on, even in the rain, or to return to the hotel. If we return to the hotel, we will have to complete this afternoon's ritual tomorrow—and we will be very late for the Pachamama Cave."

As we were debating, someone shouted "Look!" There, across a low green mountain, a rainbow had suddenly appeared. "That means we continue!" Barbara announced with the strength of a warrior. The decision was unanimous, everyone wanted to continue. I felt a pang of pride at the steadfastness and determination of the group and a bit of awe at the sudden, timely appearance of the rainbow.

"I must stop to tell you something important," Juan said, a quizzical look on his face. "Sometimes I am very slow at realizing obvious things," he told us, his childlike sincerity capturing our hearts. "You are a group of mostly women and I should have introduced you to someone right away. But now she has gently reminded me.

"This is the Mamita Putukusi," he pronounced, as if he were introducing us to one of his relatives, and pointed to the lovely green mountain across whose brow our fateful rainbow had just appeared. "She, like the Mama Simona in Cuzco, is the only female mountain in the entire area that surrounds Machu Pikchu. She wants to extend her greetings and protection to you all."

What do you say when you meet a mountain? We all took a moment to greet this female mountain deity, some silently, others out loud. "Her name means 'Flowering Joy,'" Juan explained.

We continued in the rain through the stone corridors along the north edge of the ruin until we came to an immense standing stone. As we walked, the rain slowed, and some of the clouds that had wrapped the surrounding mountains in an impenetrable mist began to recede. "Look here . . . the shape of this stone is repeated in the mountain behind it," Nina pointed out. Nina, who was very athletic, loved the physicality of this trip. She was highly perceptive of energy and wanted to apply the teachings of the Andean Path to her massage practice.

"This is the Pachamama stone. Open your *qosqos* and take in the earth energy here in this spot—connect yourself to this stone through your *qosqo*," Juan told us. Here I experienced a block. Suddenly I was not in Machu Pikchu, but back in my early prenatal chamber and I did not want to open my *qosqo*. I could sense that my mother was in a terrible emotional state, and as I took in food from her, I also received an onslaught of terror and burning feelings of shame, self-hatred, anxiety, and fear. At that moment, it seemed, I had to close my *qosqo* permanently, to protect myself from those energies, making an unconscious decision never to open it again. Now I could not open my *qosqo*, or connect to the stone.

Still, I realized how weak I felt when my *qosqo* was shut; I was keeping out the good and the bad. "There is no positive and negative energy—only heavy and refined." Juan's words came back to me as I struggled at the stone. I began to think of the onslaught of my mother's emotional state simply as *hoocha*, heavy energy. Slowly I began to feel a tiny trickle of energy flow in and out. Fear kept the door shut. Fear was my biggest obstacle.

Philosophically I loved the Andean idea that we had to be able to "eat" or become interpenetrated by all the living energies, neither rejecting nor clinging to one over another. This aligned with my previously Buddhist tendencies and was also compatible with the Jungian idea of relating to the shadow rather than cutting off from it. However, the practice of this simple principle was not necessarily easy. I wondered why I was experiencing this block here and now, when I had previously been able to work with my *qosqo* at the other sites. I resolved to ask Juan at the next opportunity. The group was already moving to the next ritual site.

As we crossed the central field of the citadel, the sun peeked out from behind the clouds, bringing indescribable warmth and happiness to our soggy group. We walked up the long stone stairway. Just as we entered the Temple of the Sun and had gathered around the glorious altar stone at its center, the afternoon sun burst fully forth from the clouds, and the group spontaneously erupted into cheers and praises to Father Sun. As we looked around the freshly rain-washed ruin, it was clear that the storm had chased the less hardy tourists away, and now, apart from a few intrepid travelers, we had the entire ruin to ourselves. It was also wonderful to witness the confirmation of our group's intuitive sense. Clearly we had read the signs correctly, and were now enjoying the benefits of our attunement.

The huge Intiwatana stone glowed white in the strong sun, as Juan began again, the ritual we had performed earlier at the Sun Temple in Pisaq. He got out his *mesa* and placed it on the altar while we made a semicircle around the stone, turning our faces like flowers toward the sun. As Juan connected each of our hearts to the altar stone with his *mesa*, this time, instead of tiny light tendrils extending out from the hearts of my colleagues, I saw large shafts of purple light. My rational mind insisted this was some kind of optical illusion made from rain and sun. Juan himself seemed to be covered in purple light as he worked, with rainbow prisms extending out at his head and feet.

As always in Machu Pikchu, I was aware of the presence of beings much larger and more evolved than myself, enormous spiritual presences that gathered and hummed and whispered to us about the vast glories to be seen on their side of reality. As we worked around the altar stone, their presence had grown steadily stronger. In fact, they seemed to make up the other half of our semicircle. This impression, I later discovered, was shared by a majority of our group.

Once Juan had finished his work with the *mesa*, the group seemed to have been transformed into a rainbow wheel of light. The hub was the center of the Intiwatana stone and each of us a point on its outer rim. An energy spoke extended out from each one of our hearts to the hub of the wheel. It was a lovely sensation. As if on cue Juan said, "Feel the bubble of the group that has just now formed itself." Those were the words that explained the sensation I was experiencing. It was the group's bubble!

Next Juan led us to the edge of the cliff behind the Sun Temple where the wind, although nowhere near the intensity of the Windgate, was blowing quite effectively. We repeated our offerings and prayers to the wind spirits, who now came streaming up the mountainside to take our *hoocha*, a cleansing before proceeding on to the next site.

"For our last ritual today, we will go to the stone of Wiraqocha," Juan told us before he led us down and out of the Sun Temple and on a steep hike up the mountainside to a wonderful perch where we could see all of Machu Pikchu laid out below us. He gestured before us to a large stone that had three small stairs cut into one side and was perfectly flat on top except for what looked almost like a head rest. I had an instinctual desire to lie down on top of the stone.

"As you know, Wiraqocha was the metaphysical God of the Inkas, like Yahweh for the Jews, or Allah for the Muslims. Wiraqocha is the invisible energy force behind all manifested forms. Many chroniclers thought the Inkas worshipped the sun as their supreme deity, but that is not the case. Wiraqocha was the object of their highest devotion. This stone is considered to be a gift from Wiraqocha. Now, for this ritual you will lie on the stone and use all the elements to help you build a tree stretching from your *qosqo* all the way up to the superior world. Not only can we take energy in through our *qosqo* but also we can extend it out into the world. To do this the whole group must help.

"In the Andean tradition there are seven levels of spiritual development, but we are only trying to reach the fourth level, and, as I have already explained, the first three levels are integrated into this fourth-level initiation. You will see here how the fourth level involves surrender and group participation. Circle yourselves around the stone and extend your bubble to the person lying on the stone to help give them more energy."

Maryann was the first one to walk up the three steps and lay her long body down on top of the stone. I was touched to see each person around the circle, some with eyes open, others with eyes closed, concentrating in an effort to help her. At first I only gazed at Maryann's form lying on the stone. Then suddenly it seemed as if a flame of life force leapt up from her *qosqo* and like ground lightning reached toward the sky. As each initiate took his or her turn on the Wiraqocha stone, I directed my attention simply to giving without expectation to each person who lay upon the stone.

When it came to be my turn, I felt again the soreness in my *qosqo*, as if it were a muscle that I had worked a little too hard that day. I laid my head and back down on the Wiraqocha stone, already warmed by other bodies, and felt a distinct buzzing underneath me. The stone itself vibrated with a very high frequency and my natural instinct told me to try to attune myself to it. I lay down and relaxed completely. The hearty support from the group allowed me to let go and drop a bit deeper inside myself. All at once, I grew twelve feet tall, then twenty-four, and after a brief spinning sensation, it seemed I had left the earth's atmosphere and my body was suddenly inter-penetrated by millions of stars. I felt frightened and out of control. I commanded my attention back into my body that was lying, as I well knew, on top of the stone.

With great effort, I fixed my attention on the exercise Juan had given us, and using all my willpower I struggled to bring the ele-ments into balance within my body: Earth. Air. Fire. Water. I felt the touch of each element at each of the centers in my body. Next I turned my attention to harness the energy of the stone and the force of the group around me, together with the elements, to grow a tree from my *qosqo*, up into the *hanaq pacha*.

Slowly, intentionally, I felt the molecules of energy responding to my will and presently I sensed heat and force gathering at my *qosqo*. I then extended the energy upward, working like an artist, like a sculptor, consciously forming the column of energy as it rose out of me and up into the *hanaq pacha*. Although it required a continuous conscious effort on my part, the exercise felt good, as if I were em-ploying a part of myself that had long been in disuse. I experienced a feeling of pride and an influx of refined energy when I got my tree to extend all the way up and connect to the *hanaq pacha*.

After each person had completed the exercise, Juan called us over to sit and talk in a circle. Against the backdrop of a red-and-gold sunset, Machu Pikchu appeared magnificent. "You see that we have repeated some of the rituals of yesterday, bringing the elements to-gether into your bubble. Now that you have incorporated the power of the Wiraqocha stone into your bubbles I will ask you to do one last thing. Sit quietly and close your eyes and I will talk you through this final meditation."

There was some shuffling around as people got situated comfortably. "Take yourself back to the end of our very first day at Huaskar Lake, where you became an Inka seed. Now, bring the spirit of water into your sacrum until you feel filled with it." Juan had an uncanny ability to allow just the right amount of time for this, not too short, but not so long that we got distracted or lost track of what we were doing. "Now feel your connection to the earth through your *qosqo*, and the sun through your heart. Finally, feel the power of the wind moving in your throat. Now, imagine that you are a plant, the stalk runs through the core of your body . . . let yourselves grow leaves and sprout a flower at the top of your head. Draw in all the elements as you need them, to help you grow." I saw my leaves getting greener and thicker as I visualized what Juan was saying. Just enough sun, a little more water, and the beautiful pink hibiscus at the top of my head began slowly to open. "Allow your flower to open, but only if it is ready," Juan instructed.

Bright eyes and faces of joy shone all around me as I opened my eyes coming out of the meditation. I could almost smell the perfume of the fragrant flowers that had energetically bloomed at the top of each initiate's head. As we worked, I could hear the chirruping of hummingbirds as they buzzed around us. This inspired Juan to tell us a story.

"Now that you have grown your flowers, I must tell you about the significance and function of the hummingbird in the Andean tradition. A large, three-inch-long Andean hummingbird buzzed overhead as Juan began his tale.

"One day the hierarchy of birds was gathered in a meadow. Everyone was there: the Kestrel, the Falcon, the Owl, the Condor, and the Hawk. The Condor told the other birds that he had taken a great flight, the largest, highest, and farthest ever, and had arrived at the very gates of the superior world. Just then, the Hummingbird flew by saying, 'That is true, brother Condor, but I have gone be-

yond the gates to the very throne of God in the center of *hanaq pacha*.'
With the other birds as witnesses the Condor and the Hummingbird
made a bet, each claiming that they could fly to the center of *hanaq
pacha*.

"On the day the flight was to be made, only the Condor appeared. All the birds had gathered to witness the competition and
they waited, but the Hummingbird was nowhere to be seen. The
other birds told the Condor that 'a bet is a bet' and, albeit alone, the
Condor still had to attempt the flight to the center of *hanaq pacha*.
The Condor raised his great wings and flew to the very border of
hanaq pacha and when he stopped there to rest, out from his feathers
came the Hummingbird, who flew to the very throne of God. That
is who the Hummingbird is," said Juan, looking at us intently.

"We can learn everything from observing nature. We see that the
condor is one of the largest and strongest fliers, but to reach the
throne of God one must possess the intelligence and unequalled joy
of the hummingbird."

This was a new idea for me. I had always experienced spiritual
growth through suffering. In fact, I realized, taking rapid stock of
myself, that I had always equated struggle with the spiritual path, not
the ease of the hummingbird's flight.

"There is a red flower here in the Andes," Juan continued. "It is
what the hummingbird most loves. On the first day of the *hatun karpay* we activated our "Inka seeds," on the second day, we gave them
water, earth, sun, and wind—all the things they need to make them
germinate. Today we performed the ritual of flowering, *wiñay*. You
are beginning to learn the practices that take a priest from the third
to the fourth level and allow her or him to become a candidate for
the fifth level. We say that when we have gathered enough nectar in
our flowers—at the top of our heads, just like the red flower—then
the hummingbird will come from the center of the superior world
and drink from us. That is the metaphor that my people have for
what you would call 'enlightenment.'"

II

Pachamama: Mother Earth

THE FOLLOWING DAY WE WERE EAGER TO RETURN TO Machu Pikchu and rose before dawn to breakfast on black tea, jam, and homemade bread before making the journey up the mountainside. We entered the ruins just an hour after sunrise, knowing it would be a full and strenuous day of hiking. Walking single file, we made one long straggly line with Juan leading and me bringing up the rear. Each of the different stone rooms of the ruin was so inviting that people began to wander off, mesmerized, and it was hard to keep everyone together. We were all more relaxed now, knowing the way. This was our second full day in Machu Pikchu, and it was feeling more and more like home.

Someone shouted and Juan called everyone to gather 'round. I ran up to the circle, pushing against the body in front of me, trying to see what everyone was looking at, but all I noticed was a clump of earthworms. "Everywhere we can look, Pachamama is teaching us, if we only have eyes to see it," Juan said with an amused twinkle in his eye. I didn't know what he meant. I looked down again and noticed that the whole bunch of worms was moving forward together, sliding one over the other, a wriggling mass of moving bodies. Then it dawned on me that they were moving together, like one seething, unified body. "We will need this piece of wisdom for something today," Juan said assuredly and, with a toss of his head, gestured for us to continue.

We passed by the Condor Temple and turned left to walk along the northern edge of the citadel to get by the quickest route to the Pachamama stone. Once the group had reassembled there, we walked behind the Pachamama stone and continued on another thirty feet to the entrance gate of Huayna Pikchu. There was a sleepy guard in a straw-roofed hut who opened a large, tattered, leather-bound book in which we all had to sign our names and the time of entrance. I supposed they wanted to make sure that everyone who went in also came out. I gazed with respect at the enormous peak as we started down the trail.

The air was warm, breezy, and rich with subtropical humidity. Glorious bromeliads clung to the sheer sides of the mountain in front of us, pronouncing their rich reds, tender greens, and ripe yellows to the surrounding lush green valley. As we hiked, flocks of small green parrots squawked and flew over our heads and once in a while a hummingbird buzzed over us, dazzling us with brilliant green, red, and purple tail feathers. I thought again about Juan's story of the hummingbird. It was a positive omen. We had to hurry. The sky was clear at the moment but there was rain in the air—you could smell it—and I knew from previous experience that the path grew treacherous and slippery in the rain.

We rushed down a long stone zigzag path and eventually arrived at the top of a flight of twelve stone steps. Juan motioned for us to stop there. "This stairway together with the stone at the bottom marks an energy line that divides the right- and left-hand sides of the path," he said. "As you know, the right-hand side of the path involves structured initiation and ritual techniques. It is the mystical side of the path, the method for going to God or Wiraqocha or whatever name you use. The left-hand path is the magical and practical application of the spiritual knowledge and power you receive, once you have had a contact with Wiraqocha by following the right-hand path. The left-hand side of the path involves performing magic, healing, and therapy. It is the more wild side of the path and can be more chaotic. Until now, we have been working almost uniquely on the right-hand side, but we are about to enter the left-hand side of the path."

I remembered Juan telling me that I was completely left side when we first met. This was not the same as the right-brain, left-brain distinctions of the Western scientific approach. Perhaps that was because the Andean Path was more body- than brain-focused. The right side of the path is the structured, organized side related to mystical knowledge, while the left side is chaotic, wild power. Now, in relation to my first two years of training, I understood what he meant. While I had developed the left side, I could not use the left-hand gifts because I did not have the right side sufficiently developed.

Before Peru, I had been a moderately orderly person. When I returned to the United States, I felt as if I had been taken apart piece by piece, but I hadn't been put back together yet. I had become spiritually disorganized, and I couldn't progress along my path without the mystical integration and ordering of the right-hand side. I thought I was trying to escape from the limitations of the rational mind. Now I realized that order and structure have their place. A natural structure helps to create order. Power is unusable if one does not have the ability to organize or channel that power. I remembered that Pachakamaq, another Andean word for God, meant "one who puts order in the universe."

It occurred to me that my first teacher, Ricardo, had been overdeveloped on the left-hand side, and was not organized either. Maybe this was why he drank so heavily and was so miserable. He was being controlled by his power because he lacked the integration and wisdom to know how to direct it.

"Please, God, put order in me," I prayed as, opening our *qosqos*, we crossed the line that marked our entrance into the left side of the path and began to descend the two-and-a-half-hour trail that led to the Pachamama Cave.

As we walked, Juan told us to breathe in the rich and living energy that was so strong in this subtropical garden. Going ever downward, we walked, talked, sang, and laughed like children. We felt light and happy, buoyed up by some invisible force, perhaps the effect of the living energy world that Juan had mentioned.

Living energy. What does it mean that the Quechua language has so many words to describe human experiences of energy? I mused as we trekked forever downward along the jungle trail. *Sami* is refined energy; *huaca* means the sacred energy of a person, place, or an object; *hoocha* is heavy energy; and *poq'po* the energy bubble; and of course *kausay*, the living energy that suffuses the world. Imbedded in the language itself is a profound understanding of the energetic nature of the universe. Obviously energy is important to the Andean Indians.

Quechua, until very recently, had never been a written language. It was an energetic language. The words could not be captured in two dimensions and set down on a page. Juan had said each word is a vibration, similar to the Sanskrit language. Each word has a general meaning ascribed to it, but that meaning can change completely, depending on the context of the sentence or the mood of the speaker. The Quechuan people, Juan told us, are masters at word games. Their language, like the people, is as mutable as mountain weather. Their ideas about the nature of reality are completely different from ours, and therefore they could do things that for us seem like magic. The Andean masters, living in a deep energetic reciprocity with nature, believe they are part of the weather, and therefore they can effect changes in it.

I remembered a story Juan had told about his master Don Benito. A reporter from *National Geographic* had come to Cuzco to do a study on the traditional use of the coca leaf, so of course he had been told to go see Juan. When Juan told him stories about Don Benito, the reporter immediately wanted to meet Don Benito and photograph him. Juan arranged the interview with Don Benito and translated for the photographer as he photographed Don Benito performing the traditional rituals with the coca leaf. It was late in the afternoon and the clouds came in to cover the setting sun, just when the photographer was taking his final pictures. He gave up, telling Juan that there was not enough light left to get the photographs he wanted. Don Benito waved his hand saying, "Oh, the light? That's only a little problem." Then Don Benito took three coca leaves and, facing the setting sun, blew on the leaves, saying a prayer into them. The clouds immediately parted, and to the photographer's amazement he was able to get his pictures. These people's beliefs, I mused, were what gave them a completely different kind of power over their world. My musings ended as at last we arrived at the Pachamama Cave.

A large natural rock overhang covered the entrance to the cave, and the niches of the five *ñust'as*, Inka princesses, were visible from the exterior. Inka-cut stones made a perfect joint with the huge extruding natural wall. Silently and with great reverence we entered the cave of the Earth Mother. Juan gestured for us to move to the very back of the cave. Clearly the cave, at one time, had gone much farther back, but now it had been intentionally filled in, so that one could enter only so far into the Mother. We sat down at a rock altar in the back of the cave, in the pitch-dark. "This is the cave of Pachamama, she who gave you life. Now you must offer her your finest energy," Juan said, his voice coming up out of the darkness, soft but serious.

Until now we had given Pachamama only our heavy energy for her to absorb and recycle. The idea of giving her my finest energy touched me. A deep humility and gratitude overcame me as I offered my refined energy to Pachamama, my gift to her. The sense of connection was instantaneous. I felt I was in the lap of an enormous and endlessly loving mother presence. She was wide and dark and soft and rich, very solid and quite different from the energy of the cosmic Mother in the church. I heard the muffled weeping sounds of the other initiates around me, as they too made this sacred offering to their real mother and received the *ayni* of her deep and encompassing love.

Now images flashed through my mind of the destruction of and disrespect for the earth committed by my North American culture, out of ignorance of the fact that she, Earth, is a living, breathing organism that needs love, respect, acknowledgment, and thanks for what she gives. As I offered, I understood more about our deep relationship with Pachamama. Like selfish children we have learned only to take from our Mother. The fact that she needs our human love, caring, and tending as much as we need her to sustain our lives came as a revelation. This is living *ayni!* I thought of anthropologists describing "primitive" religion as animism. What if these "primitives" were instead acting from a sophisticated knowledge of the energetic balance between humans and nature? What if they instinctively knew what Einstein had scientifically proven, that energy and matter are related, and their animistic worship was part of an energy exchange necessary for both Mother Earth and us?

I became deeply grateful, thanking her for the very air I was breathing, air that her plants had made for us, grateful for the rich soul-relieving beauty of her wildernesses and waterfalls, the breathtaking glory of each minute flower, each perfect detail of her creation, each pear or plum that I had ever eaten. I saw them now as gifts to me, given freely, with joy and for my happiness, expecting nothing in return. And I had never even thanked her. I could no longer hold back my feelings, and deep gut-wrenching sobs came out of me as I thanked her and thanked her and then apologized for all the years in which I had not known enough to thank her.

I thought of my own biological mother and silently began thanking her for the very bones of my body, the flesh and the blood that she had selflessly given me. Suddenly and perhaps for the first time in my life, I was grateful for the opportunity of existence, the chance to breathe and taste and smell and see and hear and feel with my heart. I felt I was going to burst, or shout or sing, but I could only sigh and weep.

My eyes, now accustomed to the dark, looked into the red eyes and tearstained faces of the other initiates. One by one our eyes met and we nodded to each other, acknowledging that somehow we were all experiencing the same thing, the deep pain and beauty of coming into a real relationship with Earth. This was the fourth-level initiation; I was becoming more and more a child of Pachamama. She loved me and I loved her and these human beings next to me, my brothers and sisters. No one had to tell me. I knew it, I felt it. We all did.

Juan called us out of the dark, out of the womb, the cradle of our mother. He called us back into the light and on to the work with the niches. We did not speak. We did not need to. We were deep inside ourselves and and yet each deeply connected through our mutual experience. The knowledge was so simple, so profound.

"YOU SEE HERE THESE FIVE NICHES?" JUAN SAID, POINTING to the stone rectangles. "These represent *ñust'as*, or female energies of nature. *Ñust'a* means 'princess' or 'royal female.' The niches contain the most sacred female energies of nature, which we are now going to incorporate into our bubbles. The first niche is red, the second black, the third golden, and the fourth silver. You will enter each niche and forget everything you know. In each niche, you will offer all your power to the *ñust'a*. When you have given her all your power, you will open your whole energy system and receive power from her," Juan instructed us. This was a difficult concept for me, as I spent all my time as a therapist trying to get people not to give away their power. But perhaps this was different, since this giving away would be a conscious act.

"When you have worked with all four niches you will go and give your heavy energy to this stone," he said, pointing to a large carved stone seat. "Then you will ask the four energies to mix together inside you and give this integrated power to the last *ñust'a*," Juan said, gesturing to a fifth niche I had not yet seen that stood to the left and outside the rectangular cubby of the four niches. "She is green. Receive her blessing."

We all nodded and began the ritual. I entered the first niche and breathed out, offering my power. A wave of fear washed over me and I felt tremendously vulnerable offering all my power to the niche and to the *ñust'a*. Would this *ñust'a* be kind to me when I was helpless inside her walls? I fought to overcome my fear and soon my inner sight was bathed in a sea of red. I saw a beautiful dancing princess in ruby red, like a Middle Eastern belly dancer, wearing a veil and golden spangles over the multilayered red gauze robes that showed seductive glimpses of her flesh. She was sensuous and moved with the agility of a wild animal. She took my energy, and when I thought I could no longer breathe, she began to pour her energy into me, filling my bubble with a deep pulsating red.

"Change," Juan told us, with quiet authority. I staggered out of the niche and flopped down in the next one. As I sat down in the niche of the black *ñust'a* I saw skulls, skeletons, bones, and decaying flesh. Many images of the destructive female force came to me. I thought of Kali. My anxiety increased and my heart was beating fast. I summoned up my courage and with a tremendous effort gave without question or doubt all my power to the black *ñust'a*. She raged and rampaged and I found myself wondering if these were my images that she was taking away from me. They were frightful.

The images disappeared and I felt the energy of the black *ñust'a* like a huge anaconda snake, glistening and powerful, nearly bursting its skin with life force, and then I began to perceive the black energy as light, Black Light. It writhed as the power rose inside my body, up my spine, trying to incorporate itself into me as I struggled against it. My mother's voice flashed through my head. Endless sentences echoed: "That's not ladylike." "Why don't you act like a girl?" "Good girls don't do that." "Good girls don't say that." "Good girls don't think that." "Good girls don't feel that!"

This energy was *not* ladylike—it was raw power. Clearly female power. Aha! I thought to myself, this must be the female power that men are so terrified of. I understood it as I gained sudden insight into the male dilemma; for in that moment I, too, feared this power. I had been trained to fear it—yet at the same time it was an innate part of my femaleness, my birthright. I felt the hackles rise on the back of my neck as fear and fascination gripped me. I wanted to fly in the face of all my cultural training, but the fear was so potent. The ensuing violent inner storm had reached a fever pitch just as Juan said "Change." Grateful, I bolted out of the niche and away from the black *ñust'a*, seeking refuge in the next niche—the golden niche. As I settled into this niche, I was well aware that my relief was only temporary. The black *ñust'a* was not finished with me yet.

In the golden niche I easily gave away my power and felt instantly surrounded by soft golden beams of light. My fear began to melt like an icicle in the hot sun, and golden heat radiated out from my chest. Slowly the inner storm calmed completely with the coming of the sun inside me. I thanked the golden *ñust'a* and moved to the next niche as Juan indicated once again, with a wave of his hand, for us to change.

Entering the silver niche I immediately felt myself pulled up into a higher frequency. A feeling of moon and stars and tinkling bells took over my inner experience. Suddenly I felt as if I were very tall and unimaginably thin, like a string of light from a star. Then I realized it wasn't me, rather I was relating to very tall, silver, female beings that said they came from the stars. They told me that they were the highest aspect of the silver *ñust'a* and that I was now ready to incorporate them. Immeasurable joy and delight filled me and I wanted to sing their silvery voices through my body. All too soon it was time to change.

Next I moved to the stone seat, thanking the *ñust'as* and asking the four energies to integrate themselves within me as I released my *hoocha*. At the next indication to change positions, I bowed very low to the green *ñust'a* before entering her niche. All at once, I understood that these niches were the residences of these nature energies, and that I was a guest entering their house; offering my power was only the polite thing to do, like bringing a bottle of wine to dinner. Somehow thinking like this made the process easier, and I gave my power much more freely to the green *ñust'a*.

I sensed that there were four little strings of energy extending out from each one of the four niches and into me. To my inner eye, I had a red, black, gold, and silver cord tying me to each niche and I was bringing them all together, to tie into the fifth niche. A tremendous sense of joy and expansion filled me as I gave my power to the green *ñust'a*, and the most exquisite and delicate shades of green from nature began to fill my awareness. She was joy, unconditional love and healing, this green *ñust'a*. Juan told us to change but I could not get up. After a few moments of self-conscious struggle, I hoisted myself out of the niche and sat to one side, waiting for the rest of the initiates to finish their exchange with the niches. I wanted some silence into which I could give a final prayer to the *ñust'as*. It had been such a powerful privilege to meet them.

Without speaking, Juan signaled us that it was time to go. There was more work to do in a cave lower down, below this one. We were going to the entrance to the *ukhu pacha*, the lower, or interior, world. After the last initiate filed out of the cave I turned back to face the niches once more. I noticed how each niche now seemed to be glowing, appearing clearer and much more sharply outlined than when we had first arrived. Was it my perception or an energetic change in the niche? Perhaps both? I suddenly received an impression of gratitude, as if we had actually served the *ñust'as*, activating them by our ritual, and that they as well were grateful for the exchange.

Embarrassed by my thoughts, I looked down at my feet, and out of the corner of my eye, from my peripheral vision, I saw four females dressed like the ruby red *ñust'a*, like Arabian princesses in red, black, gold, and silver, leaning a little way out of their niches. I didn't move my eyes, afraid the image would disappear. They bowed low, first to me, then to one another in a fluid gesture and withdrew back into their niches and out of my sight. I gasped. My eyes darted to the niche of the green *ñust'a*, and there in the center were a pair of hands in prayer position, floating in a field of deep green energy. A sense of profound wisdom and knowledge enveloped me—knowledge about hands and healing. The hands stayed there as I stared at them and although I could see no facial features, no eyes, I had a sense of being deeply looked at.

A moment later Juan came back, gathering up the stragglers, but he stopped short when he saw me. His eyes grew wide and then his whole face crinkled up in a delightful burst of laughter. "Oho, oohoo hoo, Elizabeth." He smiled through tears of laughter. "So this is what you came here for."

I TOOK A DEEP BREATH BEFORE FOLLOWING JUAN THROUGH the huge ferns and overgrown jungle plants that had nearly concealed the path down to the next cave. I wasn't sure I could bear any more. Each of the experiences today had been profound enough for me to spend weeks mulling them over, and we weren't finished yet.

We ducked through a low entrance to the cave. After my eyes adjusted to the dim light, I noticed the others had folded up their rain ponchos and were sitting on them. The floor of the cave was cold and wet. More than a dozen bats startled us, drawing a few shrieks as they flew close over our heads and out of the cave. Now *we* were the ones to invade *their* home temporarily.

"This is the only completely intact Inka temple that I know of still in existence today," Juan explained. "I say 'intact' because if you look over there in the niches, you will see that they contain the original *huacas*." As our eyes gradually adjusted to the light, we saw that dark stones, ranging from the size of a grapefruit to about the size of a football, occupied the bottom center of each one of the eight niches. "This is the place where we can have a direct contact with the *ukhu pacha*, the place of Huaskar, the last free Inka."

"Juan," Maryann asked, "what exactly is the *ukhu pacha*? Is it the unconscious?"

"In a way yes, and in a way no," he answered enigmatically. "It is a place within yourself, the place where you encounter what Jung called the 'forces of the unconscious,' but it is much more than that. It is literally a location, inside the earth; it is where, if you remember, Huaskar and Atahualpa went to live when they could not return the *ayni* of an empire. There are powerful beings and energies in the *ukhu pacha*, but they are useful only if they are first organized and contained within the self. Here, with this ritual, we put order in the forces of the *ukhu pacha.* As Jung said, 'You cannot kill the shadow.' In the Andes we don't want to kill the shadow, but we *do* want to order it. This must be experienced. To talk too much about it is to lose the thrust of our work.

"But we must prepare ourselves first," Juan said. "We have been cleansing our energy bubble and working with the practice of merging energy fields. Here, with the help of the power of this cave—which is a very powerful heavy-energy eater—we will do a deep-level cleansing of our bubbles." The group sat at attention, eager for the next instructions on this fascinating journey. Clearly we were already under the influence of this cave temple, which felt so completely different from the Pachamama Cave. There was something almost frightening about this cave. I took a deep breath, thinking that this must be my own fear of the "unconscious forces." There was a feeling of raw power here, and I knew quite well, from my time with Ricardo, that raw power attracted all kinds of junk. I, for one, was relieved that we were going to do a cleansing first. It felt appropriate.

Juan continued his explanation. "We have been talking so much about the *poq'po,* or energy bubble, because in this work we find that we truly are bound together by living energy. In the Serpent Cave, you cleansed the heavy energy from your mother and father at the moment of your conception, but here we will work with an even larger energy field. First, you must visualize all the friends, lovers, colleagues, and acquaintances you have, every relationship you have with every person you know. See it now as a web of light that ties you all together with little strings of energy."

The cave became very small and far away as I followed Juan's instruction. But I could still hear his voice as he continued. "Use the newly awakened power of your *qosqo,* the power of Pachamama and the *ñust'as,* and the power of this cave to support you as you pull all of the heavy energy from that web. Pull it from the web with your *qosqo* and release it into the *ukhu pacha.* This heavy energy will be refined energy for the beings there. Make an offering of your *hoocha* to them. You are feeding them."

Face after face came to my mind, images of my family, friends, people I loved, people I didn't even like, old boyfriends, past and present problematic situations, all of this came rushing into my awareness. After a time, I didn't want to see the faces anymore, so I stopped looking at them and they disappeared. Then all I felt was the flux of energy, as if I were holding on to a large tube through which huge volumes of dirty water was being flushed. I waited until the flux of energy ceased, and when I looked at the web again, it was sparkling like Indra's net. I opened my eyes, as if waking out of a deep dream. Baby faces greeted me around the cave and everyone began talking at once, buzzing excitedly with what they had seen and felt.

"Now we are ready for the hard work," Juan said with laughing eyes after everyone had settled down again. "First, you must go and connect yourselves with each one of the niches, exchanging energies with each stone, just as you have done with the *ñust'as.* You must start in the right-hand outside corner and work toward the center, then begin again from the left-hand outside corner and work in. The stone in the center must be the last one you exchange with. This is the stone of Huaskar Inka. At this stone you will do something different; here you will command that all the energies order themselves, by the power of Huaskar. Call on the spirit of Huaskar to help you."

"What are the stones made of, Juan?" asked Nina.

"If you try to pick one up, you will find that it is very heavy. They are meteorites."

Slowly we moved around in the dark, lining up in some kind of organic order. One by one, we approached the niches. These niches were much smaller than the niches of the *ñust'as* and were set back in the stone wall of the cave about waist high. We had just enough room to bend over each niche and wrap our hands around the *huacas* without banging our heads against the cave's low ceiling. After a short time, I noticed that people were becoming discombobulated from the impact of the *huacas* and were heading immediately to the Inka stone, so I decided to stay out of the line and help direct people, first to the niches on the right-hand side of the cave, then to the niches over on the left side of the cave, and finally the central stone of Huaskar. However, it soon became obvious that my "helping" others was, at least in part, a way to avoid the task at hand. The last person was already finished with the first niche. It was my turn.

I approached the first niche in the dark and musty corner of the low cave. I reached out my hand into the dark niche thinking of spiders and bat droppings. When my hand touched the rock, sure enough it was wet and slimy. I quickly withdrew my hand, certain it was covered in some disgusting primal goop. Nothing. My hand was completely dry. When I reached out again, I found that the stone was simply very cold, even after eleven pairs of hands had made prolonged contact with it. I closed my eyes. I was not feeling anything. In fact, I was suddenly overwhelmed by the feeling that everyone else was experiencing something and I was not. An attack of envy twisted my guts and I wanted to hide. Remembering my practice, I steadied myself, and released my heavy energy through my bubble. It was not me. It was the stone! It emanated jealousy!

As my practice gave me some detachment I realized that, rather than being overcome by it, I was holding jealousy in my hands. As I quieted my rational mind, jealousy became a tangible force that I could approach or move away from. As the game became more fluid, and I began to disidentify and experience jealousy more objectively, I felt it as a texture, an energy pattern, that could now pass easily through my bubble and into Pachamama. I remembered Juan's saying the Quechua word for ritual, *pujllay*, literally meant "play" or "sacred game." But it was time for the next stone.

I was feeling quite high about my discovery as I moved on to the next niche. As I placed my hands on the next stone, a flatter, rounder stone than the first one, I began to feel quite proud of myself indeed and felt that I wanted to tell everyone that I had figured out the secret of the stones. In fact, I wanted to shout it out to them so they would recognize my specialness, my intelligence, my brilliance. As these feelings welled up inside me and came to a peak, I understood that I was at the stone of pride. This had always been one of my downfalls. "Greek pride," my mother used to say. I only knew that in my life it had gotten me into the worst trouble—too proud to ask for help, too proud to admit a mistake, too proud to need anyone. I tried to do as I had done at the first stone and detach from the feeling, but here I just couldn't get the distance. This energy was certainly in my bubble but I had not yet learned to command it—it still commanded me. All I could do was to notice it and move on to the next stone.

As soon as I touched this dense black stone, which curiously was warmer than the others, I experienced a pleasant buzzing throughout my body. It suddenly occurred to me that it must have been nearly one o'clock, way past my lunchtime. I began to dream of what I wanted to eat—a hamburger covered in tomatoes and sloppy honey mustard and mayonnaise. My mouth began to water, and my mind became filled with images of things I wanted: what I wanted to eat, what I wanted to do, how spiritual I wanted to be, money, fame, influence. I wanted them all. Want want want want want want. One minute I saw myself speaking on a prime-time talk show, and the next, sexual desire coursed through me. Once again, the stones had fooled me. I was standing at the stone of desire. I began to play with the desire, and I realized even as I did that my desire to play only grew more and more out of proportion. Again I concentrated on releasing my heavy energy and slowly my desire began to ebb, though it did not wane completely until I left the stone and moved on to the next niche.

The next three stones were anger, fear, and shame. I felt I had done pretty well recognizing the energies and getting a little clearer on how I related to each one of these in my life. In fact, I was becoming downright cocky until my hand touched the last stone. While in deep interchange with this stone I began to realize that I had no idea if the other people were experiencing the stones in this same way. I had just assumed they were. How egotistical! Now I thought of all the parts of myself the stones had stirred up, the greed, the envy, the self-aggrandizement, and I felt a compelling revulsion at my own thoughts and my own feelings. I wanted nothing more than to get away from myself. Clearly I had reached the last challenge, the stone of self-hatred!

It was time to reconcile all this with the stone of the Inka. At least I hoped that this stone would provide some relief. I reverently approached the last *huaca*, which was nearly three times the size of the other stones. Now, with a healthy respect for the powerful effect these stones could produce, I prayed first before touching the stone. I prayed with my whole being for the Inka to help me order these forces and use their energy in my life for a constructive purpose. As I knelt before the stone of the Inka, although it was dark I could see that this stone was a lighter color, it was white rock, shot through with red and black. This stone gave off an energy that was altogether different from the others; it emanated a high-pitched vibration that seemed to shake loose the very molecules of my body. I stayed a long time kneeling before this rock in a deep energetic communion with it, unaware of my surroundings and wondering if indeed my unconscious *could* be ordered. I had a brief glimpse of a very powerful force, a force that could move magma, stirring within me deeply, slowly. It was a hand of fire that moved with the power of divine will, slowly, surely, taming these unconscious forces, putting them back in their places. As the energy exchange with the stone of the Inka drew to a close I knew there was one sure way to test the effects of this ritual: I would have to observe, over the following weeks and months, how the last part of this ritual would bear out in my life.

Finally I arose and exited the cave to find the rest of the group gathered outside, and soaking up the warmth of the strong afternoon sun. "We have a decision to make," Juan announced to our group, many of whom were still vibrating from the intensity of the *ukhu pacha* cave. "We took almost three hours coming down the trail. Now, if we want to make it up in time to catch the last bus down to our hotel, we must cut our time in half," Juan informed us, one raised eyebrow accentuating the challenge.

"Oh, no!" exclaimed Julia, a jovial, auburn-haired, heavyset woman in her midfifties who had been having difficulty all day with the physical pace we had been keeping. "That's impossible. I had enough trouble getting down here. There's no way."

"Tsk-tsk," Juan chided her, "there *is* a way and I have just now realized what it is. Do you all remember the bunch of *gusanos*—how you call, *worms*—that we saw this morning?" Heads around the group nodded in reply as we recalled one of our first experiences of the day, which by now seemed as if it had been several weeks ago. "Pachamama was showing us how to use our collective energy to move as a group. Julia, you will go in front—"

"No I couldn't possibly—" Julia protested.

"You will go in the front of the line," Juan insisted gently, looking deeply into her eyes. Then he placed his hands squarely on her shoulders and physically steered her to the head of the group. "Elizabeth, you will go behind her and keep your *qosqo* open, pushing her up with your energy and receiving an energy push from the one behind you. Each person behind you will do the same, and I will be at the back of the line. We will make an *amaru*, a snake of living energy, and it will go very easily, you will see." Juan spoke with such confidence and so persuasively that even Julia couldn't find an argument against him. Besides, it was fun to think of our group becoming a long snake of energy; it made what had been a dismal prospect into an interesting challenge and now I was actually looking forward to the hike back to the top. Thank God we didn't have too much time to think before we were off again. In fact, the physical exercise between each ritual actually seemed to help integrate the energy.

We began the line, awkwardly at first. After perhaps fifteen or twenty minutes, the group seemed to drop into a natural rhythm, and our "snake" slithered forward up the twists and turns of the mountain trail at quite a good rate of speed. I felt Julia at first resist the push I gave her. "Julia," I told her quietly, "let me help you." That seemed to be all she needed, for she was soon literally charging ahead up the trail, and we were talking and laughing as we passed through the exquisite steamy bamboo and jungle fern forest, the dirt path beneath us interrupted here and there by short flights of Inka stairs carved into the solid rock. It rained only lightly, just enough to refresh us as we hiked, and the only sounds we heard aside from our own footsteps were the strange warbling cries of the Peruvian "jungle chicken."

We didn't stop until we had reached the top, where someone sounded off the time. "Exactly one hour and a half!" Juan pronounced proudly, beaming at Julia and giving her an enormous congratulatory hug. "Thank you for leading us to the top," Juan told her. Julia could only shake her head and mutter, "I don't believe it . . . I still don't believe it." Small tears showed in the corners of her eyes as she turned to look at Juan and the group. "Thank you," she told us. "Without you I could never have done it."

"Juan," I whispered, pulling him to one side, "how did you know she could do it?" As the "leader" of our group, I had been concerned by the situation.

"I saw a woman with an enormous will," he replied matter-of-factly. "She only needed a reason to engage it, that is all." I was glad that there were teachers like Juan. We arrived at the front gate of the ruin in plenty of time to catch the last bus down to our hotel.

THE MORNING DAWNED BRIGHT AND CLOUDLESS BUT THIS was no guarantee that it would remain so. In Machu Pikchu the weather could change in minutes. We packed accordingly and after a hurried breakfast and bus ride, we again entered the fantastic ruins of Machu Pikchu in the early morning light. We followed Juan into the right side of the ruin, and soon arrived once more at the Pachamama stone that guarded the entrance to the trail. Today a big challenge loomed before us. We were going to climb to the top of Huayna Pikchu to have an encounter with the *apus*.

This time we headed up the trail, which was at times nothing more than a stairway of boulders going endlessly up into the clouds above Machu Pikchu. As we climbed, gasping for breath along the steep rock and mud switchbacks, we caught glimpses of the valley floor and the Willkañust'a River flowing powerfully through it, thousands of feet below. At certain junctures in the trail there were Inka stairs carved into the face of the rock cliff—actually more like stone ladders—which we had to ascend one step at a time without looking down or risk the nausea of feeling that we were suspended over a thousand-foot abyss.

Rounding a bend near the very top was a view almost undescribably spectacular. Soft emerald green mountains boasting shining needle-thin waterfalls and velour black or luminous white snow peaks rose above lush subtropical valleys striped with silver rivers. The magical landscape spread out before us in every direction as far as the eye could see; and everywhere a magnificent thrumming, the heartbeat of Pachamama. Messages of the tremendous aliveness of Earth herself poured in through our every sense organ—eyes, ears, noses, skin—our very cells thrilled with her resplendent vitality. There was no argument here, no reductionist philosophy or any scientific data that could persuade even the harshest skeptic among us that Earth was not clearly a living, palpitating being. Here, that turn of the mind was inconceivable, ludicrous, next to the visceral power of great Nature herself.

More exquisite still was the citadel of Machu Pikchu now far below us. A jewel wrapped in swirling mists, its long stone terraces and graceful walkways striped the mountain along its natural line. Elegant white stone staircases and rectangular buildings placed in perfect harmony with their surroundings spoke of an architecture that was a sacred song, an ode to the magnificence of the mountains' natural beauty.

When we got our breath back, Juan collected us together to give the next instructions. "You see that cave up there?" he asked, pointing up to a small black hole partially covered over by ferns. "It is another Pachamama Cave. But here we must divest ourselves of all our female energy and become young men. The top of Huayna Pikchu is a place that is completely masculine. It is a place to incorporate new masculine energy. Here we will use our gender difference to help each other. All the women in the group will come with me. Men, you stay here, and I will be back to instruct you in a few minutes," Juan commanded, leading the women up toward the dark opening. This was the first time we had ever separated into two groups. Of course our group had a few more women than men, but with Juan and the other guide it made us more or less equal—eight women and six men.

"Please, ladies, step inside and find a place for yourselves against the cave walls." We entered what looked more like a long dark tunnel than a cave; the floor was wet, and the only sound was the slow and constant dripping of water down the cave walls. Stepping carefully over the larger puddles, we found places where we could stand and lean our backs against the walls of the cave.

"Now," Juan told us from the cave mouth, "you are going to help your brothers face their most primal fear. At first, it will seem strange or perhaps even wrong to do this, but know that you are offering them the highest service. First, give all your heavy energy to the cave walls. After that, let yourself merge with the female power of this cave. Become completely magnetic, one with Pachamama. When you have done that, signal me. But be prepared. When you see the men arrive here at the entrance to the cave, open your *qosqos*. As they pass through the cave you must 'eat' all of their male power. Pull it with your *qosqos*."

A stony silence fell over the women and a feeling of apprehension filled the cave. The idea jangled against my nervous system as it collided with a deeply unconscious taboo. *This* was what men feared most about women—our power to absorb, to be magnetic! However, from deeper within my primal core, the notion produced an unpremeditated whoop of wild joy. "*Yes!*" I shouted, startling even myself with the intensity of my vocalization. And to my further surprise, the cave began to echo with the affirming cries of the other women. "Good," said Juan as he walked away.

Following Juan's instructions, we began to release our heavy energy to the cave walls, spontaneously inhaling together and releasing our heavy energy in one loud outbreath as we exhaled. After several minutes of intensive breathing a low chant began in several corners of the cave at once. "Pachamama, Pachamama, Pachamama, Pachamama." The women's voices grew louder as we joined ourselves to the power of the great heavy-energy eater, Pachamama; and when the sound reached a crescendo, I quickly stuck my head out of the cave opening, signaling to Juan that we were ready.

The energetic environment of the cave, already rich with magnetic female power, swelled as we heard the first man approach the cave. Opening our *qosqos*, we prepared ourselves to "eat" his masculine force. In that moment I knew that, as women, we were energetically built to do this—to be receptive, not in the traditional passive sense of the word but rather to absorb actively and use our magnetic power. In fact, it was when this power could not be expressed directly that women had to twist their power, becoming passive-aggressive.

As the first male came into our midst we all pulled his masculine power without reservation, inhaling deeply as we did this and quite frankly enjoying the sensation. I experienced a tremendous liberation of psychic energy having been given permission to perform this act as a ceremony, intentionally and without shame, and knowing deep inside that I was actually helping and healing my brother.

The dark silhouette of the man swayed, and he momentarily lost his balance as he groped forward through our female cave toward the outlet at the far end. He had to endure a good several minutes of this deep energetic cleansing as he made his way through the tunnel/cave that was at least fifteen feet long. As he exited the cave at the far end, the next man entered and after a few steps fell to his knees, but whether from fear or ecstasy we did not know. We continued our joyous absorption, cleansing the bubble of the second initiate, as he tried several times to rise, then crawled a few yards farther toward the exit. He was not able to rise to his feet until the first man stuck a leg and arm back in through the exit hole and hoisted him bodily to his feet and out of the cave, away from the devouring females. It was then I saw that the first man had been Juan.

Four more men passed through the cave, one at a time, each either trembling or in a profound reverie, the slow-motion movement of their limbs attesting to the fact that they were now traversing a substance more viscous than ordinary air.

When all the male initiates had passed through the cave, Juan called back to us through the opening, telling us to leave all our female power in the cave as an offering to Pachamama, and to come out the other side. Divesting ourselves of the potent magnetic force of which we had become such a part was no small task. Yet at the same time it was a relief to know that we did not have to stay identified with one type of energy, but could now slip out of it and into something else. But what else? The surprising answer lay on the other side of the cave exit.

I pushed myself through the narrow cave exit, where cool fronds of overhanging jungle ferns brushed against my skin. As I stepped out into the bright sunlight of the other side, strong male arms enveloped me in a warm embrace that was like the sun.

"Receive the new male power," I heard Juan saying. I had stepped out of one energy field and into another, completely different but complementary. I took in the comforting, protective feeling of the embrace as I realized this was a kind of male energy that I personally had rarely experienced in my life. Heartful, loving protection, security, integrity, and power all came together for me in that embrace. It was a kind of male energy that did not fear or hate the female, but stood in harmony with her.

"Take this new male energy completely into your bubble," Juan instructed, "and let yourself, for now, become totally male." Amazingly, this was not at all difficult. I wanted to identify with this kind of male power, constructive power. Certainly the men initiates had pushed their limits and this inspired me to push mine. I imagined myself now as a young boy. When I looked up, I saw I was surrounded by five more couples in deep embrace.

"Juan," one of the women asked groggily, "what just happened?"

"You have just had a real experience of *yanantin*. Let me explain. *Yanantin* is a fundamental principle of the Andean Path. It means 'harmonious relationship between different things.' As biological men and women you contain both male and female inside you. In this ceremony you were able to experience each other in your most potent forms. You women in the cave, in your ceremony to Pachamama, were polarizing your energy bubbles completely to your female side. We men, while we were still outside the cave, moved our bubbles into their most masculine polarization by performing a ceremony to the Sun. When we came through the cave to offer you our male power, you helped us by absorbing all our male energy."

"It was terrifying and wonderful at the same time," Sam piped up, looking gorgeously masculine. "In the cave I felt I was being squeezed out like a sponge. So when I came to the other side, I was empty, and completely free to absorb the pure new male energy there."

"Pure male and pure female is a perfect alchemy of powers that we call a *hapu* or 'sacred couple,'" Juan took up. "The ritual addresses not only a primal fear but a primal desire—for to be 'eaten' completely by a woman is to be taken to the sacred. Now you women will experience the challenge of letting yourself be completely absorbed by the male power. We will do that in the ceremony of the *apus.*"

"Let's go, boys," Juan said, laughing and winking at the women. I stepped out feeling vigorous and energetic, just as I imagined a young boy might feel. We walked a few feet to another opening in the rock, and, climbing up inside the rock, we came out on top of the very peak of Huayna Pikchu, an area of large gray boulders about ten feet square. The view was spectacular, and several of us stopped to take pictures while the rest of the group scrambled up through the rock. When we were all out on top, Juan pointed to a long smooth gray stone that was inclined at about a fifteen-degree angle. Here was where we would encounter the *apus.*

Juan motioned me over to the stone. Staring out over those beautiful mountain peaks, I couldn't imagine them holding anything but a benevolent energy. My earlier experiences with Ricardo and his *apus* came flooding back to me. I closed my eyes now and saw again the condors of light radiating their brilliance at the top of each peak. They held power and at the same time a challenge.

I knew that there was still some part of me that was afraid of conflict and I also knew that I did not want to fight the kind of battles that Ricardo and his third-level *apus* had put me up to. But did that mean I should shun all conflict? I was aware that one of my personal challenges was to stand my ground in the face of opposition, and even to fight back when and where appropriate, although I was often far too acquiescent. The few times I had been brave enough to stand firm, the results had been creative solutions to problems, rather than the disasters of my overactive imagination. There was still something I couldn't resolve about my own male power. Juan had explained that the third level was the level at which one learned about power and control, but had I really learned about it, or had I tried to just skip over it?

I approached the gray stone with reverence and prayed silently to receive the teaching I most needed regarding conflict. Juan gestured again for me to lie down. "You are in a bowl of mountains surrounded by the young masculine power in all of their peaks. They will come to challenge you now. You must fight them with your *qosqo*."

"But, Juan, why?" I asked, close to tears. "I don't like fighting."

"This is the warrior energy that you will need in order to accomplish your work in the world. People are not always going to agree with you, Elizabeth. You must not fear your own aggressive energy or judge it as nonspiritual. You must learn to wield it effectively." I closed my eyes and instantly I saw them coming, not frightening but powerful. The *apus* appeared as strong men in warriors' garb from throughout history—samurai warriors, knights in armor, sumo wrestlers, kung fu black belts, even machine-gun-slinging Rambo types. They came at me within the warring field of my own inner vision. One at a time. And each time, I built up a surge of energy in my *qosqo*, and, using it like an enormous fist, I thrust them back. Each time I was terrified, frightened I would hurt them and ashamed of asserting my own aggressive energy.

The *apus* were not angry or terrible in their attacks, rather they were persistent and relentless in a brotherly way, as if they were trying to give me a good workout, letting me test my mettle. Soon I was worn out. But it was then that Juan told me to work harder. "Push them back, all of them!"

By now I was sweating profusely and nearly worn down by this exhausting nonphysical battle. I recalled the night in Argentina when the bats had appeared at my window and how I had had to find a strength I didn't know I had. I called up a deeper level of reserves and focused every ounce of intent and energy I had into my *qosqo.* The next thing I knew, I was sitting up on the rock screaming my guts out. In my mind's eye I had pushed all my attackers back to their mountain peaks. They were smiling at me! In another moment, I dissolved into laughter. At last I understood that by fighting off this "male" energy I had awakened it in myself!

"Good," Juan said simply. "Next."

12

Willkañust'a: Princess of Black Light

OUR LAST MORNING IN THE MACHU PIKCHU AREA BEGAN with a blazing ten-o'clock sun that filled a cloudless sky. Because we had only one final ritual to complete before catching the two-o'clock train back to Cuzco, we had been given permission to sleep in, and the rest had been much needed. The experiences of the day before, not to mention the strenuous hiking, had been exhausting on every level. I had slept well and dreamed deeply in the arms of the great *apus* surrounding Machu Pikchu. After breakfast, we walked to the long outdoor wooden stairway of our hotel that lead us down toward the rushing Willkañust'a River. The river ran right by our hotel and its music had lulled us to sleep each night. Now, as we approached the river bank, I mulled over the possible significances of the powerful but confusing dream I had had. By the time we arrived at the water's edge I had resolved to tell Juan about my dream.

"This river is known by many names," Juan addressed the group, standing on one of the large boulders that crept up the banks of the chocolate-milk-colored waters that roared by us. The rest of us found perches on nearby boulders, mesmerized by the rush of water as it went twisting around and cascading over huge irregular rocks, their weird shapes carved out by the water's continuous pummeling. Juan had to raise his naturally soft voice almost to a yell in order to be heard above the river's thunderous roar. "It is most commonly called the Urubamba, also the Vilkanota, but the ancient Inka name tells its story best. Its ancient name is Willkañust'a: *Willka* means at once 'sacred' and 'dangerous,' *and* related with the power of the Black Light. *Ñust'a* is the Inka word for 'princess.' So the ancient name means 'Princess of the Black Light.'

"As you recall, the power of the Black Light is the most sacred and most dangerous power in our tradition because the one who tames the Black Light has power over life and death. It is really the ultimate creative power which walks hand in hand with the power of destruction." Juan paused, and significant glances were exchanged all around. This was heavy stuff.

"Another important fact about this river," he continued, "is that it physically connects every sacred temple in the Andean region. If you will recall, this river has been with us from the very first day, when we began the *hatun karpay* at the central cathedral in Cuzco. And it is the same river that was flowing past us in Pisaq and Ollantaytambo, and now again here in Machu Pikchu.

"As you know, in our tradition everything has living energy. The energy bubble of this river is most significant because, energetically, it carries the power of all the sacred places in the area, uniting them within its bubble." It was astounding to think that the Inkas could have so carefully planned the layout of their sacred temples such that they would all fall along the path of one river. How could they? Did they have a detailed topographic map of the area? Or were they working from a different perspective, attuned to another source that informed them on how to work within the design of great Nature? These questions bounced through my head like the bubbles along the surface of the sacred river. Juan was speaking again, giving instructions for the next ritual.

"By now you have learned how to connect yourself with the living energy of many sacred places, but this will be the first time we do this practice with such an important and powerful bubble as the living energy bubble of this sacred river. First, offer a prayer to the spirit of the river, then open your whole bubble to the river and allow the power of the river to clean away your *hoocha*. When you have done this, try to see each of the sacred areas we have already worked with. Connect to all of them through the bubble of the river."

I chose my stone perch close by the river's edge a little away from the others and sat down, my eyes cast downward into the racing and swirling motion of the water. I offered a prayer to the river, thanking it for its raging force and wild beauty. Then I gave it my *hoocha* easily, freely. As I felt heavy energy oozing out of me, slowly, the pouring itself became a beam or a shaft of flowing particles carrying me away into the incessant surging of the river itself. I could now experience myself as a compact static human form, or I could pour my awareness into the huge and immensely long cylinder of living energy, coursing horizontally along and slightly within the surface of the earth, like an immense snake in constant motion.

The snake! The base of my spine began to tingle and then to burn with a cool fire. Yes, it was the same energy I had experienced in the niche of the black *ñust'a*. I wondered what would happen now if I took the spirit of this river in through the base of my spine. The force was immense. A living wall of raw, wild power. A moment of terror passed over me. But this time it did not overwhelm me. I knew that I could merge with this force or separate from it, and I also knew that any power that came into me I would give away. I was learning to direct the power, but this power was not *me!*

Now that I was no longer quite so afraid, I stepped into the energy flow and the river carried me. I saw each place we had worked, Wakaypata, the central square of Cuzco, the Serpent Cave, the Pachamama Cave and the Temple of the Sun at Pisaq, the Windgate in Ollantaytambo, and each one of the temples in Machu Pikchu, with an almost surreal clarity. Yet as I recognized each location, I heard the rushing of water and understood that I was now observing all these sacred temples from the vantage point of the river herself. I felt her love for them all as she rushed merrily along, like a child reaching out her hand to touch the rails of a fence that ran alongside her path to school. The river reached out her bubble to caress lovingly each sacred temple with her grace, her power. All at once it occurred to me that my new understanding of the power of the Black Light had something to do with my dream. But I just couldn't put it all together. I had to talk to Juan.

Something pulled at my awareness, making me look up. As I separated my consciousness from the river, pulling it back into my body and looking up all in one dizzying movement, I was stunned by what I saw next. Juan was standing in a position of prayer, eyes closed and head bowed, with his hands cupped around the hands of an initiate. Powerful lines of force appeared like ripples or heat waves in the air extending out from the river and merging into his bubble. The force flowed from his bubble into the initiate's bubble, infusing it with the power of the river. It looked as if Juan had momentarily tapped and diverted the immense energy bubble of the river. Someone called my name, and rapidly the energetic perception disappeared.

"Elizabeth!" Nina called excitedly, coming up behind me. "Juan is giving us *khuyas*, power stones from the river to put into our own personal *mesa* bags." One by one, Juan charged twelve stones with the power of the river and ceremonially bestowed on us each a stone to place into our ritual bundles. He explained that this empowered stone was for use in our personal *mesas* along with the tiny square stone he had given each one of us on the first day of the initiation, to mark the awakening of our "Inka seeds." Juan explained that we could tap into the power of the river at any time by using this stone. With this, the ritual at the river was complete.

AS WE BOARDED THE TRAIN BACK TO CUZCO, I DECIDED TO get a seat next to Juan. I *had* to ask him about my dream. I knew I had to do it right away or he would be asleep and I would have missed my chance. "Juan, do you mind if I sit here?" I asked a little self-consciously. He had already given so much to us that I felt greedy asking for more. However, I knew the dream had a significance that I couldn't uncover by myself.

"Please, sit down, Elizabeth," he said graciously. "I was just going to take a little nap . . . but let's talk. Now . . . how are you?"

"I am really grateful to you, Juan. All your teaching has been such a help to me, and I can understand so much more of what happened to me when I was here before. But . . . you know, last night I had a dream . . . a strange dream . . . for some reason I want to tell it to you. Is that all right?"

"Of course!" he replied heartily. "Dreams were very important for the Inkas. In fact, they were masters of dream interpretation. Yes, please go on."

"All right," I began slowly, my face flushed with embarrassment. I took a deep breath and plunged into it. "I dreamed that I was at a gym where, in order to exercise, I had to remove one of my legs and put it in a locker. I knew that while I was exercising, the people who worked for the gym were going to shorten my leg, or trim it down, as part of a normal, routine service that they offered. I had already unscrewed my leg, put it in my locker, and gone to another part of the gym to exercise when I ran into an old schoolmate. I told her my misgivings about their practice of leg trimming, and she said, 'Well then, just go in there and tell 'em you don't want them to do it. You don't have to, you know.'

"With her encouragement I went back and found that the man who did the trimming already had my leg on a saw bench and was just about to cut into it when I approached and demanded my leg back. He grumbled but gave it to me, saying, 'Suit yourself, lady. We offer this free service and if some people aren't even smart enough to take advantage of it, well, I can't help that.' When I picked up my leg and looked at the top—it was as if I was seeing a cross-section of the place where it screwed back into my hip—I fully expected to see a gory mass. But what I saw instead was perfectly arranged muscle tissues and ligaments, surrounded by seven perfect layers of epidermis, with a beautiful bone marrow center. It looked like a flower. It reminded me of my high school days when we had once looked at plants under a microscope to see how perfectly organized their cell structures appeared; yet looking out the window at the plants outside, they looked so natural, wild, not structured or organized at all. Well, my leg looked like that! I could see the order and detail of all the physical structures of my leg and suddenly it looked beautiful to me *and* natural, all the parts organized with such artistic perfection."

"Which leg was it?" Juan asked. His question surprised me and I had to pause a moment to recall.

"It was the right leg," I told him.

"Ha!" said Juan.

"Ha?" I asked.

"Yes. Just as I thought." And without hesitating for one moment he launched into an immediate and profoundly compelling dream analysis.

"First," he said, with the relish of an artist getting out his favorite paints, "the right leg represents the right-hand side of the path, which you have purposely removed because it interferes with your exercise—or so you think. The right-hand side of the path has to do with structure. Second, your intervention to stop them from shortening your leg—your old schoolmate—represents the power of discrimination that you have developed to know what you want despite the 'norms' or pressures from society.

"Third, the fact that you give your leg up and then get your leg back—transformed—by the end of the dream shows that you are going through a process of renunciation and reclamation with the right side of your nature. You must first renounce it, in order to see its beauty. That you are able to see your right leg as a 'flower,' as a beautiful part of nature, by the end of the dream, is *very* important. The dream says that now you are able to see that the right-hand side, all that has to do with the rational, structured, ordered aspect of your humanity, is natural and sacred too. It is not an enemy or hindrance to your spiritual path, but actually a part that must be accepted and reintegrated if you are to step forward on your path. This points to the mystical power of the critical mind."

I was left breathless by Juan's interpretation of my dream. He had hit the mark so hard that I literally felt as if I'd just had the wind knocked out of me. I asked him to explain it two or three more times slowly, so that it could sink in. "You Americans tend to think that the critical mind is your enemy. That all you have to do is to open your intuition and everything will be all right. Nonsense! Certainly it's true that the West has overemphasized the importance of rational thinking to the detriment of other kinds of knowledge, for example connecting with the wild and more chaotic nature of the left-hand side of the path. But why go from one extreme to the other? You must not 'throw the baby out with the bathwater,' is that not the expression?" Juan said, laughing.

Although I was not a big fan of the theorists who located consciousness within brain hemispheres, the right-hand side of the path did seem related with what was generally conceived of as "left-brain functions," and the left-hand side of the path, with the more creative "right brain," as Juan had described it. Clearly the Andeans centered themselves in the body rather than the brain. Juan continued his fascinating elucidation.

"In order to attain the fourth level you must develop the powers of the left and right sides both, together! You must have discernment. When you first came to me you were totally left sided. To be totally left sided is dangerous because it leaves you open to the great problem of the mystical delirium."

"The mystical what?" I asked.

"The mystical delirium. The danger of identifying yourself with the archetypal energies that you are discovering. As the ego begins to stretch to contain the larger spiritual identity, it goes through an intense period of contraction and expansion. First you think that you are nothing, and then you think that you are everything. This is fine as long as the initiate recognizes this process and does not take either extreme too seriously, or act on it in any way. Unfortunately, many initiates at this point begin to think that they have attained some absolute truth just because they have connected with a power larger than their individual self. But this power is still filtering through the individual egos. Many an inspired teacher may rise up suddenly, but they burn out quickly like a falling star. They cannot contain or sustain their power.

"This is a very dangerous phase when one is tempted by the powers that are called *siddhi*s in Eastern traditions. Here we call it the mystical delirium. The power of the critical mind is just what is needed as a counterpoint to this potentially disastrous time. Your dream is an excellent sign. It marks a vital, ahem, *step* for you, so to speak." Juan's eyes twinkled with laughter and he looked at me like a proud father.

"Furthermore, in our tradition and particularly with regard to dream interpretation, we see the body as an oracle. Do you know how a person traditionally becomes an initiate on this path?" Juan asked.

"I have heard that they are struck by lightning. Chosen by nature herself," I responded, remembering stories I had often heard at Ricardo's *mesa*.

"That's correct," Juan affirmed, "but did you know that they had to be struck by lightning three times? The first strike kills the initiate, the second strike dismembers the body, and the third strike fuses the body back together again, but in a new configuration. If we look at this ancient initiatory experience metaphorically, we see that the ego dies, is taken apart, and finally, reconfigured into a more appropriate form that can hold more energy. The Andean masters also say that if you move the body of someone before they have been struck three times they will die."

"But Juan, why is it that so often here in the Andes I find that these 'metaphors' have a physical as well as a psychic reality? Maria, from Ricardo's group of apprentices, once told me a story from her childhood. She was raised in the jungle, and one day during a storm her eleven-year-old sister was struck by lightning. Trying to protect her, the family had moved her inert body out of the storm and watched as, sure enough, lightning struck twice more in the exact place where she had fallen. Her sister died. Maria has always felt that her sister would have survived had they known enough to let the process complete itself."

"It is a very good point, and one that your group should take deeply into consideration. For if we use this example again in the metaphoric sense, we can find in it the wisdom that, while undergoing a deep process of initiation, one must remain still, not making any large life movements, decisions, or changes until the process is finished."

"Juan, what happened there at the river?" I asked, unable to resist the question. "What is this power I found in the black niche and then again in the Willkañust'a River? At first it terrified me, but now . . ."

"Now?" he asked, looking deeply into my eyes with his great intensity.

"Now I feel calm about it. I don't feel that it pulls at me, rather that it could just move through me. I don't know how to explain it." I looked down, feeling silly, embarrassed by my inability to articulate my experience.

"Good," Juan said. "Do you know that the first belt is the energy belt that is related with the Black Light?" I nodded. "But it is only when the Black Light is pulled up to here," he said, touching the point between his eyebrows, "and guided by the force of consciousness, the mystical power of the rational mind, that it becomes useful. You know the black hat ceremony of the Tibetans?" he asked me.

"No," I said, "what is that?"

"I think it must be a ceremony related to this same esoteric practice. I have heard that the black hat is actually made from the pubic hairs of yoginis. It is a metaphor for the same idea—bringing the life-force energy of the lower center up to be directed by the higher consciousness."

The train chugged along and we each retired to our own activities, Juan to his long-overdue nap, and me to chew on all that had just been said. We arrived in Cuzco late in the evening and Juan headed for home, asking me to relate our conversation to the group over dinner.

Back at the señora's house, we all greedily consumed our delicious hot meal and stayed chatting into the evening. I related my dream and Juan's interpretation. I shared our conversation about the mystical delirium that lead the group into the heavy subject of power, abuse of power, and the seduction of power. Nearly everyone in the group had had a profound experience with this, either as the victim or the perpetrator, and most often both.

Everyone agreed that neither position was really satisfying and that acting either as a victim or a perpetrator was based on fear. Fear was the problem. I had seen this as a family therapist on many occasions. Fear made people do the damnedest things. Each person in the group, at some point or another, had had to fight through an overwhelming fear that came upon them before leaving for Peru. In fact, the trip had inspired such a profound fear that it had forced some people to go and make out their last will and testament. Others had had dreams of dying, accidents, or being killed.

The difference for this group was that they all had the psychological wherewithall to know that these feelings were pointing to an important, life-changing experience. A real initiation. The experience would be a psychological or egoic death as opposed to a literal shedding of the physical body. The funny thing was that something in us all was desirous of that kind of death. As we talked, I realized that I, too, had felt the same feelings that day on the Santa Cruz boardwalk when my own inner voice had alerted me that should I go to Peru, my life would never be the same. The threat of death and the challenge of a new kind of life, a new beginning, an initiation. It had all been right there in that moment. At last, we were forced to go to bed for, fittingly, the next day we had to be up early for our ceremonial visit to the Temple of Death.

13

Temple of Death

WE ARRIVED AFTER THE USUAL BUMPY AND DUSTY UP-
hill ride to a ruin on the outskirts of the city, still yawning
and stretching from our early-morning wake-up call. It took only
forty minutes to arrive at a beautiful ruin known for its water fountain, called Tambomach'ay. It was a large temple consisting of three
tiers of highly refined Inka stonework built into the side of a hill.
On top there were five large niches. In front of the niches a gushing
current of water flowed through an Inka aqueduct and fell in a large
cascade down to the second level where another channel separated the
water into two streams. The two streams fell again into a large stone
pool at ground level. The source of the water was not visible and I
assumed it came from underground. Juan gathered everyone together
at this pool to address the group with this morning's teachings.

"What you were discussing with Elizabeth last night, the power
of the Black Light, is said to hold the key to life and death. Therefore the *paqos* who can master that power hold the force of creation
and destruction—life and death—in their hands. I have met many

masters who have shown me many powers, but to gain complete mastery of this force, I have found no one. At least not yet."

We were standing quietly taking in Juan's words, the tangible gravity of the issue weighing heavy on our minds. He gestured for us to follow him up the short stone stairway to the higher level of the temple. Power had to be wielded with truth and wisdom, or it could be used for selfish aims or for destruction. Juan's comments had taken me back to our conversation at dinner that had brought up images and feelings in all of us of the many instances or lifetimes of abusing power ourselves or being at the mercy of someone else's abuses. Psychologically, and from my own experience, I knew that abuse of power came down to the one thing: ultimately being unable to tolerate my own helplessness, my own limited and imperfect power. This was terrifying, and when I was that afraid, I wanted to attack others, verbally, emotionally, or even with thoughts.

I realized that to follow this path demanded a deep examination of one's own shadow, to reconcile oneself with one's own helplessness, one's own vulnerability, one's own sadism, jealousy, envy, anything that could make one use power in a harmful way. I understood now why certain esoteric knowledge had been kept very secret.

"You come from a culture that denies death. But here, in my poor country, we live side by side with death every day. Still that does not mean it is any easier to deal with death if you are Peruvian and raised only with a strictly Catholic background. These ideas about purgatory, heaven, and hell only serve to frighten us, kill our curiosity, and keep us away from exploring one of the great mysteries of human life . . . death," Juan said casually. I was rather surprised at his ease in discussing the subject. He went on.

"But if it is indeed possible to acquire the mystical power over life and death, then we have to understand what death really is," Juan continued, speaking the unvoiced thoughts of the group out loud. "My master Don Benito was, like most Quechua Indians, a very funny man, and so he taught me about death in a very beautiful and humorous way. Would you like to hear the story?"

"Yes!" Barbara and Maryann chimed their emphatic reply together. Others nodded their heads vigorously. I, for one, was fascinated by the subject, but rarely found others who would readily discuss death. I was glad Juan had a story about it. As a therapist I had discovered that somehow difficult topics were always easier to ingest when they came in the form of a story. Juan began his tale.

"When Don Benito died I was devastated. He was nearly eighty years old when I first met him and I worked with him for more than ten years before he died in April of 1988. My own father and I were very close and shared much of our work, but he was an academic. He and I did not discuss spiritual matters. Don Benito, however, was like a spiritual father to me. He taught me everything he knew, and I loved him with all my heart.

"Like most Andean masters, Don Benito knew when he was going to die. Just one week before his death he called all his students together. Through a strange mishap, I was not given the message that he had called for me to come, and so I was not there to say good-bye to Don Benito, or to receive his final words or gifts to me. Therefore, when I was told that he had died, I was traumatized. I threw my *mesa* against the wall and swore that I would never use it again. If all my training had only brought me to this suffering, then it was not worth it, I told myself.

"Luckily, however, months before, I had made an appointment with a student from Lima to give him the *hatun karpay* initiation, the training that you are receiving now. That student arrived in Cuzco and would not let me out of the commitment. Now who is the teacher and who is the student in this case, I ask you?" Juan said smiling, his humility making him all the more adorable. "So finally, I had to take him through the ceremony, starting as you have done at the cathedral and then moving on to work at the Illia Pata—you remember, the platform of light, where we first worked with your *qosqos*.

"I was standing on the Illia Pata when Don Benito appeared to me, smiling and nodding approvingly at my teaching, and then he disappeared. I saw him as clearly as I see you all standing before me now. Then, here at the Temple of Death, he appeared to me again and told me, laughing and smiling in his usual way, that I must not be caught by the illusion of death, but rather that to understand death I must reach beyond it.

"Now you must reach beyond death," Juan repeated as his eyes held mine in a vise grip. We were now standing on the upper level of the temple in front of five stone niches. The temple covered a large area of about seventy-five square feet with the most refined Inka stonework we had yet seen. I marveled at the beauty of the channel of water that crossed in front of us and cascaded down to the lower level where it separated into two streams of water and fell into a pool below. From the pool, another Inkan aqueduct took the water across the dirt road and into a little river on the other side. There it flowed into another ruin that appeared to have been completely razed. Nothing more than the stone foundation remained. I noticed that this stone foundation was situated directly across from the niches in front of which we were now standing. I had always heard that Tambomach'ay was a water temple, nothing more. Juan was now telling us that its function was actually quite different.

"You see how the water comes down the main channel there," he said, pointing to the hearty current flowing in front of us. "Then it separates into two streams." I nodded as my eyes followed his point- ing finger. "This separation represents the moment of death, the separation of the body from the spirit, or the human bubble of liv- ing energy from its casing. Now, you see how the two streams of water fall into one pool, at the bottom where we began, and then cross the little river on the other side of the road?" Heads bobbed up and down as we looked where he pointed. "You can see how that channel of water goes toward the temple on the other side of the river," he told us, referring to the stone foundation as a temple. "This is a metaphor. It represents the journey the soul takes after death, across the river."

I nodded vigorously. "Like the Greek river Styx!"

"Exactly," he said, beaming at me. "The temple on the other side represents the place we go when we die. Now, here you will con- nect yourself to the living energy of this temple by entering into each of these five niches and letting yourself become filled with the energy of the place. And once you have done that, come and stand here, facing the temple across the road. Use your *qosqo* to build a bridge of living energy from this temple over to that temple."

I closed my eyes and stepped into each niche, intending that my bubble connect with the energy bubble of the temple. I felt the familiar goosebumps just before the flow of energy came from the temple into my body. I nodded to myself, I was connected.

I turned to face the ruin on the other side. Using my *qosqo* I began to draw in living energy from the environment around me and from the niches. Slowly I began constructing a bridge of energy. Like a spider, I was forming it out of my own body, weaving it together. As it grew out from my belly center, I directed it toward the temple on the other side of the road. My perception began to shift and I could not only see but also taste with my *qosqo* the sensation of the living energy on the other side—at the Temple of Death. Why, this place wasn't dead at all!

My mind and heart were shocked to recognize that this place—the Temple of Death, or what I had thought of as death—was really another realm of living energy! It was just a different, more refined kind of energy. There were beings and activities and lives going on within this other temple. The living energy from my *qosqo* was bridging not only two physical places but also two realms. My living energy connected to the living energy on the other side. I realized that if I chose to, I could travel across the bridge I had just constructed and visit the "other side."

"Shall we go?" Juan's voice interrupted my deep trance. My eyes flew open to see his smiling face. "Yes," he said, reading my thoughts. "Another day you will cross that bridge." We moved on past the tourists snapping their cameras. "Elizabeth," Juan said, sharply piercing my trance state again with his intensity.

"Yes," I answered sleepily, finding it difficult to return to the ordinary world.

His manner softened and he began laughing at me. "You must learn to become invisible." I felt burdened by his request. I was just learning to use my *qosqo* and to pull the energy lines, and to understand death and power, and now he wanted me to learn to become invisible as well? I gave Juan a shriveled look, which only caused him to roar with laughter, making me feel even smaller. "I mean that you can be having a very strong mystical experience inside you, but just looking like a tourist on the outside—that is invisibility."

We got on the bus and headed back to Cuzco. In the afternoon, there would be one more ritual to complete. As we bumped along the unpaved road that took us from the Temple of Death back to the Inka capital, I asked Juan to explain more about the Andean energy system, so different from the more familiar Hindu system of the chakras.

"The Andean system is simple, really," Juan explained to his busload of students, faces and bubbles glistening from the recent experience at the temple. "It is more similar to the Taoist system than the Hindu. Rather than chakras, or 'wheels of light' as described by the East Indian mystics and seers, our priests see that we have four energy belts or bands that surround the body. We even have a special kind of *paqo* with special *khuyas*, or stones that are tools used in a ceremony to open these *chunpis*, or energy belts. In the Hindu tradition one must study for a very long time to open the chakras, but in the Andean system you can work with the *chunpi paqo* and have an immediate experience."

"But, Juan, who is going to be our *chunpi paqo*? Do you know one?" I asked.

"Yes," he answered, nodding humbly. Then he pointed to himself. "Me. Don Andres Espinoza of Q'eros first trained me in the art of the *chunpi paqo* in 1982. Then Don Benito gave me the ritual again when I completed the Great Initiation, and I was able to find an old set of the stones in the marketplace. This afternoon, after lunch and a rest, I will come to your house and we will perform the ceremony of opening the belts."

We arrived back at the house and the señora greeted us at the door with the barking of dogs and the smiling faces of Panchita and little José, Panchita's assistant, all very happy to see us. She had lunch already waiting for us.

Around two o'clock, after we had lunched heartily on a delicious quinoa soup and *lomo saltado*, a Peruvian dish of beef, rice, potatoes, tomatoes, and garlic, and topped off our meal with an aromatic cup of Cuzco-grown black tea, we napped or wrote in our journals while we waited for Juan to reappear. By two-thirty I decided to go look for him and was heading down the creaky wooden stairs when I looked up and noticed that the sky had clouded over considerably. Toward the southwest, in the direction of Apu Ausangate, it was almost completely black. I was heading through the courtyard toward the front door when I heard the bell. It was Juan.

"*Hola, Maestro,*" I said with somewhat cheeky irreverence, holding open the old plank door for him to step through.

"*Hola,* disciple," Juan riposted, both of us chuckling as we exchanged the cheek-pecking customary greeting.

"C'mon upstairs. Everyone is waiting," I told him, bounding forward across the courtyard and up the stairs in a few large leaps. By now my lungs were accustomed to the altitude. I walked down the hall tapping on each door like a drill sergeant, announcing that Juan was here, and that all had to come out and present themselves. When I had knocked on all six doors and received the appropriate muffled replies from within, I went back into the main hall. Juan was nowhere to be seen.

Thinking he had stepped outside to smoke a cigarette, his habit knowing that I did not allow smoking in the house, I walked out to the outer stairway. And there I found him staring intently down the valley at the brewing storm. He was not smoking.

"Juan?" I said softly. There was no response. I walked out onto the landing and down a few steps to where he was standing, and as I looked in the direction he was staring, a huge bolt of lightning flashed in front of us. I jumped back a little, startled by the sudden flash. Juan was staring, still as a mountain. The flash had not caused him even the slightest twitch of an eyebrow.

He whispered something to me, but his voice was lost in the first large drops of rain that began to pummel the corrugated tin roof covering the stairway over our heads. I bent forward, straining to hear what he said. His gaze never wavered from the valley as I cocked my head forward to catch the words, "Open your *qosqo*," he told me. My ear was next to his lips as I reached for the next nearly inaudible command. *"Eat the storm."*

A thrill of terror and excitement ran through me at the brilliant outrageousness of his directive. Immediately I turned my body, imitating Juan's posture, and faced the storm. Tentatively at first, I commanded my *qosqo* to open, and reached out into the gray swirling mass of clouds, the thick pelting rain and wire-thin, curling metallic strips of flashing lightning. There was tremendous power here. I could see it with my eyes. But what was more fascinating, I could now also taste it with my *qosqo*. There was a warm, roiling sensation, and an electrical surge. My awareness somehow joined with the storm, as I thrilled to the rush of the wind, the surge of lightning, and the delicious rain-rich air.

I began to pull the storm into my *qosqo* as if I were feeding on the very force of the storm itself, bringing it into my body. Was it my imagination or was the storm responding to us? It seemed as if the storm, delighted by the attention it was getting, was actually drawing nearer. Or were we pulling it? *It was probably just moving this way anyway,* my rational mind chimed in.

As a child I had always loved thunderstorms, which were plentiful in the midwestern lands of my upbringing. Now, instead of simply enjoying the storm, I was being taught how to connect with its power. This was wonderful! Amazing!

"Elizabeth? Juan? Where are you?" The initiates voices called from inside. Putting a finger to his lips, Juan smiled and winked at me as we both turned to walk up the stairs and into the parlor.

When everyone had gathered in the parlor, Juan began to unwrap a beautifully woven white alpaca cloth edged with a sharp black stripe and tied together at the four corners with colorful long-fringed tassels. Within that cloth was another cloth, mostly black with bright pink geometrical designs. I immediately recognized the special colors of the Q'ero Indians, and the exquisitely spun alpaca, woven left-handed for spiritual protection. I knew that Juan had trained with the Q'eros, a group of Andean Indians who still lived in villages at fifteen thousand feet and were considered to be direct descendants of the Inkas, and that his other primary masters, aside from Don Benito, had been Don Andres Espinoza and Don Manuel Q'espi of Q'eros. But I didn't know any more about it than that.

Upon opening the inner Q'ero cloth, Juan revealed five whitish-brown curiously carved stones, each about the size of a large egg. Each stone had one or more strange protuberances. The first three were flat on the bottom with rectangular bases so that they could stand up, with their protrusions shaped like one, two, and three elliptical breasts pointing to the sky. The fourth stone was more rounded with four protuberances, and the fifth stone was larger, about the size of a small apple and shaped like a five-pointed star. The stones looked as if they had originally been white but had browned with age. I wondered how old they were.

"These are the sacred stones, the tools of the *chunpi paqo*. See the cross engraved here?" he said, pointing to the base of the one-humped stone. There, visible, was a perfectly carved Christian cross. "The cross shows that this particular set of stones was probably carved sometime in the seventeenth century." We stared at the stones in amazement. They were beautiful and seemed to pulsate softly with living energy.

"That means the *chunpi paqos* were still practicing their art long after the Spanish conquest," Barbara stated in a rather grave voice.

"Precisely!" Juan corroborated. "That is why there are still *chunpi paqos* practicing their art today. And the fact that this set of stones bears the Christian cross shows again the flexibility and inclusiveness of the Andean system." It was fascinating to think that the Inkas had developed an entirely different way of seeing, interpreting, and working with the human energy system that dated back from before the arrival of the Spanish, and that they had maintained their art and even included Christian symbols into its practice.

"Now," Juan began again, gathering everyone's attention by brandishing the first, one-humped stone in the air in front of us. "In the Andes we believe that at the moment of conception three different powers are brought together: the power of matter, the power of the individual soul, and the eternal power of the spirit. These three powers meet here," he said, pointing to an area on the head just above the hairline. "When we are children this area is still very open and we receive lots of pure living energy or 'white light' through this opening. But as we grow, this energy center closes. We will use this stone to open the center once again.

Juan worked with these sacred stones to open each one of our energy belts. He began with the black belt at the base of the spine, which was related to water. Then he moved up to the *qosqo,* the center for the red belt that surrounded the body and was related to the earth. Next he used his special stone to open the belt around the heart center, which was gold and related to fire and the sun. The energy belt at the throat was silver and related to the spirit of the wind. Finally he used the fifth stone to open the point between the eyebrows that was purple and was related to the finest energies of the superior world. He used a different stone to open each energy belt.

As Juan worked patiently with each person and the rest of us watched, the storm was building. I had to get up several times and shut the door at the top of the stairs that was burst open again and again by powerful gusts of wind. As evening fell and the room grew dark, the storm had now become so active that the short but continuous strokes of lightning created nearly enough light to see by. No one moved to get flashlights or to turn on any other form of light. The effect of the lightning on the faces of the initiates, as Juan worked with each one, was magnificent. It seemed that nature herself was adding her power and blessing in celebration of our ceremony.

Juan worked tirelessly, repeating the prayers at each change of the sacred stones, and then stopping to make one long prayer, as he began anew with the next initiate. Soon it was to be my turn and I was intrigued to discover whether or not I would see the things Juan had described or if I would even feel anything at all.

By the time it was my turn, everyone else had gone off to their rooms, either too relaxed or in too altered a state of perception to be able do anything else. Juan took a moment to stand outside and absorb more living energy from the storm before coming back inside to me. He bowed his head and began to pray again as he held the first *khuya* tightly in his hand. I closed my eyes, wanting to hold a state of open attention.

I felt the cool smooth touch of the first stone as he placed it on my head, and I immediately felt a warm tingling in the roots of my hair all around the stone. Goose bumps went down my arms. All at once I felt a soft sort of "pop" and a flash of light. *Must have been the lightning*, my mind chimed in.

"You feel it?" Juan whispered to me. I nodded because I could not speak. Once again I had slipped into a deep trance. He changed the *khuya* and I felt warmth move toward the back of my head where it seemed to fall into two pools. "Feel the separation of the fields?" he asked. I nodded, I didn't even have to try, it was so easy to feel. I felt the gold and silver cords pull down from the back of my neck, gold on my right, silver on my left. The *khuya* was moving down my spine, but my awareness moved before the *khuya*. It raced to the base of my spine, which opened in a lovely green flower, the exact color of the green *ñust'a*. Then the green raced back up my spine and melding with the silver and gold became a living, shining black.

Juan's *khuya* had just reached the base of my spine. "Open?" he asked me, to know if I felt the base center was open. "Yes." My tongue had loosened and I was able to whisper. I observed the intensely pulsating Black Light. The black was shot through with gold and silver, but it wasn't the color that made the black appear luminescent. Rather the gold and silver gave the black dimension and volume. The Black Light crackled and whipped at the back of my neck. "Now mix the three together," Juan told me.

"Done," I replied softly.

"Aha, you got ahead of me," Juan laughingly teased. "Okay, bring the Black Light back down to the center at the base of your spine." This Black Light was sassy, a capricious power, and I had to exert quite a bit of my will to direct it back down to the base of my spine. Juan quickly drew the black belt around my pelvis by tracing his *khuya* around my hips, making sure the belt was connected front and back. I could feel the belt as if I had it on, as if I were branded with it. From the center of my lower belly he drew his *khuya* up to the spot about three inches above my belly button and directly over my diaphragm, my *qosqo*. He pressed the *khuya* slightly in.

"Open?" he asked. A pulse of red flowed into my *qosqo*, and before he started to work the *khuya* I already felt the red belt around my waist begin to "turn on" almost by itself. He worked the *khuya* around the left side of my torso connecting it to my spine, and coming back to my belly. Then he worked the *khuya* around the right side of my torso and held it against my spine. "Connected?" he asked. I now had a red belt of pulsing energy surrounding the midsection of my body. With eyes closed I nodded.

He moved the *khuya* up to the middle of my chest and a warm golden fire awoke in my heart. As he moved the *khuya* around my body, actually circling around the upper part of my shoulders, I saw golden fire spread out from my heart and surround my entire chest area, forming a belt of deep gold light. Juan's *khuya* moved up to my throat and I heard the singing of the silver *ñust'a* in my ear as I saw and felt the silver light gather in my throat area. He changed the *khuya* and began tracing a circle around my throat, connecting the belt of silver front and back. Juan then traced a line with one of the protuberances of the *khuya* from my throat up the middle of my face. He stopped at the point between my eyebrows.

"Now, absorb the purple energy from my *khuya*," he told me. Again, it happened almost by itself. And I couldn't tell what had come first, his words or the purple light. It was a gorgeous deep violet—my very favorite color since childhood. Not dark, but a bright rich violet. The color seemed to be illuminated from within just as the Black Light had been, a sort of incandescent purple. The color itself was pure joy.

"Yes, that's right. Enjoy it," Juan told me. Only then did I realize that a deep smile had come over my face as I took in the purple energy. "Now, release all your heavy energy to my stone," Juan said, turning the stone around so that the opposite central bump now rested against my forehead. I let *hoocha* flow out, and I felt lighter and my mind grew pleasantly empty. "Now you can absorb all the purple energy," Juan invited. I stood for a long time feeling the beautiful colors in my energy bubble. My bubble felt different. It felt fat and round and full and healthy! I told Juan. He laughed and nodded, saying, "Go and gather the others. There are a few more things I have to tell you before I go."

When we had rather groggily assembled once more, Juan spoke to us as a group. "Your bubbles have now become fully charged, which means that many small attachments to your energy bubble have been broken. Your relationships with people may change, and you may be certain that people's reactions to you will change. Be aware that you may now receive a lot of projections from others," Juan warned us. "Because your bubble is full and is harmonized with nature, you may draw jealousy and projections of the shadow from others. Remember, you must eat their heavy energy, this is the practice you have now embarked upon. Now I will tell you more about our path, for tomorrow is our coronation ceremony.

"The point here is to become a 'seer'—*qawaq* in Andean terms. If we look at the great traditions of our times," Juan said with a new depth and clarity, his eyes glistening as he warmed to his subject, "the Greeks were primarily concerned with concepts. In their view, theoretical knowledge and the construction of beautiful conceptual structures such as mathematics were of primary importance. The Jews, however, were most preoccupied with precepts, the Ten Commandments of Moses and moral law that has, in a general sense, been of utmost importance in the Jewish tradition.

"The Andean prophets, however, put a different emphasis on things. For them *perception* is the most important thing. Yes, concepts and precepts are important too, but for us *perception* is primary. This means that a person of real development is able to see the world of living energy behind all manifest forms.

"Western culture is a very visual culture. You put a lot of emphasis on appearances and the information you receive through your physical sight. Even the Hindu tradition calls the spiritual eye the 'third eye,' referring to the physical eyes as the other two. But the *qawaq* eye is called the 'seventh eye' in our tradition, and I will tell you why. With the ceremony of the sacred stones we have opened your four energy belts and each belt has a center, or an 'eye': the base of the spine, the belly, the heart, the throat. These we consider to be the first four 'eyes.' Add your two physical eyes, and that totals six. Once these six eyes are open, then you are ready to open the point between the eyebrows. This is called the seventh eye. In our tradition, to become a seer means that all your seven eyes are open and you can see or perceive with your whole body, with your whole energy bubble. This is a very highly evolved degree of perception that very few of even our fourth-level priests have achieved.

"Don Benito was one of the few. I have been telling you that Andean mystics base themselves in a reality of living energies and the direct apprehension of that energy world. To explain this more clearly, let me tell you a little story about Don Benito." We nodded our agreement, and Juan continued.

"In 1986 I was in touch with a group of people who were very involved with the teachings of the Mayan calendar. There was a date they had discovered for a great world transformation. This date was supposed to be in August of 1987. The group asked me if the Andean prophets concurred with their date. I told them I would investigate. So I went to the little village of Huasao to find Don Benito.

"We were talking inside his house when I told him about this date and what the significance of it was supposed to be—a time of transformation for all humanity and for the whole world. Don Benito listened very carefully to me and then, without saying a word, he got up and went outside. After a few minutes I went to see where he had gone and I found him standing outside his house, looking down the valley toward Cuzco. He was standing very still and so I did not disturb him but went back inside the house. When he came back in, he simply shook his head, and said, 'No. Not yet.'

"'But Don Benito,' I protested, 'how do you know? How can you be so sure, when my friends have spent months and made many mathematical calculations to arrive at their date?'

"Don Benito only laughed, and said simply, 'I know because I saw. The energy bubble of Cuzco is only halfway up the mountains.

To indicate the time your friends are talking about, the bubble must be at the top of the mountains. This time has not yet arrived—but it is coming. Tell your friends.' Don Benito seemed to be indicating that in regard to predictions and prophecies, dates are uncertain, changeable, mutable. We have to depend on something more immediate, like the direct perception of energy."

"But, Juan, you haven't really told us all about the prophecies. How does it all fit together? What exactly are the prophecies? What do they say?" Maryann asked, urgently.

"I have been researching and gathering the prophecies over the last twelve years. This is difficult because there are no written records, only the oral tradition. The prophecies speak directly to this time period in history as a time of transformation, what we in the Andes call the *taripay pacha*. Literally it means the 'age of meeting ourselves again,' but it refers to the potential for a golden age of human abundance. This is a time when human beings must really begin to work together. But it is also a time when miraculous occurrences can and must take place. Let me explain.

"August first of 1993 marked the end of the *pachakuti*—a cosmic transmutation—preparing the earth for the first phase of the *taripay pacha*. This initial phase is supposed to last from 1993 until the emergence of the fifth level of consciousness. We have been talking about the fifth level but what you don't know is that a fifth-level priest will be a person with miraculous healing powers. They must be able to heal every person of every problem or illness, with just one single touch. And they must be able to do it every time."

"Could that be someone who has tamed the power of the Black Light?" I asked nervously.

"That is highly possible," Juan concurred, and continued his narrative. "The second phase will last until the manifestation of the Sapa Inka, a priest of the sixth level of consciousness and someone who must show extraordinary leadership, social engineering, political prowess, someone who can rebuild the Inka empire but to a much greater glory than it achieved in ancient times. The full-blown form of the *taripay pacha* will begin when the sixth-level priests emerge, which could be around 2012 or so. The dates are uncertain because this is only an opportunity, we—humanity—must do the work.

"This time period, from 1993 to 2012, represents a 'critical period' in the development of human collective consciousness. These nineteen years mark the time when a significant percentage of humanity can and must pass from the third to the fourth level. We must be able to leave fear behind and learn to share our cultural gifts and achievements. If we can truly learn to live *ayni*—sacred reciprocity—and to share all of our accumulated knowledge without fear of each other, then we can discover our wholeness, like putting together pieces of a puzzle that make up our human family, our *ayllu*. It is up to the people of the earth, us, to maximize this critical period in order to bring in the *taripay pacha*. We must not waste this opportunity!

"You are now entering upon the ninth day of your initiation and you should realize that achieving the fourth level means that you can enter a synagogue, a Hindu temple, a Catholic church, a Muslim mosque, a Tibetan lamasery, a Buddhist temple, or an Andean cave with the same feeling of the sacred in your heart. The capacity to do this indicates someone who has just begun to arrive at the fourth level—someone who can see, feel, and recognize the *huaca*, the sacred energy, of people or a place or an object directly. They are able to see through the symbol, beyond it, moving into direct energetic perception. This is the real meaning of being *qawaq*, a mystical seer. The Andean prophets come to an understanding of what is happening and what will happen, their prophecy, through a direct perception and interaction with the world of living energies.

"Tomorrow we go to the Temple of Wiraqocha for the coronation ceremony. That is the place to talk about the complete prophecy. You have been accumulating wisdom, experience, and most importantly energy over these past eight days. If I had told you the prophecies earlier, it would have been only so many words to you. Now, perhaps, you have the ability to understand not only the words but also the implications of what I will tell you tomorrow. Rest well tonight. I will come for you with the bus early tomorrow morning. Be prepared. It is a long, long ride."

14

Inka Mallku: The Fifth Level

WE STOOD AWESTRUCK BEFORE THE MASSIVE INKA temple, its square columns of pale peach-colored stone and adobe rising easily fifty feet high into the deep blue Andean sky. Ten giant squared-off pillars stood before us, commanding our attention and respect. Resembling giant human figures, they formed the central wall of the main temple. We followed Juan to the base of the stone giants, and stood in an expectant circle around him. The group's silence was rich with awe and wonder. Everyone had been looking forward to this moment.

"Now I will tell you about this place . . . and about the full prophecy concerning the return of the Inka." Juan spoke slowly, quietly, and in his usual matter-of-fact tone. "This is the Temple of Wiraqocha, built by Wiraqocha Inka, the eighth Inka and the father of Pachakuteq. Wiraqocha is the Andean name for God in the same sense as Yahweh or Allah, referring to a metaphysical or invisible creative intelligent force behind all the visibly manifested world. The eighth Inka is said to have received the revelation of this wisdom and

so took the name Wiraqocha Inka. He built this temple in the fif-
teenth century to honor his God.

"Wiraqocha Temple is the most important temple, even more
important, more powerful, and more sacred than Machu Pikchu. On
the first day of the *hatun karpay*, we began at the *qosqo* of this sacred
geography, at the cathedral on the central square of Cuzco, and from
there we went to the base of the system at Machu Pikchu. Now we
are at the top of the system. Curiously enough, the altitude at
Machu Pikchu is 8,400 feet, on the main square of Cuzco it is
10,800 feet, and here at this temple we are at 11,800 feet above the
sea. In the Cuzco area we worked most strongly with the *kay pacha*—
the *apus* and the beings and energies of this world. In Machu Pikchu
we worked very strongly with the *ukhu pacha*, or interior world. Here
we will work most strongly with *hanaq pacha*, the superior world." I
found it curious and fascinating that there was so much implicit
structure in this ten-day ritual.

"In Inka times," Juan continued, "there was not just one but
twelve royal families or lineages, related to the twelve kinds of people. Because of the preservation of this coronation ritual through
the oral tradition, passed down by people like Don Benito and his
masters, we still know what ritual was used during the Inka times to
choose the new Inka ruler. Here at this temple you will see that there
are twelve houses or temples for each one of the royal families.
When it came time to choose the next *sapa* Inka, meaning 'sole lord,'
or 'high king,' all twelve families would gather here and present their
candidate, usually the one among them who was the best and most
efficient worker at all of the most important things an Inka had to
do—including spiritual work." We glanced around at the twelve
temples trying to imagine what it would have been like to witness
this event during Inka times.

"Because the Inkas had a centralized power system, governing
economic, social, and spiritual administration, the candidate chosen
to represent each lineage had to be the best economist, as well as the
best at social organization, *and* the most spiritually developed. In this

way, the Inka culture promoted the exact opposite of the extreme specialization that we see in Western culture today. In Inka times you had to be master of all tasks.

"Each family would present its candidate, and then perform many collective rituals to empower and support their candidate. Each candidate, supported by his community, would join together with the other candidates and perform the ritual that we are about to undertake. At the end of the ritual process, which moves from one end of the temple complex to the other, one of the candidates would literally begin to glow or shine with a brilliant light that could be seen by all those present. This candidate was the next *sapa* Inka, chosen in effect by Wiraqocha—by God himself."

Audible exclamations could be heard from the group and someone commented, "Can you imagine if our presidential elections worked like that?"

"Another thing we know is that the Inka ruled together with his *qoya*, a female mate of equal spiritual development. You will see the evidence for this during the ritual itself. Okay?" Juan asked, looking around at the faces and searching for signs of comprehension before he continued. "You must now realize that the word *Inka* refers to a spiritual level or condition. The *sapa* Inka, the one who shines during the ritual, is a priest of the sixth level. The ability to glow is considered, in Andean terms, an indicator of someone at the sixth level of consciousness, like Moses for example. We believe that the Inka rulers starting at the time of Wiraqocha and ending with Huaskar Inka were all chosen in this manner. The prophecies say that after August 1, 1993, the world has undergone the cosmic reordering necessary to create the conditions for the return of spiritual beings of the sixth level."

"But Juan, I thought we were just getting initiated into the fourth level. What about the fifth level?" Maryann inquired.

"The *hatun karpay*, or 'great transmission,' is the ritual that takes us from the third to the fourth level. But here at this temple, the ritual we perform today will allow us to become candidates for the fifth level, a level of spiritual development that must precede the prophesied return of the *sapa* Inka and *qoya*. As I was telling you yesterday, the prophecies of the Andean masters say that we are now in the initial phase of the *taripay pacha* and during this time—approximately from 1993 to the year 2000—at any time, priests of the fifth level can emerge. Male priests of the fifth level are called Inka *mallku*, meaning people that belong to the Inka lineage, and the females are called *ñust'a*, which means 'princess.' "

Juan paused to take a puff on his cigarette, giving us a moment to digest this wealth of information. "The indicator of a fifth-level priest is that he will have the ability to heal any disease, injury, or illness at a single touch, and he will heal each and every time. Today we have some excellent healers, but sometimes they can heal, other times they cannot. Why? The emergence of the Inka *mallku* will mark a vital step in the spiral of human evolution and humanity must be prepared for this transformation, because it will indicate that we, as a race, have gone beyond the limits of the individual karma that each person's disease may represent, to move into the level of group karma."

"But, Juan," Barbara piped up, "where do these prophecies come from?"

"These are the prophecies of the contemporary Andean masters and they tell exactly how and where each Inka *mallku* and *ñust'a* will appear. The only thing they don't specify is when. There were only two of my masters who carried the full prophecy, Don Benito Qoriwaman of the Huaskar lineage, and Don Andres Espinoza of the Inkari lineage from Q'eros. With my research and study under these two masters, the lineage of the first Inka, Inkari, and the last Inka, Huaskar, have come together. In all my twenty-five years of study in this mysterious tradition of charismatic priests, I have seen over and over again, even in the indigenous rebellions of the seventeenth century, the recurring theme of the return of the Inka. It shows the deeply devotional and steadfast nature of the Andean Indians that was never conquered by the Spanish.

"The Q'ero Indians were discovered to be direct descendants of the Inkas," Juan told us. "They are the keepers of the 'spirit of the Inka,' the ones who have, over nearly five hundred years, maintained the Inka ways. These modern Inkas possess what you would call an 'eco-religion' and for them, contrary to the West, a deep spirituality interpenetrated with nature is the only basis upon which a true political leader can stand. There are now only a few hundred Q'ero left."

"Juan, wasn't it your father who discovered the Q'ero in 1955?" I asked, remembering the words of the guide who had first given me Juan's name.

"Yes," Juan replied humbly. "It was also my father, along with several other anthropologists, who worked to free the Q'ero from their enslavement by the landowners and give them back their land in 1959." Obviously there was much to the story of the Q'ero Indians that was yet to be revealed. Juan continued his explanation.

"After my master Don Benito gave me the fourth-level initiation, he told me about the entire ten-day ritual of *hatun karpay*, including the coronation ritual. As he was talking, a strange thing happened. Rather than hearing his words, I began to see pictures in my head of all the places he was mentioning. That was when I realized he was not speaking to me in Spanish or Quechua, but in that strange language he had spoken to me on the very first day we met. It was the second and last time I ever heard him speak it.

"At the time he told me of it, Don Benito said that the coronation ritual had nearly been lost, because for more than fourteen years there hadn't been enough fourth-level priests to play the full ritual. *Pujllay* is the word for 'ritual' in Quechua, and it literally means 'sacred play.' So you can see that our act today of 'playing the ritual' is actually a way of preserving it.

"You must also realize by now that this spiritual work is a collective effort of human energy in collaboration with nature. Here in the Andes, we have never forgotten that we are a part of nature, and for us to evolve to our crowning glory we must participate within the greater natural order of Pachamama. The rituals that we learn in undergoing the *hatun karpay* teach us to put our energy bubbles together with each other and with the energies of nature. But for my master, the *hatun karpay* was only a step on the way to becoming a candidate to the fifth level."

We were just getting used to the fourth level, it was hard to imagine trying for the fifth. "The prophecy says that the place of the emergence of the first fifth-level priest, the Inka *mallku*, will be at the Q'ollorit'i Festival. This makes enormous sense because it is a collective ritual involving more than seventy thousand people and it is held at the foot of a glacier."

"You mean the prophecies say this place—Q'ollorit'i—is the actual location where the first Inka *mallku* will appear?" Maryann asked, her eyes bulging.

"That's correct," Juan replied. "My master sent me to Q'ollorit'i for nine years before I understood the real significance of the festival. Each year, I would go back to Don Benito and tell him, 'Master, I saw this, I saw that.' Each time he would just shake his head and say, 'You must go back again next year.' Now I will give you the benefit of my nine years of experience.

"Q'ollorit'i is a gathering of a huge number of pilgrims, each coming with a deep sense of devotion, from all around the Andean area. They bring their icons and dancers, and great dance competitions are held between groups of various regions. At the end of three days one enormous procession is held. Finally in the ninth year, and with the help of my wife, Lida, I was able to perceive with my seventh eye that one enormous collective bubble of living energy was being formed as a result of the group ritual. When I went back and told this to Don Benito, at last he smiled at me and said, "Now you are beginning to understand."

"And indeed, now I do understand that it is this enormous collection of human psychic energy, together with the natural power of the place, that can create the conditions for the emergence of the first Inka *mallku*. Every pilgrim who attends the festival is consciously, or more often unconsciously, playing his or her part in the fulfillment of the prophecy. It is through our collective energy that great miracles are possible. We are lucky, because we have the conscious knowledge of what we are doing. At the festival there are public and private rituals that have to do with the fulfillment of the prophecy, but all the rituals involve the use of collective human energy in collaboration with nature. You will see as I tell you the exact details of the prophecy."

Nina signaled for Juan to pause as she changed the cassette in her tape recorder. No one wanted to miss a word of what we were about to hear. Juan cleared his throat and began. "Once the first Inka *mallku* rises at Q'ollorit'i, which could be any time now, he must follow a specific travel route to the village of Urcos, and there, at the door of the church, he must meet and recognize another Inka *mallku* who has risen simultaneously here, near the Temple of Wiraqocha. These two must then travel together to Cuzco where they will meet and recognize the third Inka *mallku*, who will rise at the public ritual of Corpus Christi on the main square in front of the central cathedral of Cuzco, the ancient Temple of Wiraqocha in Cuzco.

"These three together must then travel to Lima where they must recognize the fourth Inka *mallku* and the first *ñust'a*, the female fifth-level priestess who will arise simultaneously at the enormous public ritual of the Lord of Miracles, near the ancient Temple of Pachakamaq. These five together must travel by sea to Arequipa, where they will meet the second *ñust'a*, who will rise at the Festival of the Virgin of Chappi. The six will then travel over the altiplano to Lake Titicaca, to meet and recognize the third *ñust'a*, who will rise at the Festival of the Virgin of Copacabana. The seven must then travel together back toward Cuzco and recognize the fourth *ñust'a*, who will rise from the Festival of the Virgin of Paucartambo. The eight must then meet with two more fifth-level couples, who will come from the North. Exactly where this couple will come from is as yet unknown. The twelve must gather here, in the Temple of Wiraqocha, and perform the coronation ritual. But rather than using the tools of the Great Initiation as we are doing, they will have the new initiation, that will come as a natural result of attaining the fifth level.

"The vehicle of this new initiation must be the royal hummingbird, the only bird of the Andean system that has direct access to the center of the *hanaq pacha*. Also, once one person attains the fifth level they can—and must, by the law of *ayni*—transmit their level to any other prepared candidate. So you see, I am not worried if you or you," he said, pointing to Peter, Justin, Sam, and then Nina, "attain the fifth level before me, because you must share it with me." Juan's eyes sparked with delight and pride at the ingeniousness of his tradition. It really was quite an astonishing and yet sensible philosophy, so profoundly different from the individualistic way of thinking of our Western culture. I had never heard of a spiritual tradition like this, which cooperated in the name of spiritual advancement. Juan went on with his explanation with unparalleled eloquence.

"When these twelve Inka *mallkus* meet here in the Wiraqocha Temple, they will perform the coronation ritual that will bring about the emergence of the new *sapa* Inka and *qoya*, who will possess the fully developed power of gathering and redistribution, making them able to reunite the people of the four corners of the ancient Inka empire. Whether the *sapa* Inka and *qoya* will shine forth from among the twelve *mallkus* present, emerge from a group of passing tourists, or come from amongst the farmers of the town of Raqchii, no one knows. The Andean masters do say that these leaders of the new era can come from anywhere. It is no longer necessary to be an 'Inka of the blood,' rather you must be an 'Inka of the soul.'"

"But Juan, what will the *sapa* Inka and *qoya* do? Will they really be able to change anything? They may be recognized here, but what about in other countries?" asked the ever-practical mystic Barbara.

"They will be known by their deeds," Juan replied simply. "Remember, a true *sapa* Inka and *qoya* are of the sixth-level consciousness. Not only must they shine, but they must be able to gather power and redistribute it, the ancient meaning of the word *Inka*. The *qoya* and *sapa* Inka will be able to fill the ancient Inka empire with *kausay*, with 'living energy,' once again. Remember, too, that the masters predict a world that must surpass the Inka empire of old—so they must be even more powerful than before. The masters say that the emergence of the *qoya* and *sapa* Inka and their subsequent achievements will signal the arrival of the mature stage of the *taripay pacha*, a kind of *plenipotencia*, or 'heaven on earth,' and with that, the meta-physical city of Paytiti—similar in meaning to the Shambhala of the Tibetans—will manifest on the physical plane. It is truly the predication of a golden age for humanity and certainly that is something worth working toward. No?"

Juan's question was greeted with a dumbfounded silence. All the initiates could do was to nod their heads in agreement with his last statement, but I knew that, among this thoughtful crowd, the revelation of the full prophecy was bound to stir up some heated discussion. In this magical moment, however, somehow everyone's disbelief seemed momentarily suspended, as if the group's innate skepticism were put on hold to consider the possibility the prophecy held out to us.

"You mean to tell us that those twelve Inka *mallkus* are going to come about as a result of the ritual that we are going to do here now?" Maryann asked.

"Yes, we are helping to create the conditions for this," Juan answered.

"Well, what are we all standing around here for?" she exclaimed. "Let's do it!" Maryann's powerfully positive declaration helped to break up the stiffening that had set in to the group.

I believe the group actually was experiencing a state of shock, something like the shock of an underprivileged child receiving his first shiny new Christmas toy. *Could this be true?* we asked ourselves. For in our heart of hearts we all believed or wanted to believe in the possibility, but, like the child, we had all lived another reality and we knew about the pain of disillusionment that was the price of our hope.

Now we turned to follow after Juan, who led us past the tall figures and behind them to another area of the enormous temple complex. Soon we were standing in the middle of an area about the size of two football fields, with six large stone-and-adobe houses on each end. In the center was a large open courtyard that contained an occasional pile of dark gray stones, some part of the ruin that was being reconstructed.

Each stone house or temple had, similar to the huge figures, a stone base about ten feet high and another ten or fifteen feet of adobe wall above that. The houses were rectangular and the walls inside showed six niches on each of the longer walls and two niches built into the walls at either end. Most of these temples were missing at least one wall, and a few only had one wall left, but the stone foundation showed the original shape of the temples.

"Each of these twelve temples belonged to one of the twelve royal families of the Inkas. Here, each one brought their candidates for the coronation ritual," Juan informed us. I looked around at the exquisitely designed buildings, still quite lovely after more than five hundred years. If I closed one eye and sighted down a straight line I could see the front wall and roof of each of the twelve temples. They appeared to have all been built in perfect alignment with each other, or, knowing the Inkas, they were probably built along a natural energy line.

"In our tradition we believe that each place holds the energy of the people that lived and worked in that place. To begin the coronation ritual, each one of you will choose one of the twelve temples. You will go to that temple and do a ritual of energy exchange with the temple, offering your prayers and releasing your heavy energy to the holy earth spirit of that temple. Then, once you have cleansed your *hoocha*, you can begin filling your bubble with the living energy of the royal lineage associated with the temple you are standing in.

"Once you have done that, you will walk slowly from your temple to this central courtyard, concentrating on carrying with you a cord of energy, extending from the temple to here. Elizabeth, you will stand here in the center." My heart jumped as I was singled out of the crowd. I felt embarrassed, almost guilty, and my face grew hot. I was certain I must have turned a deep shade of crimson.

"You will pull power from the temple through this cord of energy and push that energy into Elizabeth's bubble," Juan described. I wasn't so sure I liked this idea. "Elizabeth, you will pull all of these cords with your *qosqo* and concentrate the energy in your bubble. Then when you feel you are filled with *kausay*, you will let us know, and you and all of the group will start to build a collective column or pillar of energy, just as we did at the Wiraqocha stone in Machu Pikchu—you will build this column of energy using the energies of the temple, high enough so that it reaches all the way to the *hanaq pacha.* Understood?"

Everyone looked confused. "Where do we go?" one of the initiates asked. I smelled trouble. Something pushed me to act. Rapidly I divided the group in two and then in two again, making four groups of three.

"There are twelve temples and twelve of you. You three go to the far right-hand side of the complex and each choose one of those three temples. You three go to the west side, and so on," I told them. In short order we had distributed and dispatched the initiates and they were on their way to their temples. Juan gave me a nod and wink that said "Good work."

I stood in the center of the courtyard feeling alternately silly and proud, and lucky to get to experience this "hub of the wheel" position. Juan had explained to me before that this was the position of *taqe,* the joiner of energy fields. Simply by gathering a group of twelve and bringing them down to Peru I had begun the work of a *taqe.* I didn't really understand what *taqe* meant, but I figured, as usual, Juan wanted me to have the experience first and the explanation would come later. I knew it was part of what I had to do to become a fully developed fourth-level priest, the only road to becoming a candidate to the fifth level. There were many other tasks required, but Juan had only told me small bits and pieces. I had not yet had the time to ask him.

Sometimes I wondered if this was all just a bunch of silly ideas that had no basis whatsoever in reality. But I couldn't believe that because, whether it seemed rational or not, there was something very compelling to me about the prophecy. The idea of the collective spiritual work fascinated me, and the concept that we could create miraculous changes in our world if we were able to cooperate a little better was for me an undeniable truth.

I had seen families, and individuals' lives within their families, change radically and for the better with a little bit of guidance and a lot of willingness on the part of the individuals. I guess I could never be a family therapist if I didn't believe that. But certainly not every family changed for the better, and not every time!

I thought now about the new family I was creating with this trip, a spiritual family, an *ayllu*. My heart suddenly grew warm as I imaged each member of our group clearly in my mind. I held each one to my heart and felt very tender love, like a mother's love, toward each one. I knew in that moment that they were all very dear to me.

A sensation in my *qosqo* snapped my attention back into my body. I felt as if my *qosqo* were opening, almost by itself, and reaching around for something. The cords! I could actually feel them attached to each person as I now sensed with my eyes closed. They were drawing near. Again, I felt the sincere affection that connected me to each one of the initiates, and then I slowly realized that this actually helped me to gather their energy, to find the cords and pull them into my *qosqo*. For a brief moment, I caught a glimpse of the generations, including the Inka lineages, that supported each initiate in his or her spiritual work, but even this tiny glimpse was quite overwhelming and I had to focus my attention quickly back on gathering and concentrating the energy in my bubble as Juan had instructed me.

I was nearly bowled over by the influx of energy, and I had to adjust my stance physically to keep from falling over. I squinted open my eyes and saw that all of the initiates were now standing around me in a circle and for an instant I could see red lines of energy coming out of their *qosqos* and into me! I closed my eyes and concentrated more deeply. I tried to push my bubble up into the sky. Nothing happened. In fact, I felt as if there were a lead wall above my head that I couldn't penetrate.

After what seemed like a long time, but was probably only minutes, I had exhausted myself with the effort of pushing up. I felt dizzy and so decided to try stretching my energy bubble deep down into Pachamama in order to regain my equilibrium. Curiously enough, the further down I pulled my bubble, the higher up it floated, easily and naturally, until, to my inner sight, the very top of our bubble—a huge group bubble—almost touched the sky.

I seemed to lose consciousness for a moment and then— pooophf! I heard a brief sort of popping sigh and I was covered in a glorious sensation, as if it were snowing soft luxurious feathers down all around me. I was enveloped by the smoothest, most silky sensation of energy I had every experienced, which seemed to be emanating from above. I heard the group sigh, as if everyone had let out their breath softly and simultaneously, and I had a sense of resting much more deeply inside my physical body, as if some part of me felt relieved. I had been unsure, until now, that I could feel such a complete and exquisite peace and still exist within the boundaries of a physical body. Somehow this fact was extremely relieving and relaxing to my mind *and* body.

"Enjoy this," came Juan's voice softly. "We are having a touch with the fifth level. Pull down this purple energy from the *hanaq pacha.*"

It wasn't actually until he said the words that I noticed that this most exquisitely soft energy was a glowing purple color—the same incandescent purple I had seen during the ceremony of the energy belts. With Juan's suggestion I could now pull this purple *sami* down the long column of energy that we had created and cover the whole group, or see that the whole group was already covered in this beautiful field of rarified energy. I was floating . . . high . . . and at the same time exceedingly grounded.

"Inka mallku pacha bandera . . . bandera," Juan was singing the song in the strange atonal pattern of the Q'ero Indians, a song that was an invocation to the Inka *mallkus* to come here to this plane. The group imitated the sounds Juan was making and the song reverberated soft and strong, seeming to resonate through all the temples. Our song brought this part of the ritual to a close.

"Wonderful! Wonderful!" Juan was glowing as he exclaimed his delight, and he quickly came around the circle to hug each one of the initiates, making *ayni* with his joy. Juan had a habit of hugging us any time he had a particularly profound mystical experience during one of our rituals. I only now realized what he was doing. He was actually giving or transferring to us through his bubble, the energy of his experience, in an effort to help us along our paths. After all, it didn't matter who reached the fifth level first, as long as someone did.

"Now you have had a touch with real power," Juan told us excitedly. "Power in the Andean tradition," Juan continued, "is a good thing. Really it is only the difference between things that you can do and things that you cannot do. We are not afraid of power. It is good to have power. If you have the power to love, you must demonstrate that power. If you claim to have that power you must show it by loving well. If you have the power to build a very large *saiwa*, a column of energy, as we just did, you must demonstrate this by using the power to some purpose.

"You Americans will be surprised to find out that the more energy you can give, the more you are open to receive an even more powerful energy. Your consumer society trains you to accumulate, but it is really the opposite of what you might think. You think power is something you must hold on to. This is not true, for the more you give away your power, the more *huaca*, or sacred, you become. You are too concerned with keeping things. This is your biggest downfall. The surest way to gain is when you are able to exchange energy with another living system. This is what keeps you and Pachamama alive.

"Look at it on a simple level. When you appreciate someone, you are giving them some of your living energy. Receiving your energy, they will have more and be better able to give you some back later. This is a natural self-sustaining process of interdependence. When fruit ripens it wants to be picked and eaten by animals and people. Fruits are the kisses of Pachamama, she wants to give them to her children because of her great love. The fruit sustains the body of the person or animal, and the seeds can go into the ground through the feces of the animal, and the fruit can live again in another place on the earth. So by eating her fruit you are helping to keep her alive. We keep nothing. We are here in the *kay pacha* to learn to do *ayni*. We must become very good at *ayni*."

Certainly we were all beginning to realize that the power we could generate collectively was much greater than anything we could experience or do individually. This seemed to be a key aspect to the prophecy.

For the next part of the ritual we stood at the end of the long temple of tall stone figures. Juan had explained that when one stood facing north, the right side of the temple was gold and the left side was silver. He told us to form two lines of seven each, including Juan and myself, and move in a kind of snake dance through the tall pillars of the temple, stopping at each of the little windows to stand opposite our partner initiate and connect *qosqos* through the stone window. Then we would proceed to the end of the pillar and cross over to the opposite side of the temple at the open space between each pillar, changing sides of the temple with our partners, and in this way progress from one end of the temple to the other, weaving a sort of braided snake dance with our bodies.

Each time I connected with my partner at the window, a pulse of red passed back and forth between our *qosqos* and I wondered what effect our ritual was having on the temple itself. I imagined what our ritual would look like from above if I could see it energetically, a gold line of energy on the right, a silver one of the left being woven together by red through the middle. In my mind's eye I saw that the shape formed a caduceus!

When we got to the far end of the temple, Juan told us each to go sit in a little niche in the far wall and concentrate on becoming either completely gold or silver, depending on which side of the temple we ended up on. I went and sat in the golden niche, turning on my golden belt and feeling this color slowly take over my entire bubble. I became golden light. I thought about the Inkas creating life-size figures out of solid gold and silver and I wondered if perhaps these figures had carried an esoteric significance that related to the energy belts or to this ritual. Regardless, it felt wonderful to become completely gold, and I luxuriated in the sensation and only reluctantly gave the niche up to the next initiate who came behind me.

Once everyone had passed through either the gold or silver

niche, this portion of the ritual was complete and Juan told us that it was time for the third and final part to the ritual, a work with more *ñust'as* and the final *karpay ayni*, or interchange of personal power. This last part of the coronation ritual was to take place in the most sacred part of the temple complex. This was the final exchange that would make us all equals and, we hoped, prepare us to become candidates for the fifth level.

It was incredible to think about what these prophecies were predicting: an end to personal or individual karma, an end to fear and poverty, and the beginning of a time of sharing, and the development of amazing new human abilities! The idea that even one human being could develop the capacity to heal so completely was astounding. But the prophecy was clear. This was the time for miracles. I thought about all the world's problems, wars, poverty, the ecological crisis. I was sure I had said more than once, "It's going to take a miracle to fix this."

For me, all of my experiences in Peru had forced me to put the word *impossible* out of my mind. I had learned that we humans are highly creative and malleable creatures that are constantly inventing and modifying the reality that we see. Certainly my study of psychology had taught me that, and now my study of this spiritual tradition, as strange and wild as it was, had further prepared me to recognize the potentially miraculous nature of individual human beings, groups of human beings, and of reality itself.

Juan was right. If I had come to Peru and heard these prophecies before going through all the experiences of the last five years, it would have sounded like no more than another idealistic fairy tale or theory of utopia. But these prophecies that were based in such practical and simple principles as sharing energy, tolerating differences, and learning to harmonize and use diverse energy fields gave useful tools and step-by-step instructions on how to go about bringing in a utopia, or at least a better world. Although the outcome seemed miraculous, it all made plain and simple sense, saying that we humans are heading for a miracle just by developing more of our humanness.

If an acorn contains within itself a plan for something as implausible as an oak tree, then why couldn't humanity also have an innate plan, a preset wiring for a greater and more highly evolved human being, and therefore, society? Why couldn't these prophecies become a reality?

We walked along what looked like an old cow path, or perhaps more accurately a llama path, lined by two low stone walls, until we came to a third area of the temple complex. In this large field, all that was left of the temples were four stone foundations, two perfectly round and two rectangular. Juan gestured us over to the field next to these stone foundations and there we saw five beautiful Inka stone fountains only about two feet high, which gushed water into an Inka aqueduct. Surrounding this water temple we saw again the very highly refined stonework that marked the most sacred places of the Inkas. Juan explained that we were going to perform another water ritual, but this time one of purification before entering into the most sacred area of the whole temple complex.

"Just as in the Pachamama Cave in Machu Pikchu, here are five more *ñust'as*, or female nature spirits. I am not asking you to take a bath, but you can connect yourselves to each *ñust'a*. Try to taste the energy of each one of them as you give them your power and incorporate their energy into your bubble."

I approached the *ñust'as* with great respect and sat before each one, not bathing my head in the water until I felt a kind of permission had been granted. I splashed my face and head, and touched the water to my throat, heart, belly, and sacrum. I offered my refined energy to them and waited for them to return the *ayni*, and with the influx of energy, I felt connected to each *ñust'a*. Again I had a slightly different sense of female energy with each one. The first *ñust'a* seemed calm and clear, the second more rambunctious with a wide energy that was very earthy, the third was sensuous and wild, the fourth wise, and the fifth stately and elegant, like a princess. I took in their power and offered my heavy energy to Pachamama.

As I stepped away from the last *ñust'a*, Juan pulled me aside. "You will go fifth in line, carry the *mesa* and give the prayer for the new initiation." He placed his *mesa* firmly into my two hands and walked away. I did not question him or protest, but stood very still. Again he was offering me a great honor, but a part of me wanted nothing more than to turn and run away.

I knew that for the next step in the ritual, two males and two females would take their places inside the male and female temples, the two stone rectangles and two stone circles in the top part of the temple. Here, these four priests would be giving the initiation of the final interchange of personal power. I was to be initiated first, carrying the *mesa* through the four temples and receiving the blessing of first two male priests and then two female priestesses. I was then to invoke the spirit of Wiraqocha on behalf of each candidate, so that they might someday receive the new initiation, the initiation that would make them priests of the fifth level. For this there were no instructions. I had no idea how I was to do this part of the ritual. It was then that I realized, not only was Juan giving me an honor, it was also a test.

The two males and two females were chosen by group consensus in front of the water temple of the *ñust'as* before entering the most sacred area. They went to take their places inside their respective temples. There they would connect with the power of the place and act as transmitters for the energy of the temple to pass through their bubbles and be received by each initiate. I went first, carrying Juan's *mesa* in my trembling hands, only pretending that I knew what I was doing.

Peter was in the first temple, and I heaved a sigh of relief as I approached him, for he knew how to get out of the way and allow energy to move through him. I stepped over the low stone foundation into the temple and stood before him, bowing my head. He placed his hands on my head, and immediately a large rectangle of energy began to construct itself around us. To my inner eye, it was as if a rectangular building made of pure energy had erected itself, enclosing us inside our own private temple. It grew higher and higher in direct relationship with our intention to raise the *saiwa*, the column of energy, until it touched the *hanaq pacha*. As the energy transfer was complete, the image of the rectangle around us began to dissolve and Peter released his hands from my head. The ritual was simple and lasted only a few minutes, seeming to have its own organic timing. I bowed to the priest and exited the rectangular temple.

I moved on to the next temple with anticipation. As we were short on men, Ivan, Juan's son, would be giving the initiation here. He had been fully initiated by Juan several years before and I felt very good with him. Although this was not a personality test, I did feel better receiving initiations from those whose bubbles seemed better able to hold and transfer the energies. Nothing they ever taught me about in graduate school had prepared me for this kind of perception. This seemed to have to do with the integrity of the individual's energy field, which of course had everything to do with personal integrity. There were powerful lessons to be learned here. I offered my openness and again felt the rectangular structure erecting itself around us, and a very satisfying exchange of energy took place between Ivan, myself, and the temple.

I approached the next temple, the first round female temple, with trepidation. The priestess was in a weakened condition. I could see that her bubble was not holding energy, but this had been the election of the group. I had no say. I could only go along with the unfathomable group logic. I offered a prayer and bowed my head to receive the energy. It came in very diffuse at first until I consciously augmented her energy with mine. Immediately the tower went up around us tall and strong and round this time. I realized that her earth energy was low but with a little help she did an excellent job of transferring the energies. That was what this group work was all about anyway, I reminded myself. My personal opinions or judgments only got in the way. I bowed to her and went on to the next circular temple.

I entered inside the ring of stone and was immediately struck by the beauty and depth of this temple. I bowed my head to receive the energy from the priestess, who had by now taken on archetypal proportions. Connie, a hot blaze of red hair and emerald eyes, already resembled a fairy princess, and here in this temple she radiated all of her elfin glory. Immediately a high circular wall encompassed us with a very deep feminine sensation. I felt the potent love and willpower of this priestess, who worked so beautifully from her heart center. We took the sacred communion with the land together, and I moved into the fifth position, standing outside the last of the stone circles, with the *mesa* grasped tightly in my now trembling and sweating hands.

I stood holding out the *mesa*, deep in prayer, as I waited patiently for each member of our *ayllu* to travel through the temples, receiving the initiations as I had just done. One by one the initiates came to stand with me. They made a circle around me, as I wondered how I was to do what had been asked of me. Without instructions, I would just have to do what came to me. I took a deep breath and began to prepare myself. Maryann was on my right and I knew in my *qosqo* that I would begin with her. I felt energetically drawn to begin at my right, then move counterclockwise around the circle.

All the initiates had now gathered in the circle, and my heart was beating with the responsibility and the sacredness of the moment. As I stood there with the *mesa* held level with my heart, I began to hear a soft voice speaking to me from out of the *mesa*. I was some-how instantly aware that it was the voice of Don Benito.

"The moon, the stars, the wind, the ocean, the trees, and the birds are in this mesa." The voice was coming from one of the small round *khuyas* in-side the *mesa*, and blowing directly into me like a warm breath. *"The universe is in this* mesa," the voice continued. And as it was speaking, I felt my awareness expand and expand to touch each one of the things named, until I felt as large as the universe itself.

"Offer the universe to each one, for that is what there is to offer," the voice came again and for the last time. The words seemed to float out of the *mesa* one by one and infuse themselves directly into my heart, until there was nothing left of me, just a vast sea of stars, galaxies, and planets. I held the *mesa* above Maryann's head and waited for the soft lightning bolt that I watched descend from *hanaq pacha* to touch the *mesa*. I was just there, like the telephone repairman—less, really, a

simple human conduit—there to connect this lightning bolt into the top of each person's head in the circle.

As I placed the *mesa* on top of Maryann's head, I could feel her crown open energetically, like a flower, to receive the current of force. She sighed and rocked back and forth very lightly on her heels as she adjusted to the new sensation. I waited until the flux subsided and went on to the next person. As I worked with each one, I received insights into them, seeing each person on a much deeper level. I felt compassion for their joys, struggles, and learnings.

When I came to Juan I did not hesitate, but placed the *mesa* bundle on his head. I saw a strange series of fluxing images, some glorious, some horrific. I wondered if they were his past lives. The "slide show" of stills ended with an image of Juan wearing a brilliant headdress composed of three different-colored rays shooting out from the top and sides of his head. As I faced him, a long red ray shot out of the left side, just above his left ear, and went up into the sky. From the top of his head came a golden ray moving straight up, and from the right side, a silver ray. I marveled at this, made a mental note of the colors and placement, and went on with my work.

By the time I had completed the eleventh initiation my arms and body were charged with energy. I felt very alive but not stiff, and deeply peaceful. Into a rich group silence the words were urged out of me, "I feel that I have at last really met each one of you." Another deep moment of silence overcame the group, and, without warning, throats opened and everyone sounded and held a different note together, making a sudden and beautiful harmonious music. And it was over.

THAT NIGHT WE CAMPED OUT UNDER THE WATCHFUL GAZE of the huge pillars of Wiraqocha. The valley was silent and the night sky, perfectly clear, with huge fistlike stars jutting out against an exquisite black velvet background. After a quiet dinner in the dining tent some ventured out to walk the ruins again, while others just crept from the dining tent to their private tent and went off to sleep. During dinner, a few people spoke of their profound experiences during the ritual; others maintained a glassy-eyed silence. All had been deeply affected. No doubt or skepticism about the prophecies was spoken.

I walked over to the *baño* tent—a delightful construction like a large canvas bag that you had to zip yourself into and out of—set up by our wonderful crew. It was by far the best yet in outdoor peeing. When I came back, the dining tent was deserted. Juan was standing alone outside, smoking a cigarette and staring at the stars.

"Juan, what did Don Benito teach you about the stars?" I asked, not wanting to waste this valuable moment to get in a few of the questions I had long been waiting to ask.

"The stars? Oh . . . I am afraid I was a very bad student for that. I know that Don Benito was constantly talking to his guiding star," Juan told me, looking forlorn at his lack of information.

"How?" I pressed.

"He had a great stone bowl, like the two stone platters we saw in the Temple of the Cosmic Mirrors in Machu Pikchu. He would put water in this stone dish and spend hours each night, looking at his star in the reflection of the water," Juan answered.

"I knew it! Then the cosmic plate did serve as some kind of interlink with the cosmos," I exclaimed.

"What?" Juan's face crinkled in confusion.

"You remember . . . I told you about how Ricardo's *apus* gave me this cosmic plate and sent me to Argentina to sell it?"

"Ah, yes," Juan replied.

"Well, that plate looked almost exactly like the ones in the Temple of the Cosmic Mirrors in Machu Pikchu!" I said, getting excited again. "It must be like the one Don Benito had."

Juan considered my face for a long moment before responding. "Don Benito told me that every fourth-level Andean master knows when he is going to die. When you die you travel through the sky, back to your guiding star. That's why it is very important to study your star. It is very important to know the way back to your star.

When you die, you go into *hanaq pacha,* and all your energy gets absorbed back into your star. But while we are here, all our most important instructions come from our guiding star. The real guidance for the path of our soul comes from our star."

"But, Juan, how do you know which one . . . out of all those . . . is yours?" I asked, sweeping a hand toward the brilliant starfield above our heads." It seemed overwhelming.

"The same way you know which is your *apu* . . . you must have a vision, an experience, or a feeling of being personally related with a particular star. Traditional Andean initiates call their *apu* their 'guiding star,' it is like the idea that you Californians have of a 'spiritual guide,' or something like that. As you progress on the path, your guiding star changes. For example, when you first arrived in Cuzco, you had a vision of Apu Ausangate, your guiding star for the third level," Juan explained.

"But, Juan, I also had that vision of Jesus, remember?"

"Yes, which means that you were already a candidate for the fourth level. But, because you had the vision of Ausangate, that means there was something important at the third level that you had not finished yet. Do you know what that might be?" Juan asked me with a perspicacious smile.

"Yes." I hung my head, and admitted, "Conflict."

"Conflict is the task of the third level. In our tradition there are three stages of relationship and they are all described energetically with very specific Quechua words. *Tinkuy* is the encounter between two bubbles of energy. *Tupay* refers to the next stage of challenge or confrontation between the two people, two villages, or even two nations. The third level is full of *tupay,* or confrontation. All of the experiences you described with Ricardo's group and his *apus* fall into these first two categories. You went to his *mesa,* he and his *apus* accepted you, *tinkuy.* And then the *tupay* began."

"But, Juan, I hated that. It seemed so . . . so juvenile . . . so ridiculous," I responded, becoming agitated.

Juan held a hand up, gesturing for me to calm down. "How can you say that it is ridiculous when we are talking about something that is a necessary step in your development? *Tupay* is not bad. In fact, challenges make us stronger, allow us to test the potency of our bubbles, and to discern in what areas we are undeveloped. Don't many full-grown adults in your culture engage in *tupay*?"

"Yes. Lots," I agreed.

"*Tupay* only becomes a problem if it never progresses to the third stage of relationship, *taqe*," the master pronounced.

"Just what is *tah-kay*?" I tried imitating the sound he had made.

"*Taqe* literally refers to the capacity to join together or integrate diverse fields of living energy. That is the third stage of relationship that, in the higher levels of our tradition, must follow a *tupay*. You remember the very simple example I once gave you of the two Indians who met on the road?" I nodded. "That meeting is *tinkuy*. Then they decide to have a race to the top of the mountain. That is the challenge, or *tupay*. The winner of the race then *must* teach or train the other how he won. *That* is *taqe*. In Inka times it was considered cause for great shame if a leader did not have the capacity to bring a relationship to the third stage. The ability to join together diverse ideas, peoples, communities—bubbles of different kinds of living energies—was a highly prized cultural value amongst the Inka."

"The Inkas had some ideas that we could sure use today," I told Juan.

He nodded. "The Inka social structure was by no means perfect, but they had some very refined aspects to their culture."

"But, Juan," I insisted, getting back to my original question, "we are talking about 'guiding stars.' What I want to know is how the literal stars in the sky fit into all this."

Juan shook his head, laughing at me. "In some way, it is the same thing. The stars are part of the *hanaq pacha*, the superior world. When you move into the fourth level, as you know, you become one with Pachamama. This means that your energy bubble literally resonates with the spirit of the entire earth. At that point in your development you can no longer be under the tutelage of an *apu*, but you must come under the tutelage of a being from the *hanaq pacha*. This could be Jesus, one of the other saints, or Inkas that live in *hanaq pacha*, or it could quite literally be one of the stars in the sky. Remember, for us the stars are *beings*, not just sterile hunks of matter."

This explanation brought heaven and earth together inside me. With the Great Initiation I had just begun to feel as though I belonged to the earth. Now I was starting to understand my relationship to the heavens as well. After all, the stars were just another part of nature, like mountains or plants or trees. They *must* possess and emanate their own kind of living energy as well. In the same way that I could connect to the energy bubble of a river or a mountain, I could connect with the living energy of the stars!

15

The Return of the Inka

THE NEXT MORNING DAWNED WITH A TONE PRECISELY opposite to that of our sacred and profound ritual of the day before. The engine of our bus had died overnight and we would now have to wait hours until the engine oil—which had apparently frozen in the chill temperatures after sunset—had once again unthawed. If that didn't work, the drivers would have to walk hours to the nearest town and bring another bus.

Like it or not, we were stuck at our campsite in the town of Raqchii, at this holiest of holy Inka shrines. I, for one, liked it. This "misfortune" allowed us time to relax and absorb the feeling of this magnificent temple. It also gave us a chance to go deeper into our conversation with Juan about the Andean tradition and the meaning of the prophecies.

But the real prize of the morning was that, at breakfast, Juan opened his mysterious *mesa* bundle for the first time and showed us what was inside. I had always assumed its contents were a closely guarded secret, until it had occurred to me simply to ask Juan if we could see. Perhaps it was the higher altitude or the vital energy of the temple itself that had made me brazen. Before breakfast I saw Juan sitting by the campfire, his *mesa* at his side. "Hey, Juan, what's in the bag?" I had asked presumptuously. Expecting to be rebuked for my curiosity, instead he nodded at me.

"Come." He gestured me over with his orange plastic camping cup. "I will show you." I walked over to the campfire where he and the rest of the group were huddled around, waiting for breakfast and trying to keep warm in the freezing morning air. Before our eyes, Juan opened his mysterious pouch. The circle pressed around Juan more tightly as everyone jostled for a good view. It appeared that, unbeknownst to me, each member of our group had had the same burning curiosity I had.

Carefully Juan unwrapped the expertly folded bundle that, like a large cloth origami, held its shape by a magic folding pattern. The small square ceremonial cloth, called a *lliklla*, was made of a fine weave of beautiful black-and-pink alpaca. The cloth had a woven edge of bright pink, with two thin panels of pink-and-white snow-flake designs at the outer edges, followed by two large black panels, with another pink-and-white panel in the center. Inside this first *llikl-lla* was another plain gray cloth held together with a long silver pin.

Juan opened the second bundle to reveal the curious contents: a two-inch-long Christian cross made of dark *chontah*, a very hard wood from the Amazon jungle; several seashells like the type used in *despachos*; four tiny real gold and silver crosses; two tiny images of saints I didn't recognize; and any number of small oddly shaped stones, some round and black as a marble, others flat and white like quartz, still others that looked like ordinary river stones, or stones you could find on any city street. I recognized a round gray stone, the one that had carried Don Benito's voice to me during our coronation ritual.

"These are all my *khuyas*, gifts from my masters, including this," he said, holding up one of the gold crosses. "This is a gift from one of my greatest masters—my wife," he told us laughing. Yet despite his laughter I knew that Juan was quite serious. I had not met his wife, Lida, but I knew that he considered her a very spiritually powerful person, and he had told me that Andean priests always worked in couples, sacred alchemical couples. He had also said that it was Lida who unlocked the secret of Q'ollorit'i for him, but he had never fully explained this comment. I decided to take the opportunity to ask.

"Juan, yesterday you told us that one of the first places the fifth-level priests—the ultimate healers—would appear is at the Festival of Q'ollorit'i. It must be a very sacred and important place. What is this festival all about anyway?"

Juan took his time to return the contents of his mesa into the smaller cloth, and then to refold the entire bundle, while he considered his answer. "Ah, Q'ollorit'i," he finally responded as he now sat surveying his folding job with satisfaction.

"Q'ollorit'i is held every year on the last full moon in May or the first full moon in June, depending on the year. The site of the festival is an important sanctuary at the foot of a huge glacier at about sixteen thousand feet altitude."

"Is that where the bear-men go?" I asked. During the time I lived in Cuzco, I had seen men dressed in what to me looked like strange Halloween costumes, black-and-brown fringed garments, wearing masks. When I asked about it I was told they were "the bear men" going to a festival held once a year on an ice peak.

Juan chuckled, "Yes. These are the *ukukus*. They have many functions at the festival, but really they make up part of another entirely different spiritual path, separate from that of the Andean priest, yet related. They are spiritual warriors in training and they are part of the prophecy too."

"How?" Peter asked.

"They come every year as the keepers of order at the festival, and you must watch what you do or you may feel the bite of one of the *ukukus'* leather whips," Juan warned us. This made me think of the leather whip I had seen and heard used years ago at Ricardo's *mesa*.

"But do they hurt you?" I asked Juan, rather frightened.

"No, no. They will simply let you know when you are disrespecting the rules in the sanctuary area. Remember, more than seventy thousand people attend this festival. Once you get close to the sanctuary, the crowds can be quite intimidating and the *ukukus* are there to keep order. You will find them very friendly and funny too. The *ukukus* are our sacred clowns. It is a curious contradiction, for while they are the keepers of order, they are also sanctioned to break the social rules by acting a little crazy. They speak in very silly, high-pitched voices and are constantly playing gags on one another.

"But it is the *ukukus* that go up on the glacier and stay there all night, to prove that they have the power to keep company with the mightiest forces of nature. If they survive the night, they have gained the right to cut and carry down a piece of the glacier with them; often a huge chunk of ice cut in the shape of a cross. By this test they have shown that they can incorporate the power of the *apu* into their bubble. They then melt the chunk of ice and bring it back to serve as holy water for the people of their village. In fact they are carrying the power of the *apu* back to their people. All this and more is the training that prepares them to be part of the spiritual army of the *sapa* Inka. For you see, they, too, are awaiting the Inka's return. In this way they play their role in the fulfillment of the prophecy as well." Juan sat back as we marveled at this further elucidation of the prophecy.

"What a job!" Sam exclaimed. "I thought being a computer programmer was hard. I'm glad we are not following the path of the *ukukus*, it seems dangerous."

"It is," Juan replied. "Almost every year one or more *ukukus* die on the glacier. Their bodies are considered offerings to the mountain spirit."

"It sounds like human sacrifice," Justin commented.

"Every culture has their own form. I understand that in your culture many young and middle-aged men die of stress and heart disease. Are you not sacrificing your men to the god of money, status, power?" He had a point.

"Of course, on the more mundane level," Juan continued, "the *ukukus* remain at the festival after everyone has gone, to clean the area, returning it to its original pristine condition. In this way they are the guardians of the sanctuary area and servants of both the *apu* and Pachamama," Juan informed us.

These *ukukus* sounded more like clowns than spiritual warriors, in fact they seemed downright playful. Perhaps this was what I was learning more than anything else here in the Andes, that spirituality and play went hand in hand. The most religious event for the Andean people was not a somber and grave affair, but was carried out with great joy. I asked our bus driver, Eduardo, who we had learned that morning was also a *paqo*, his opinion on this.

"Oh, the *apus* would not have it any other way," Eduardo said as he poked the fire. He was a slight yet square, handsome man with jet black hair. "They would not enjoy something solemn. We have festivals to honor them and what they love best is a good party. You see, each *apu* has a different kind of personality. Some are more firm and serious, like Apu Salkantay. While others are wild partiers, like the Mamita Veronica." I knew that the ice-capped Veronica, like Mamita Putukusi, was one of the rare female mountains, visible on the road to Machu Pikchu.

Eduardo was encouraged by our interest. "If you need more authority in your personality, or if you need to learn how to have more fun, you can go on a pilgrimage to the *apu* that possesses the characteristics that you most want to incorporate in yourself. But at the festivals, all the *apus* want to see us enjoying ourselves. What father does not want to see his children happy?" Eduardo asked, turning the questioning back to me. He had a point. I liked the idea that the Andean gods wanted their people to be happy. I believed that God wanted us to be happy. This seemed like a very healthy spiritual system.

All at once a realization struck me. The fearsome and punishing God of the Judeo-Christian system was like Ricardo's *apus*—a frightening supernatural being that punished and rewarded. But this was related only to the third level of spiritual development! At the fourth level you made friends with the *apus* and they acted as your allies, you faced your fear of authority and developed a more responsible and mature relationship to it!

This was what I found so comforting about the Andean Path. The more I practiced it, the more I realized that what Juan said about it was true: there really was no rigid dogma or rules that one had to follow. There was only one simple rule, sharing, and a simple structure that, for me, made sense. Juan never exerted any pressure or force to make someone do a ritual that was uncomfortable for them. He carefully encouraged us to move beyond our limitations, but in a graceful way; he was never domineering or demanding, he only invited us to partake of what he was offering.

Juan, in a real way, seemed to embody the Andean system that was so flexible, so inclusive. Rather than imposing its rules and structure on its practitioners, it seemed instead to reveal an innate, organic structure that, within time, one would just discover naturally anyway. I now understood this religious system as a sort of spiritual road map, but instead of speed limit signs and patrolling police, it had an occasional large friendly-looking sign with an arrow saying "Why Don't You Try This Way and See What Happens?" Everything about it was fun, and it encouraged personal discovery and direct experience. Yet the mystical teachings explained so much about life. They addressed an area where there had been an enormous hole in my education.

"Have pilgrims been going to Q'ollorit'i for a long time?" Barbara asked Juan as she stirred a heap of chocolate into her hot water and passed the can over to him.

"There is a myth about the origins of the Q'ollorit'i Festival, and there are many different versions of it. Let me tell you the version that I know, and it will give you some idea, at least about the entry of the Christian aspects into the festival." And without further ado, Juan began the tale.

"The story goes that around the year 1780 there was a young llama herder here in this valley who was sent out with his brother to tend the herd. The elder brother was lazy and unkind, and left his little brother to do all the work. It is said that the young llama herder tried his best on his own, but it was just too much work. After several exhausting days, another young boy appeared to the llama herder and said he would help him tend the flock. Within a short time, and with the help of this mysterious friend, the herd had miraculously flourished. The boy's father wanted to reward his young son for his good work. The boy insisted his friend be rewarded also. When the father asked his son what his friend wanted, the boy gave his father a piece of his friend's tattered tunic, saying, "All he wants is some more of this cloth to make himself a new tunic." The father went off to Cuzco, a long walk in those days, to purchase more of the cloth.

In Cuzco he discovered that the cloth was actually a fine canonical material used only to make the robes of the priests. The story came to the attention of the Archbishop of Cuzco, who sent his curate from Ocongate, the village nearest to the sanctuary, to investigate what appeared to be a heinous act of sacrilege. When the local authorities approached the boy and his friend, who were standing near a large rock, the friend ran away, seeming to disappear into the rock in a blinding flash of light. They say that the image of Christ appeared at that moment, etched into the stone. The young Indian llama herder was said to have died of shock and was buried under the rock. We know that since at least 1780, this has been an important place of pilgrimage, but we suspect that it was a sacred site much before that. Unfortunately most of the *khipus*, the knotted cords that were the only records of the Inkas, were destroyed by the Spanish.

"Recently another interesting theory has emerged amongst the scholars of Inka history. The year 1780 also coincides with the powerful uprising of Túpac Amaru, which overtook the entire Andean area and almost ousted the Spanish. There are those who would argue that the vision of Christ in the rock, although first seen by a humble Indian boy, was really a ploy on the part of the Catholic Church to help squelch the Indian rebellion.

"That may be. However, one thing the history books will not tell you is that every Indian uprising, from the Taki Ongoy movement of the sixteenth century to Túpac Amaru and the national Inka movement of the eighteenth century, up to the campesino rebellions of the twentieth century, all have, at their core, the messianic expectation of the return of the Inka. All the leaders of these movements have, of course, been very charismatic *paqos*. In fact the leader of the Taki Ongoy movement was from this area, an Andean priest named Juan Ch'oqne, whose guiding star was the Pleiades.

"The Pleiades!" I started. I had had a childhood obsession with the Pleiades. "Juan, I have always heard that people call Q'ollorit'i the Star-Snow Festival and someone once told me that was because it had something to do with the Pleiades."

Juan shook his head. "Yes and no. This occurred because of a mistranslation of the ancient word *qollo*, which means 'pure white,' as *qoyllur*, which means 'star.' It just so happens that the constellation that watches over the festival is the Pleiades, but this is because of the esoteric and energetic significance of the constellation. The Pleiades serve as *taqe* for the festival. *Taqe* means a 'joiner of energy fields,'" Juan explained to the group, winking at me. "The Pleiades emanate the powerful cosmic influence of joining diverse living energies together into a collective whole, which truly embraces the energetic and spiritual meaning behind the whole Q'ollorit'i Festival. And for the Andean masters, they represent the seven levels of psycho-spiritual development, pointing to the fact that there is an unrevealed seventh level, beyond the emergence of the sixth-level *sapa* Inka and *qoya*."

"Juan, what does it mean to have the Pleiades as your guiding star?"

"To have the Pleiades, the seven sisters, as one's guiding star is highly auspicious. It may signify that one has the possibility of reaching the seventh level in this lifetime!" My mind boggled at the mere idea of the fifth-level priests who could heal any disease. I couldn't even begin to imagine what it would mean to achieve the seventh-level consciousness.

"What does that mean, Juan . . . for a human being to reach the seventh level?" I *had* to ask.

"Little is known about the capacities or duties of seventh-level priests beyond the fact that they will be able to resurrect their physical bodies, as Christ did. Christ is a very important figure for the Indians of today, perhaps as important as the Inkas of old. In fact, the image of Christ in the rock is very meaningful for them. The sanctuary building at Q'ollorit'i was constructed around the stone only recently, to enshrine the image of Christ, and electric lights were put in within the last few years. Twenty years ago only five or maybe ten thousand pilgrims came there, but over the last eight to ten years the quantity of pilgrims has increased dramatically. I think the prophecy is what explains this best. More and more people are drawn to this spot. They may not know why, but they come because they are called," Juan said, pointing to his chest to indicate the origin of the call.

"Certainly that's why all of us are here," Barbara said as other heads around the circle bobbed up and down in agreement.

"Then I must tell you that you have all now become a part of the prophecy. There is another piece that I have not yet told you. I think this must be the time. Would you like to hear it?" Juan asked.

"Yes!" came the resounding collaborative sound of the group, that was nearly a shout.

"I told you that over the last years the ritual at Wiraqocha Temple had almost been lost because there were not enough fourth-level priests to perform the ritual. Do you remember?" Everyone nodded. "Well, I think you all understand by now that this prophecy of the Inka's return is based in a collective spiritual effort. You each now possess a *mesa* that can be used to help you gather your spiritual family. You each have the opportunity, having now nearly completed the great initiation, to become *taqes*, like the Pleiades—joiners of energy fields—to bring your own spiritual group of twelve here to Peru, to undergo the *hatun karpay* initiation.

"Although she may not yet know it, Elizabeth and I are already working in the part of the prophecy that says when the time is ripe, twelve groups of twelve fourth-level priests will come together to perform the ritual in Wiraqocha Temple, and this will give the boost needed to help create the energetic conditions," Juan said, shaking his finger at us and repeating, "to create the *appropriate* conditions for the manifestation of the first Inka *mallku* in Q'ollorit'i. Each group of twelve will have someone who will serve as *taqe*—a joiner, or hub of the wheel."

I imagined the ritual we experienced when we created the column of energy in the center of the twelve temples of the royal lineages of the Inka, played out with, instead of only one person in each temple, an entire trained group of twelve fourth-level priests. What we had accomplished with a mere group of twelve was awesome; what we could accomplish with a group of 144 was something I couldn't quite wrap my mind around, but the possibility was tantalizing. The idea of the collective intention of 144 trained energy bubbles focused on a specific goal made my hair stand up on end. It presented the possibility of enormous potential energy, yet I knew it would not be an easy task.

Time had flown by as we were talking. Eduardo announced lunch, and as the steaming plates of food were passed around the circle, the group was left to ponder the notion of becoming one of the twelve *taqes*, the hub of a group of twelve. It was an awesome responsibility. We heartily wolfed down the delicious and much-needed food, which had been prepared for us in this most awe-inspiring seat of nature's sacred power, each lost in our own musings.

It was an ambitious project but one that appealed to my sense of adventure, my sense of service, and my sense of community. The structure of this kind of enormous ritual was really one of community effort and interdependence. I saw a tremendous amount of work as well as a real opportunity for growth. I was sure this kind of a challenge would present me with every possible chance to face my own stumbling blocks and to find out what it would take to overcome them. I knew that the same would be true for the others who chose to become *taqes* as well. There was potential for real spiritual learning involved here.

I understood from Juan that the forming and maintaining of an *ayllu* was one of the tests of a true fourth-level initiate and one of the necessary steps before attaining candidacy to the fifth level. This, too, was a fascinating part of the challenge, because I had always had a notion, since childhood, that it was possible to heal with a single touch.

I remember being fascinated by movies that discussed miraculous healing, and even an episode of *Star Trek* in which one of the aliens was capable of this level of healing. In Andean terms this person would be described as an Inka *mallku*, an ultimate healer, a person who had fully developed the powers of the heart, mind, and body. I was fascinated by the fact that a bunch of Andean priests somewhere on a mountaintop in Peru had dreamed the same dream that a TV producer, or that I, a child in Minnesota, had dreamed. Could it be that many others held this dream as well, somewhere inside them? Perhaps this kind of vision came from our collective dreaming.

But if what Juan was saying about the *sapa* Inka were true, then the Andean people had experienced a sixth level being within the recent past—their Inkas. Perhaps this made it easier for the Andean people to remember their true human potential. Our Christ, obviously someone who had in Andean terms reached the fifth level and gone well beyond, had lived two thousand years ago. And it was certainly a fact that profound atrocities had been committed in his name since then, including the killing of hundreds of thousands of Andean people. Although we had occasional outstanding examples of human beings, like Gandhi, or Martin Luther King, Jr., it seemed we humans just hadn't refined ourselves to anywhere near the level of the Buddha or Jesus Christ.

How were we ever going to "grow up" as a society, as a race? I was haunted by that question. It just seemed to me that we had so very far to go in order to evolve beyond the level of fear and the accompanying desire to dominate—the third level. We had to reconcile ourselves to our deepest fears. All of the attempts at evolving that I had seen in the United States, either in the New Age movement or in the psychology movement, never produced anyone who had truly gotten beyond the third level. Power always seemed to turn into domination rather than harmonious attunement.

It seemed to me that this was the truly great challenge of our age. No culture or society so far had been able to get beyond the third level collectively. In our culture we are fascinated by opposites and yet we can't reconcile them. Here in the South, men and women were different, yet complementary. The Inka concept of *yanantin*, resolving opposites into complements with each retaining their own uniqueness, was wisdom we desperately needed. The Inka ideal of the three stages of relationship maturing at *taqe* was also phenomenal. The Inka culture seemed to have a lot of what we lacked in the North, yet I knew that South Americans didn't have everything either. Each culture had to share their knowledge, their piece of the human puzzle, just as the prophecy said.

"We cannot control the prophecy—we must let ourselves be carried by it." Juan spoke into the thick silence of the group, mute with the possibility and challenge of what was being presented to them.

"There is a tremendous power gathering, but it is a wave for us to ride. I think in the place you come from, California, there must be a very great understanding of this. Your surfer culture must know something about the power of nature. A surfer cannot try to control the power of the wave. If he tries to do so, it will surely be his downfall. But he can have a great experience if he has the strength and agility to stay on top of the wave as it is breaking. In this work, the person with a rigid or self-serving ego will certainly be swallowed up by the wave. It is only those with a very agile ego that will be able to stay with the wave of the prophecy as it continues breaking."

Eduardo announced that our yellow bus was finally cured and ready to take us back. We packed ourselves inside and headed down the dusty road, destination Cuzco. Still the group was silent, pondering, digesting. The next day we would be flying back to the States. Our great initiation was complete. Juan had reminded us again and again: "*Initiation* means *beginning*." Now we were prepared to begin our work.

I could only dream of what lay ahead. There was so much more work to do. There were the twelve groups of twelve that had to be gathered. I had had enough experience with groups and with the human problems surrounding commitment that I knew it would not be an easy task. There were all of those festivals that I had not yet attended, the places of the prophecy, the many lessons of the fourth level that I had only just embarked upon. I dreamed of attending the Q'ollorit'i Festival, and of one day going to Q'eros to meet Don Manuel Q'espi himself, Juan's eldest remaining teacher. The many miles of the pilgrimage that remained lay before my feet. Deep within my heart I now held a wish, a deep wish for myself and all of humanity: that we would live to see the return of the Inka, that we would work tirelessly together to create the conditions for the coming of a better world. The one thing I knew was that now and for the rest of my life, for the sake of my children and my children's children, I would use all of the power of my heart, mind, and body to work for this miracle. For I had tasted the sweetness of this dream, and now nothing less would satisfy me.

Afterword:

THE MYTH OF INKARI

This is a Creation myth of the Q'ero people. It was collected in 1955 by Oscar Nuñez del Prado, father of Juan Nuñez del Prado, and tells of the beginning of the Inka empire and the expectation of the Inka's return.

During the time when the sun did not exist, there lived a people on earth whose power was such that they could will stones to walk, or convert mountains into prairies with a single dispatch of their slingshot. The moon irradiated their shadow-world, lighting dimly the activities of these people known as the nyauwpa machu—*the ancient ones.*

One day the Roal, the supreme creator spirit and chief of the apus *(spirits of the mountains), asked the* nyauwpa machu *if they would like him to bequeath to them some of his power. Full of arrogance they replied that they had their own and did not need any other. Irritated by their response the Roal created the sun and ordered him to shine forth on the world. Terrified and nearly blinded by the brilliance of the celestial body, they sought refuge in little houses, the majority of which had their doors oriented toward the sun's daily rising. The sun's heat dehydrated them, slowly turning their muscle into nothing more than dried meat adhering to the bone. Still, they did not die, and now they are the* soq'as *(dangerous spirits) that come out on certain afternoons at the hour of sunset, or on the evening of a new moon.*

The earth became inactive and the mountain spirits decided to forge new beings. They created Inkari and Qoyari, a man and a woman filled with wisdom.* They gave to Inkari a golden staff, and to Qoyari a spindle as symbols of power and industriousness. Inkari received the order to found a city in the place where his golden staff clove upright in the earth. He tried the first throw, but the staff only fell on top of the ground. On the second throw, the staff stuck into the earth at an oblique angle, caught between black mountains and the banks of a river. Even though the staff had fallen sideways, Inkari decided to found a town there, called Q'eros. The conditions were not very propitious so he thought it convenient to build his capital nearby in the same region, setting himself hard at work in the ruins now know as Tampu. Tiring of this dirty and sweaty work Inkari desired to bathe himself, but the cold was too intense. So he decided to bring forth the thermal waters of Upis, constructing baths there that still exist today.

Inkari built his city in spite of the apus' *mandate and they—to make him understand his error—permitted the* nyauwpa machu, *who watched Inkari full of bitter envy, to take on new life. Their first desire was to exterminate the son of the mountain spirits, and to this end they took gigantic blocks of stone and rolled them down the slopes in the direction of the place where Inkari was working. Terrified, Inkari fled in the direction of Lake Titicaca, where the tranquillity of the place allowed him to meditate. He returned once more in the direction of the Willkañust'a River. He dallied in the peaks of La Raya and from there he hurled his golden staff yet a third time, where it lodged plumb in a fertile valley. Here he founded the city of Cuzco, and lived there a long time. Q'ero could not remain forgotten, so he sent his firstborn son to go and populate the town. The rest of his descendants were sent to various places where they gave rise to the royal lineages of the Inkas.*

---

*Inkari is a combination of the Quechua word *inka,* meaning "ruler," and the Spanish word for "king," *rey: Inka-Rey.* Qoyari is a mix of *qoya,* meaning "queen," and the Spanish *rey.*

Having completed his task, Inkari decided to set forth again in the company of Qoyari to teach his wisdom to the people. Passing again through Q'eros, he disappeared into the jungle, but not before leaving witness to his passing by his fingerprints, which can still be seen in in the ruins of Mujurumi and Inkaq Yupin, until the time when the Inka returns.